HISTORICAL ARCHAEOLOGIES OF COGNITION

Dedicated to Henry Glassie, and to the memory of James Deetz (1930–2000)

Historical Archaeologies of Cognition

Explorations into Faith, Hope and Charity

Edited by

James Symonds, Anna Badcock and Jeff Oliver

Equinox Publishing Ltd

equinox

SHEFFIELD UK   BRISTOL CT

Published by Equinox Publishing Ltd.

UK: Unit S3, Kelham House, 3 Lancaster Street, Sheffield, South Yorkshire S3 8AF
USA: ISD, 70 Enterprise Drive, Bristol, CT 06010

www.equinoxpub.com

First published 2013
First printing in paperback 2017

British Library Cataloguing-in-Publication Data

A catalogue record for this book is available from the British Library.

ISBN-13 978-1-84553-534-6 (hardback)
         978-1-78179-636-8 (paperback)

Library of Congress Cataloging-in-Publication Data

Historical archaeologies of cognition : explorations into faith, hope and charity / edited by James Symonds, Anna Badcock and Jeff Oliver.
     pages cm
 Includes bibliographical references and index.
 ISBN 978-1-84553-534-6 (hardback)
1. Archaeology and history--Case studies. 2. Archaeology and history--Philosophy. 3. Social archaeology--Case studies. 4. Cognition and culture--Case studies. 5. Material culture--Social aspects. 6. Material culture--Psychological aspects--Case studies. 7. Faith--Social aspects--Case studies. 8. Hope--Social aspects--Case studies. 9. Charity--Social aspects--Case studies. I. Symonds, James, Ph. D. II. Badcock, Anna. III. Oliver, Jeff, 1973-
 CC77.H5H563 2013
 930.1--dc23
                          2013000985

Typeset by ISB Typesetting, Sheffield
www.sheffieldtypesetting.com
Printed and bound by Lightning Source Inc. (La Vergne, TN), Lighting Source UK Ltd. (Milton Keynes), Lightning Source AU Pty. (Scoresby, Victoria)

Contents

List of Contributors

Anna Badcock, ArcHeritage, Sheffield; abadcock@yorkat.co.uk

Jeffery F. Burton, Manzanar National Historic Site, National Park Service (US); jeff_burton@nps.gov

Gillian Carr, Institute of Continuing Education, University of Cambridge; gcc20@cam.ac.uk

Brent R. Fortenberry, Department of Archaeology, Boston University; brent.fortenberry@gmail.com

David Gadsby; hampdenarchy@gmail.com

Laura McAtackney, School of Social Justice, University College Dublin; mcatackl@hotmail.com

Harold Mytum, Centre for Manx Studies, University of Liverpool; h.mytum@liv.ac.uk

Jeff Oliver, Department of Archaeology, University of Aberdeen; j.oliver@abdn.ac.uk

Greig Parker, Glamorgan-Gwent Archaeological Trust, Swansea; parker.greig@gmail.com

Travis G. Parno, Department of Archaeology, Boston University; tgparn@bu.edu

Jonathan Prangnell, School of Social Science, University of Queensland; j.prangnell@uq.edu.au

Kate Quirk, School of Social Science, University of Queensland; kate.quirk@uqconnect.edu.au

James Symonds, Department of Archaeology, University of York; james.symonds@york.ac.uk

Samuel Walls, South West Archaeology, South Molton, Devon; samwalls@swarch.net

Carolyn L. White, Anthropology Department, University of Nevada, Reno; clwhite@unr.edu

Timo Ylimaunu, Archaeology, Faculty of Humanities, University of Oulu; timo.ylimaunu@oulu.fi

List of Figures and Tables

Figures

Tables

1 Finding Belief, Desire and Benevolence in Historical Archaeology

James Symonds and Jeff Oliver

Introduction

Our lives are guided by faith: faith in our families and friends, faith in those who work with us or on our behalf, faith in the religions that shape our beliefs and morals, faith in the secular institutions that govern our day-to-day actions, and faith in the technologies that sustain us and the material world. We keep faith, lose faith and sometimes doggedly adhere to faith. Faith is belief that is held without evidence and cannot be disproved. Faith is intangible, but is also palpable and faith, or loss of faith, has been central to every war in human history.

Hope is more than a wish, it is desire tied to expectation. Hope reveals itself in the trivial, the everyday, the present and the momentary, it looks to the future, but is grounded in the inheritance of the past. Hope may be found in the most desperate circumstances amid poverty or oppression; it is an expression of defiance, a rejection of rationality, a rebuttal of the taken-for-granted. In some situations hope is lost, while in others hope can be a way of thinking, a strategy for survival.

Charity draws upon altruism to extend compassion to individuals beyond our immediate kith and kin. It strives to produce social cohesion, yet often sets individuals and groups apart in the institutions, buildings and landscapes that it creates. By its very performance charity segregates the needy and draws a dividing line between donors and recipients, or the haves and have-nots. The act of charitable giving is commonly motivated by a desire to ameliorate inequality, hunger or desperation, but may also create a dependency, which serves to reinforce steeply asymmetrical power relations. Where there is wealth there will also be poverty. The extent to which this disparity is tolerated in any society is determined by the dominant political ideology and mediated by charitable acts.

Faith, hope and charity run through our day-to-day lives. Such highly charged emotions and actions are an important part of being human but tend to be fleeting, and often leave few or no tangible traces. This conundrum led the 2007 Contemporary and Historical Archaeology in Theory (CHAT) group conference in Sheffield to consider how evidence of faith, hope and charity might be recovered in the material world. The optimism with which this question was framed illustrated a confidence in archaeological theory and methods. Both organizers and contributors were clear that even seemingly intangible aspects of the past are knowable and, moreover, that the traces of past human behaviour which have survived into the present day may be put to use to inform debates in the contemporary world.

What Can Be Known? Archaeology and the Limits of Inference

The aims and scope of archaeology are constantly changing, shifting and unfolding in response to societal interests and concerns. In the 1950s the Oxford don Christopher Hawkes was clear that archaeological knowledge had its limitations. In an invited lecture delivered to members of the American Anthropological Society at Harvard University, he responded to Walter Taylor's call for a 'conjunctive' archaeology, which implored archaeologists to embrace more holistic anthropological approaches and to move beyond simplistic 'where and when' questions, and the obsessive chronicling of cultural materials (Taylor 1948).

Hawkes' response was steeped in Old World conservatism and functionalism. According to the 'ladder of inference' that he devised it was relatively easy to work from archaeological phenomena to the techniques that produced them, or to reconstruct subsistence practices and economic activities using ecological evidence and material remains. Evidence for social structures, religious practices and aspects of spiritual life were, however, deemed to be far harder, and arguably impossible to reveal without the assistance of textual sources (Hawkes 1954). A generation later, issues of chronology, typology and cultural diffusion had become largely redundant with advances in independent dating methods and the radiocarbon revolution (Renfrew 1973). The New Archaeology of the 1970s brought a spirit of unbounded optimism which spread, *ex occidens lux*, with an almost evangelical fervour. Henceforth social structures and many aspects of human activity were deemed knowable, so long as the right data were assembled, and suitably robust hypothetico-deductive methods deployed (Binford and Binford 1968:21; Watson *et al.* 1971).

However, such optimism did not extend to all corners of the discipline. In particular the unhappy relationship between mainstream American processualist archaeology and historical archaeology has been ably charted by Laurie Wilkie (Wilkie 2005). Thus while some historical archaeologists were content to follow the prehistorians on their faculty, and to search for testable hypothesis and generalizing laws that could explain artefact patterning (e.g. South 1977), others followed a more humanistic path. Anne Yentsch and Mary C. Beaudry have described how the paradigmatic shift in material culture studies in American historical archaeology began simultaneously, as a group of individuals experimenting with new analytical approaches who were known to one another without actively collaborating (Yentsch and Beaudry 2001). For example, the attempts to capture cultural forms and social values in the changing styles of gravestones (Deetz and Dethlefsen 1967) or folk housing in middle Virginia (Glassie 1975) sprung from the belief that artefacts and other culturally modified materials embodied and reflected human beliefs and cosmologies.

The common thread that links Beaudry, Yensch and a host of other North American historical archaeologists who were trained in the 1970s, and have subsequently risen to prominence, is the influence of their tutor, James Deetz. In his classic study of early American life, *In Small Things Forgotten*, Deetz skilfully combined structuralist analysis and semiotics to expose how 'world views' such as the 'Georgian Order' had permeated through all levels of daily life among eighteenth-century mercantile capitalists in New England and the Chesapeake. Drawing upon the intellectual vigour of his colleague and life-long friend Henry Glassie (1975), who had used structural anthropology to explicate changing worldviews expressed by architecture, Deetz was clear on the potential of anthropological archaeology: 'In the seemingly little and insignificant things that accumulate to create a lifetime, the essence of our existence is captured' (Deetz 1977:161). Put simply, Deetz believed that everyday objects were 'freighted with both social and symbolic significance' (Deetz 1994:xix) and therefore served to 'carry messages from their makers and users' (Deetz 1977:4).

In Deetz's view, the role of the archaeologist as public intellectual was clear: archaeologists were code-breakers and their job was to decipher the semiotic codes that had been used to encrypt these ancient messages. The past existed as a series of distant events and was separate from the here-and-now. The process of archaeological interpretation forged links in a chain of being that actively reconnected the past—and by implication all the values and traditions that it had set in motion—to the present. To be truly effective, however, archaeologists had to do far more than simply decode and reassemble these scraps of information. The act of transcribing the contents of a probate inventory is in itself no more edifying or informative than simply reading aloud the contents of a supermarket till receipt. Archaeologists are fact-finders, but they must also be interpreters and storytellers, capable of creating meaning, captivating an audience and projecting their ideas across time and space. In the 35 years since the publication of *In Small Things Forgotten*, historical archaeology has out-grown its narrow focus on North American East Coast historic sites and is now a truly global endeavour, being undertaken on every continent. The very best examples of today's historical archaeology create intimate material histories, which expose constructions of race, class and gender, and have the capacity to challenge taken-for-granted knowledge and received political histories.

Deetz and Social Archaeologies

Although still hugely influential, Deetz's view that material culture is 'not culture but its product' and that '[our] world is the product of our thoughts' (Deetz 1977:24) has been criticized in recent years on the grounds that it relegates material culture to a position where it merely *reflects* a separate cognitive realm of culture (Stahl 2010:154). An alternative view takes the stance that 'humans and things cannot artificially be sieved apart, but rather must be treated as *a priori* ontologically mixed' (Webmoor 2007:564; Webmoor and Whitmore 2008).

It is impossible to know what James Deetz would have made of this ontology. It may be that an opportunity to move beyond dualities would have offered new and potentially liberating ways of seeing the world, even for one so steeped in structuralism. Reading between the lines of Deetz's definition of material culture, penned in the 1970s, it is possible to find evidence of some marvellously unconventional thinking. Whereas one of Deetz's most famous definitions of material culture opens in a straightforward way, suggesting that material culture is 'the vast universe of objects used by mankind to cope with the physical world', the definition soon takes an interesting turn:

> Our body itself is part of our physical environment, so that such things as parades, dancing, and all aspects of kinetics—human motion—fit our definition. Nor is the definition limited only to matter in the solid state. Fountains are liquid examples, as are lily ponds, and material that is partly gas includes hot air balloons and neon signs. I have suggested in *Invitation to Archaeology* that even language is part of material culture, a prime example of it in its gaseous state. Words, after all, are air masses shaped by the speech apparatus according to culturally acquired rules (Deetz 1977:24–25).

Deetz's definition of material cultural, as a carrier of information, in some senses almost an avatar, shaped by human action and capable of action, comes close to Alfred Gell's conception of material agency, where materials serve to gather and project a secondary form of human agency (Gell 1992, 1998). The power and effect of artefacts, as described by Deetz, also brings to mind the web of relations proposed by actor-network theory, in which human and non-human actors are intertwined. We can only wonder how he would have responded to the idea of non-human agency, as expressed by Bruno Latour (Latour 1993), or to Ingold's pleas to abandon the 'Cartesian ontology', which artificially divides thought and action (Ingold 2000:165), in favour of a position that seeks to understand how the flows and combinations of materials and actions shape and re-make the world through practice (Ingold 2007).

This volume pays tribute to the foundational work of Henry Glassie and James Deetz, and their conviction that everyday objects can inform us about human thoughts and actions, and that deep insights in human cognition can be gained by comparing and contrasting a range of artifactual, documentary and other sources of evidence. Given their mutual commitment to interrogating material culture for what it can potentially say about different forms of belief, it seems only fitting to extend these insights to the archaeology of faith, hope and charity. Archaeology, like all other disciplines, twists and turns, as theories and methodologies come to prominence, before being questioned and modified or discarded by new generations of scholars. There has never been a 'monolithic corpus of interests among archaeologists', but the diversity of approaches to archaeological reasoning has usually been celebrated rather than bemoaned by practitioners, and upheld as evidence of a vibrant and dynamic field (Webmoor 2007:564).

The Organization of this Volume

The essays in this volume are divided into five sections, and explore different aspects of belief, desire and benevolence. In Part I, *Landscapes, Power and Belief,* Brent Fortenberry and Travis Parno offer a new and challenging interpretation of life in seventeenth-century Jamestown. By closely examining the evidence of four artefacts, which may have formed part of a Catholic rosary, they question whether these finds have the potential to destabilize traditional historical narratives. Working from the premise that such objects were 'props in a complicated and diverse theatre of emerging colonial identity', Fortenberry and Parno argue that a multi-vocal approach is needed to expose the range of possible meanings that artefacts may have held. Four possible interpretations are advanced to explain the possible meanings of the artefacts from a 'variety of angles', which recapture the complexity of life in the early colonial fort. The significance of this chapter is twofold. First, it exposes an unsettling ambiguity, which threatens to challenge the received historical narrative of the colonization of Virginia by English Protestant settlers. And second, it exposes the craft of interpretive archaeology, revealing how archaeologists often implicitly create an 'interpretive hierarchy' in which less favoured interpretations are 'glossed over in favour of a single, polished conclusion' (p. 18).

Evidence from a less well-known colonial context is presented by Timo Ylimaunu, in Chapter 3. When founded in 1621, some 14 years after Jamestown, the town of Tornio, in modern-day northern Finland, was the most northerly town in the world. Tornio was established by the Swedish Crown in an attempt to control the lucrative Lapland trade in salmon and furs. Ylimaunu demonstrates how formal town planning, and the design and siting of churches were used to produce a closely defined social order within the town. Ylimaunu's study extends through time into the early nineteenth century, when Finland became annexed to Russia as the autonomous Grand Duchy of Finland. The power of church architecture continued to be used at that time, projecting the sovereign ideology of the Swedish state on one side of the border, and power of the Russian Emperor, expressed through Russian Orthodox architecture, on the other. Ylimaunu's contribution combines Foucaultian notions of surveillance and social control with carefully assembled empirical evidence. The chapter also, importantly, serves to remind us that the colonization of the New World was only part of a far wider story of seventeenth-century European exploration and colonialism, and opens up a new area of study focusing on the internal colonization of peripheral lands in northern Europe.

Almost forty years ago the Marxist thinker David Harvey argued that geographers could not remain objective in the face of capitalist appropriations of urban space, which served to dispossess workers and create poverty (Harvey 1973). In Chapter 4, David Gadsby investigates the twenty-first-century redevelopment of a city which has featured prominently in Harvey's work—Baltimore, Maryland. Gadsby exposes the tensions that have emerged in the real estate-driven regeneration of post-industrial Baltimore, and argues that the cynical consumption-driven approach to urban renewal encourages the citizens of Baltimore to 'simultaneously celebrate and destroy its industrial past' as the memories of the working-class construction of the city are sanitized, and confined to museums and developer-sanctioned murals. Taking up Harvey's call for 'the right to the city', Gadsby contends that heritage discourses can be reused to revitalize urban communities and that 'the power of archaeology (can) change the way people think, and in turn ... change the way they talk to each other about the past' (p. 53).

Part II of the volume, *Faith in Fashion*, contains a pair of essays which explore clothing and items of personal adornment. Buttons, clasps and low-value items of jewellery are frequently found in archaeological excavations. These items are dutifully described and catalogued by historical archaeologists but, as Mary Beaudry has shown in her study of needle-working paraphernalia (Beaudry 2006), the significance of such small finds is all too often overlooked or taken for granted. Carolyn White takes a trans-Atlantic perspective on clothing and artefacts of personal adornment, comparing excavated assemblages from eighteenth-century domestic sites in Portsmouth, New Hampshire, and London, England. White's chapter takes an innovative approach to colonial entanglements by exploring the relationship *between* the materials and fashions of the colonizing country and the colonized land. Her findings in part reflect the different archaeological techniques used in America and England, with small-scale carefully sieved interventions in New Hampshire producing information on individual households, in contrast to the data from large-scale development-led excavations in the City of London, which provided a more impressionistic view of city life and fashions. Significantly, American Independence is not visible in the New Hampshire archaeological assemblages. It seem that, rather than resorting to homespun items and locally produced goods to reduce reliance on British imports, the residents of Portsmouth continued to follow British fashions and trends into the late-eighteenth century (White 2010).

In Chapter 6, Greig Parker explores fashion and ideas of luxury and decency among Huguenot refugees to London. The Huguenots, Protestants who fled religious persecution in France and the Low Countries between the mid-sixteenth and the early-eighteenth centuries, feature prominently in histories of the metropolis, and are credited with bringing new skills and manufacturing techniques to the city. The stereotypical representation of the Huguenot family portrays silk weavers and merchants in Brick Lane and the East End streets of Spitalfields but, as Parker shows, Huguenot merchants also settled in the west of London. The production and marketing of luxury goods by west London Huguenot merchants promoted a 'Catholic version of French culture', which was characterized by 'opulence, extravagance, and excess' and at odds with their Protestant religious convictions (p. 78). According to Parker, dalliance with luxury goods created tensions in the west London Huguenot community, and exposure to wealthy clients from the middle and upper echelons of English society led to a decline in group cohesion and, ultimately, to the assimilation of the refugees into the 'polite society' of the host community.

In her book *Middle-Class Culture in the 19th century*, Linda Young charted the spread of a transnational 'culture of gentility' to all corners of the British Empire (Young 2002). The promotion of the British Empire's values of Christian faith and respectability are examined in Part III of this volume, *Colonial Entanglements.* Starting in the southern hemisphere, 'as far from the centre of Empire as it was possible to get', Jonathan Prangnell and Kate Quirk lead us through the religious landscape of gold rush Queensland, Australia. Unlike earlier forms of Protestant religion, Methodism eschewed the idea of predestination. The promise of salvation through self-restraint and self-improvement appealed to the ragged collection of hard-rock miners and families who hoped to strike it lucky on the banks of the Burnett River. Excavations within the short-lived late-nineteenth century boomtown of Paradise have revealed porcelain vessels and a ceramic assemblage dominated by the teawares of a 'polite' society. Here was respectability and, judging by the lack of alcohol bottles, temperance amid a devout Methodist congregation. Keeping up appearances clearly mattered in Paradise and, although the majority of the 97 houses identified by the archaeological survey had rubbish middens to the rear, the five houses linked to Methodist households, including the Mission itself, had buried their household refuse in pits, or taken it to the town dump, leading Prangnell and Quirk to comment that 'a concern with order, neatness, cleanliness, and outward appearance' reflected the Methodist missionary ideology (p. 95).

In Chapter 8, Jeff Oliver investigates the complexity of the 'colonial experience' in a detailed a case study from south western British Columbia. Unlike Prangnell and Quirk, Oliver focuses on the impact that colonialism had on indigenous peoples. Drawing upon recent developments in postcolonial theory, Oliver makes the important point that faith in the binary oppositional outcomes of European acculturation *or* indigenous resistance, miss out on the 'hybridized, fragmented and shifting realities' of colonialism (p. 98). The establishment of large hop-growing farms transformed the cultural and agricultural landscapes of the Fraser valley in the years following 1858. The Coast Salish population were dispersed and re-located, and many became wage-labourers in the newly laid-out hop yards. Some, such as 'Billy' Sepass, Chief of the Scowkale Indian reserve, embraced elements of European culture and crafted a new hybridized identity, becoming a successful 'Indian' farmer. At a broader scale, the diverse indigenous communities living in the valley took stock of the physical changes in the landscape that discriminated against them collectively and responded by assuming a new group identity, the 'Stó:lō' ('river people'), which deemphasized older kin-based social formations in favour of emphasizing regional community ties. The new world created by colonialism drew upon European ideas of property, profit and individualism. Rather than seeing this as an entirely negative and one-sided process, Oliver argues that the population of the Fraser valley responded to these alien concepts by devising 'new ways of thinking and acting, new traditions, and new possibilities for getting ahead' (p. 111).

Resistance and responses to social control are explored further in Part IV, *Confinement and Resistance*, this time in twentieth-century contexts. For more than a quarter of a century studies of peasant resistance have been influenced by the work of the Yale anthropologist and social scientist, James C. Scott. In *Domination and the Arts of Resistance* (Scott 1990), Scott devised the term 'hidden transcript' to describe spoken or enacted critiques of power by subordinate groups, behind the backs of those who have power over them. In Chapter 9, Gilly Carr makes use of this idea in her study of resistance and the V-sign campaign in Channel Islander German internment camps during World War II. Following the BBC's 1941 'V-for-Victory' campaign, which encouraged civilians in the Nazi-occupied territories of Europe to adopt symbolic forms of resistance to boost morale, the use of improvised 'V' signs proliferated in the Channel Islands. In an extraordinary account of everyday resistance in the face of a substantial occupying garrison in Guernsey, Carr describes the tracing of letter 'V's on dusty windows, the dropping of V-shaped pieces of paper on roads, and the wearing of V-sign badges, concealed on the underside of jacket lapels. In 1942 and 1943, some 2,200 men, women and children were deported from the islands and were confined as potential future hostages in civilian internment camps in southern Germany. Covert forms of resistance continued in the camps and took new directions. Under the duress of constant scrutiny by camp guards, internees used their bodies to enact 'V' signs, through hand gestures, or in at least one case, through the deliberate trimming of a beard and moustache into a V. As the war progressed, attempts to fashion 'V-for-Victory' signs made increasingly audacious use of the metal tins, parcel string, cellophane and cardboard packaging, which entered the camps through the delivery of Red Cross parcels, enabling a 'subtle language of resistance to internment' (p. 129).

A no less shameful World War II 'relocation', this time of 120,000 Japanese Americans by the US government, occurred on the West Coast of the United States in 1942. Jeffery Burton describes the incarceration of 10,000 Japanese Americans in the make-shift Manzanar camp, located in the high desert east of the Sierra Nevada in California. In this case the perceived threat of insurgency and/or sabotage by Japanese Americans in the months following Pearl Harbor led to the detention of whole families, many of whom were American citizens, without charge or trial. Burton describes recent archaeological work at the camp by the National Park Service, which has helped to create a National Historic Site. Although the massive watch towers and barbed-wire fences that once surrounded the camp have long since disappeared, the features surveyed by Burton convey an eerie 'remembrance of desolation and exile' (p. 137). At one level the recovery of artefacts that illustrate the mundane materiality of daily life in the camp, such as the thick military-style dining plates and large containers for institutional food, has helped to disprove the local myth that the camp had been a well-provided for 'holiday resort.' But more importantly, the physical traces of activities, games and contributions to the war effort, such as the making of camouflage nets, attest cultural resilience. The most remarkable imprints of faith and hope may be found in the numerous internee-built ornamental landscapes of rock-alignments, gardens and ponds, which reflect undiminished 'Japanese ideals of order, beauty, and harmony' (p. 141).

In Chapter 11, Laura McAtackney explores a more recent, but no less infamous place of confinement, the Long Kesh/Maze prison in Northern Ireland. This prison was in operation for thirty years from 1971, and was central to attempts by the British and Northern Ireland governments to control civil conflict by confining the perpetrators of violence during the bloody years of 'The Troubles'. McAtackney's essay sets out to examine how the abandoned site has evolved from 'a place associated with injustice and death to a potential symbol of hope' (p. 147). In the years since the signing of the Good Friday Agreement in 1998, many of the more prominent buildings and structures associated with the state security infrastructure have been demolished or removed. As regeneration proceeds, however, there has been a growing 'public ambivalence' towards the hasty removal of sites associated with the conflict, and a belief in some quarters that this difficult heritage needs to be more properly addressed. Focusing on the Hunger Strikes of 1981, which left ten Republican prisoners dead after an orchestrated campaign of defiance, McAtackney reveals how the materiality of commemoration spread through west Belfast, from wall murals of Bobby Sands and the other dead men, to the nailing of small wooden 'H's with 1981 written on them to trees, referring to the notorious 'H Block' at the prison. Although still heavily contested, with attitudes divided along sectarian lines, the hospital site within the prison has nevertheless undergone a symbolic transformation from a functioning medical installation to a sacred site. Perhaps the most remarkable aspect of this transformation has been the piece-meal removal of wire springs from 'Bobby Sand's' metal-framed hospital bed by visitors to the site, who have been keen to acquire powerful and potentially subversive 'sacred artefacts' with a tangible link to the Irish Republican martyr.

The final section of this book, Part V, considers the archaeology of *Death and Remembrance,* a subject which featured prominently in the work of James Deetz. Harold Mytum, an archaeologist trained as a Reader in the Anglican tradition, offers an overview of the links between theology and practice in commemorative traditions, suggesting that when combined with other sources of evidence the study of memorials can reveal shifting trends in popular faith. Mytum draws upon his extensive experience of graveyard survey to offer a range of detailed case studies, from eighteenth- and nineteenth-century sites in New England, Britain and Ireland. Mytum begins by making the important point that in an age imbued with Christian faith, grave monuments were far more than a 'postscript to life' and 'were active in providing exemplars of lives lived and evidence of faith in action' (p. 162). Fundamental differences are revealed between Protestant graves, which celebrated the persona of the deceased and warned the living of a predestined judgement to come, and Catholic graves, which were more active localities and encouraged visitors to pray for the soul of the deceased. Mytum goes on to explore shifts in the selection of symbols and biblical texts for inclusion on gravestones. In all of the areas studied, symbols on gravestones were invariably concerned with the process of judgement and redemption. The precise form of individual monuments, however, was determined by a range of historically contingent factors, such as the dominant local theological tradition, carver preference, the social and economic status of the deceased, and their ethnic origins and political affiliations.

In Chapter 13, Sam Walls surveys the changing memories and meanings of World War I, as expressed through public commemorations and memorials in the city of Exeter, Devon. Walls departs from the conventional approach to studying war memorials, which often focuses upon individual monuments or particular types of monument, and provides a view of the wider commemorative landscape and the interactions between contemporary and successive war memorials. This richly contextual approach uses documentary and iconographic information to expose the tensions and competing interests of the various committees charged with creating monuments for the county, and the city in the post-war period. All of the monuments to the Fallen of World War I in Exeter attempted to avoid the mistakes of the South African War Memorial, which had been unveiled within the cathedral in 1903, annoying some non-Anglicans, but their strategies differed. After initial attempts to commemorate the war by renovating the cathedral cloister or adding a new wing the hospital proved unpopular, the Devon War Memorial Cross was proposed by Lord Fortescue, the Lord-Lieutenant of the county. This monument was designed by Sir Edwin Lutyens, carved from specially quarried Dartmoor granite, and was unveiled by the Prince of Wales. In contrast, the Exeter and Devon War Memorial, promoted by the Mayor of Exeter, was an elaborate octagonal column supporting four seated figures, and 'Victory' trampling a dragon and holding a laurel wreath to the heavens. This monument was designed by John Angel, a local architect, and was far more closely linked to the history of the town, including a town crest, and a ship's motto. It was also carefully sited close to Exeter Castle and the City wall, creating a link to earlier conflicts.

Together, the essays in this volume show that Henry Glassie and James Deetz were correct to suggest that the thoughts and deeds that shape our daily lives can be recovered by archaeology. This ability to recover evidence of faith, hope and charity through material remains is not time or period specific. Nevertheless, it can be said, and said with some confidence, that the richness and variety of evidence available to historical archaeologists far exceeds the relative paucity of evidence surviving from more distant periods. Rather than being seen as a hindrance, this should encourage historical archaeologists to engage more productively with the study of cognition. This volume does not attempt to provide a straightforward method for recovering evidence of thought processes. In working through the various archaeological examples of faith, hope and charity, which have been presented by the authors, however, it does implore us to open our minds to all possibilities. At one level this may mean stepping back from our modern rational habit of drawing distinctions between the natural and the supernatural, or the practical and the 'ritual' (Brück 1999). At another, it means that we need to invest far more effort into understanding the very basic question of what it means to be human.

Bibliography

Beaudry, M.C. (2006) *Findings: The Material Culture of Needlework and Sewing*. New Haven, CT: Yale University Press.

Binford, S.R. and Binford, L.R. (1968) *New Perspectives in Archaeology*. Chicago: Aldine Publishing House.

Brück, J. (1999) Ritual and rationality: Some problems of interpretation in European Archaeology. *European Journal of Archaeology* 2 (3): 313–344.

Deetz, J.F. and Dethlefsen, E.S. (1967) Death's head, cherub, urn and willow. *Natural History* 76 (3): 29–37.

Deetz, J.F. (1977) *In Small Things Forgotten: An Archaeology of Early American Life*. Garden City, NY: Anchor Books.

Deetz, J.F. (1994) Foreword. In A.E. Yentsch, *A Chesapeake Family and Their Slaves: A Study in Historical Archaeology*, xviii–xx. Cambridge: Cambridge University Press.

Gell, A. (1992) The technology of enchantment and the enchantment of technology. In A.

Gell (1998) *Art and Agency: An Anthropology Theory*. Oxford: Clarendon Press.

Glassie, H. (1975) *Folk Housing in Middle Virginia: A Structural Analysis of Historic Artifacts*. Knoxville, TN: University of Tennessee Press.

Harvey, D. (1973) *Social Justice and the City*. London: Edward Arnold.

Hawkes, C. (1954) Archeological theory and method: Some suggestions from the Old World. *American Anthropologist* 56 (2): 155–168.

Ingold, T. (2000) Making culture and weaving the world. In P. M. Graves-Brown (ed.) *Matter, Materiality, and Modern Culture*, 50–71. London: Routledge.

Ingold, T. (2007) Materials against materiality. *Archaeological Dialogues* 14 (1): 1–16.

Latour, B. (1993) *We Have Never Been Modern* (trans. C. Porter). Cambridge, MA: Harvard University Press.

Renfrew, C. (1973) *Before Civilization*. London: Penguin.

Scott, J.C. (1990) *Domination and the Arts of Resistance*. New Haven, CT; London: Yale University Press.

South, S. (1977) *Method and Theory in Historical Archaeology*. New York: Academic Press.

Stahl, A.B. (2010) Material histories. In D. Hicks and M. Beaudry (eds.) *The Oxford Handbook of Material Culture Studies*, 150–172. Oxford: Oxford University Press.

Taylor, W. (1948) *A Study of Archaeology*. Washington, DC: American Anthropological Association (American Anthropological Association Memoir 69).

Watson, P.J., LeBlanc, S.A. and Redman, C.L. (1971) *Explanation in Archeology: An Explicitly Scientific Approach*. New York: Columbia University Press.

Webmoor, C. (2007) What about 'one more turn after the social' in archaeological reasoning? Taking things seriously. *World Archaeology* 39 (4): 563–578.

Webmoor, T. and Whitmore, C. (2008) Things are us! A commentary on human/things relations under the banner of a 'social' archaeology. *Norwegian Archaeological Review* 41 (1): 53–70.

White, C. (2010) 'Beholden to foreign countries': Trade and clothing in Portsmouth, New Hampshire. In C.D. Dillan and C.L. White (eds.) *Trade and Exchange: Archaeological Studies from Prehistory and History*, 113–128. New York, Dordrecht, Heidelberg, London: Springer.

Wilkie, L. (2005) Inessential archaeologies: problems of exclusion in Americanist archaeological thought. *World Archaeology* 37: 337–351.

Yentsch, A.E. and Beaudry, M.C. (2001) American material culture in mind, thought, and deed. In I. Hodder (ed.) *Archaeological Theory Today*, 214–240. Cambridge: Polity Press.

Young, L. (2002) *Middle-Class Culture in the 19th Century: America, Australia and Britain*. New York, NY: Palgrave Macmillan.

Part I

Landscapes, Power and Belief

2 Catholic Artefacts in a Protestant Landscape: A Multi-Vocal Approach to the Religiosity of Jamestown's Colonists

Travis G. Parno and Brent Fortenberry

Four Artefacts: A Snapshot

In 1997 Jamestown Rediscovery Project archaeologists uncovered a lead crucifix, a small brass religious medallion and two jet beads, all objects generally associated with Catholic rosary use (see Figure 2.1). The cast lead crucifix (912-JR) was found in two pieces in Pit 3, a feature contained in the southeast bulwark of the fort. The crucifix's proportions are extremely vertically skewed: it measures approximately 61mm high and only 12.5mm wide. The upper portion shows the figure of Christ hanging beneath a horizontal plaque, which likely held the 'INRI' inscription, an abbreviation of 'Iesvs Nazarenvs Rex Ivdaeorum' or 'Jesus of Nazareth, King of the Jews'. Beneath Christ, a woman, likely Mary, kneels in prayer. At the base of the crucifix rests a skull and crossed bones, also known as the 'death's head', a symbol of the eternal life promised by Christ's crucifixion. The crucifix is not equipped with a hole for the purpose of stringing on a rope or chain and no clear means of attachment can be found on the back of the piece. Crucifixes were, however, often used as tokens of pious vigilance and placed in one's hat, clothing, or simply stashed away in a pocket as a private devotion. Such items were also commonly attached to the fronts of Bibles or collection boxes (Luccketti and Straube 1998:22).

The brass oval medallion (609-JR) and the two jet rosary beads (516-JR and 504-JR) were found in plough-soil contexts. The medallion measures approximately 9mm across and 10mm high with a 5mm hanging loop from which the artefact can be suspended. One side of the icon portrays the image of Jesus' head, while on the reverse the image of Mary's head appears. The rosary beads are oval in shape and are multi-faceted. Both are about 12mm vertically (along the bore) and about 11mm in diameter (Luccketti and Straube 1998:22–23).

Beginnings

While seemingly of little consequence given the breadth of material culture recovered from James Fort, these artefacts' lack of abundance and size hides their true nature;

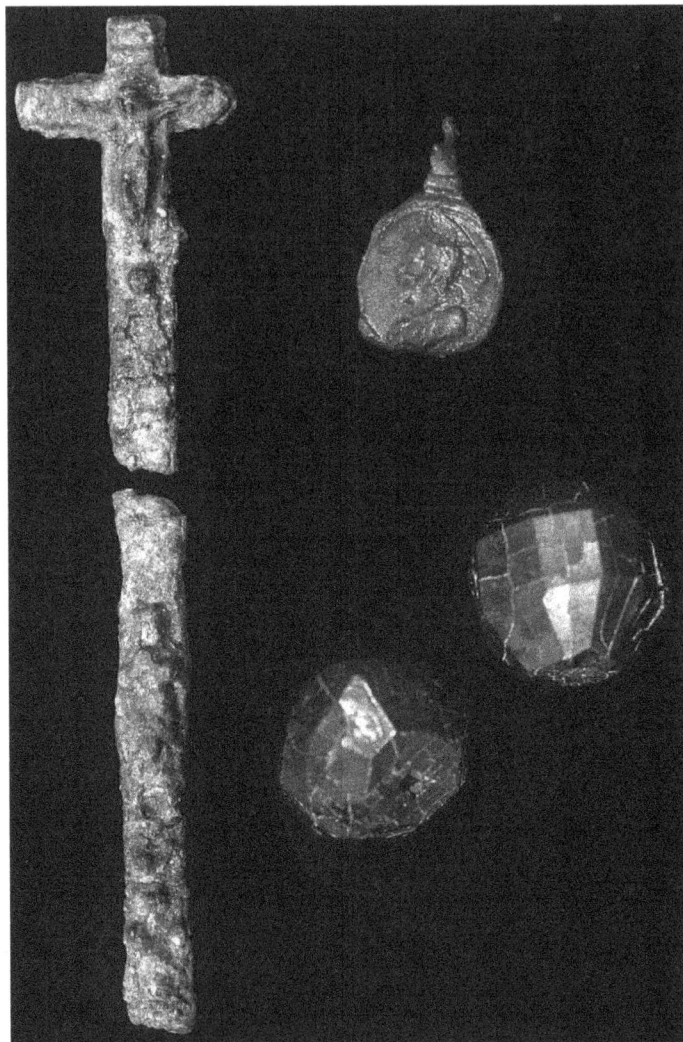

Figure 2.1   A lead crucifix, brass medallion, and two jet rosary beads discovered at James Fort in 1997 (courtesy of Preservation Virginia).

there is little doubt these objects were props in a complicated and diverse theatre of emerging colonial identity. Faced with the fires of political and religious conflict that were burning in seventeenth-century Europe, many intrepid colonists ventured forth to the fringes of the known world. Interpretations of the material culture left behind by these colonial movements, as with all components of archaeology, often prove frustrating and inconclusive. While historical events are generally documented in extensive detail, disconnects often exist between the written word and lived experiences. In recognition of this reality, and the polyvalent nature of meaning and identity, we argue that a multi-vocal approach is necessary in any attempt to access these entangled moments. Moreover, we recognize that due to the dialogical nature of fieldwork, interpretations and publications, the possibilities of the past are only bound by our own imaginations and interactions (after Joyce 2002).

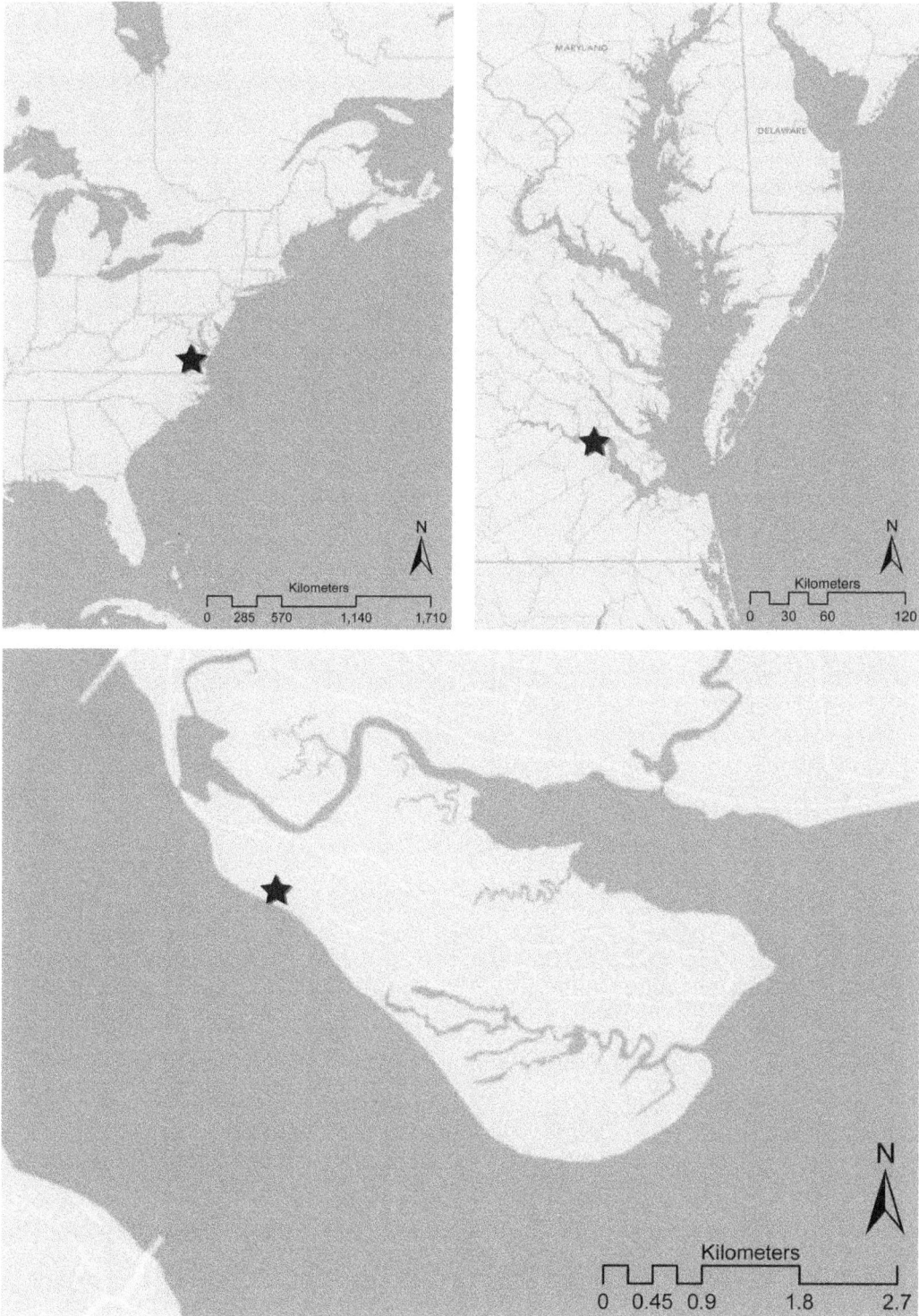

Figure 2.2   The location of James Fort (indicated by the star) at three scales: eastern seaboard of the United States (top left), Chesapeake Bay (top right), and Jamestown Island (bottom) (image by authors).

The notion that objects possessed multiple meanings has edged its way into the archaeological vernacular (see further Loren and Beaudry 2006). Nonetheless, the painstaking consideration of each possible narrative during the interpretive process is typically glossed over in favour of a single, polished conclusion. This immediately establishes an interpretive hierarchy which positions the archaeologist, providing the 'answer,' and the reader, receiving the 'answer,' at odds, thus illustrating one of archaeology's greatest challenges: trust. We must trust the archaeologist to present the most comprehensive and accurate story. While in many cases we might yearn for a nice, neat portrait of history, the past, like the present, was necessarily messy, complex, and often difficult to articulate. So too is the process of archaeological interpretation. Joyce highlights the need for disclosure of the push and pull elicited by fervent internal debates and scholarly sparring over then late-night pints (2002:58). These thoughts culminate in one simple question: if the past has multiple meanings then why not present them?

In this spirit our discussion returns to the four small artefacts mentioned above. What possible roles did they play in the constellation of life at James Fort? If the settlement was based on the recently adopted state religion of Anglicanism, then how were these 'illegal' artefacts tolerated? Are these objects tangible evidence of Catholicism at Jamestown? Or were they instead intended as resources for exchange with native populations? Perhaps these small finds lost their religiosity during the transition across the Atlantic and were folded into a new colonial understanding of décor and personal adornment. In all likelihood, the historic conditions were a much more complex combination of these and other meanings. It is for this reason that we will present a collection of interpretations from a variety of angles in an attempt to recapture the multitude of political, economic and religious aspects of colonial life at Jamestown.

England's Changing Religious Landscape

In the century prior to the English settlement of Jamestown, Europe was embroiled in religious controversy and struggles of faith. The Protestant Reformation, built on the foundation of religious scholars such as John Wycliffe, John Hus and John Calvin, and catalysed by the posting of Martin Luther's *Ninety-Five Theses* on 31 October 1517, blazed through Europe, fuelled by widespread disgust with the crumbling Catholic Church. The ensuing centuries witnessed constant struggles between the monarchs of Europe and the Roman papacy.

In England power shifted in a new direction. When King Henry VIII's demand for an annulment of his marriage to Catherine of Aragon was rejected, the king placed himself at the head of the state-established Church of England, thereby creating the first Anglican Church. This break from the church was essentially a political action as Henry continued to enforce laws requiring the observance of many Catholic practices and beliefs, going so far as to burn many Lutherans at the stake. This politicized religiosity was a recurring theme among the English monarchy throughout the sixteenth century.

Edward VI's rise to power ushered in a period of national Protestantism, overturning many of the laws upheld by Henry, but Mary I's bloody reign reversed these policies with her vicious attempts to restore Catholicism as the state religion. Queen Elizabeth I's ascension to the throne in 1558 brought about another shift, making Protestantism the national religious standard.

Despite her devotion to the state religion, Elizabeth's cloak of Protestantism was one that was never worn constantly or completely. Her reign was hailed as a new religious era by the supporters of the Church of England, but Elizabeth's political conservatism prevented her from making many of the sweeping changes desired by her Protestant constituents (Haigh 1998:28–30). She faced pressure from Protestant radicals in the House of Commons to abolish certain remnants of Catholic practice, such as bowing at the name of Jesus, making the sign of the cross at baptism, and wearing a ring in the marriage ceremony (Brigden 2000:242). But it was not the influence of the Commons with which Elizabeth was concerned; it was the votes of Catholic nobles in the House of Lords that caused her political hand to waver (Haigh 1998:31). This imbalance manifested itself in the swinging pendulum of royal decrees made throughout her reign as Elizabeth worked to garner support from both religious groups. Thus, despite the establishment of the Anglicanism as the state religion, the queen was, as Haigh has written, 'soft on Catholics' (1998:36).

On 24 March 1603, Queen Elizabeth died and James I was declared king of England. The departed queen left in her wake a country in religious and political turmoil and one greatly in need of reform. James met his country's crisis with tact and flexibility. He went to great pains to distinguish between peaceful Catholics and those who were seen as insurrectionists. Throughout his reign, he allowed the Catholic minority to worship in private and increase slightly in numbers while enacting various anti-Catholic laws that were not severely enforced (Coward 1980:109–111).

The lack of an exhaustive anti-Catholic policy allowed the illegal religion to survive, and even prosper, in what Hill has termed the 'dark corners of the land' (1975:3–47). These were places in which Anglican parishes were not as strong and few Protestant ministers practised. Additionally, with the advent of the Jesuit ministry, Catholic Reformers pushed for a private religiosity through the medium of the rosary. They identified the local practices of rosary devotion, created a new standard of rosary, and distributed it to the English Catholics in the form of the Society of the Rosary. Outlined in the form of a handbook, the organization provided a ritualistic practice that could be normalized, placed at the heart of daily devotion, and controlled by the Jesuits (Dillon 2003:452–463). The accessibility and adaptability of the Catholic religion in England allowed it to persevere into the seventeenth century and onward.

New World Religiosity at James Fort

It is quite clear from this brief outline that the English religious landscape was by no means dichotomous; rather, the line between prescription and enactment was constantly being renegotiated. There is little doubt that such an environment of uncertainty had a great influence on the religious outlook of the Jamestown colonists. With the funding of the Virginia Company of London and the blessing of King James I, the colonists set sail from England in search of the New World. In May of 1607, after nearly four and a half months at sea, they reached the east coast of North America. By June a proper palisaded fort was completed, offering the colonists a semi-impermeable barrier from the unforgiving surrounding environment. Throughout the early years of the colony a mixed group of councilmen, most of whom desired to cement their own influence and agenda on the affairs of the fort, governed Jamestown and its residents (Kelso 2006:9–27).

Of specific significance to this discussion are the rumours surrounding the religious affiliation of Edward Maria Wingfield, the first president of the council at Jamestown. Wingfield was an alleged Catholic or Catholic sympathizer. Many of these charges related to Wingfield's lineage. His father, Thomas-Maria Wingfield, was an open Catholic who served as Huntingdonshire's parliamentary representative during the reigns of Edward VI and Mary (see Morgan 2011:95). Although Edward Wingfield possessed all the trappings of nobility, he apparently never acquired the skills required to lead a fledgling colony. Following his removal from office as council president on the 10 September 1607, Wingfield drafted a letter of apology to the Council of Virginia entitled 'A Discourse of Virginia' (Haile 1998:183–201). In his missive, he mentions the charges against him—that he 'combined with the Spaniards to the destruction of the colony' and that he was 'an atheist' because he 'carried not a Bible' (Haile 1998:197). The disgraced Wingfield continues on in his own defence, writing that although he admired 'any noble virtue and prowess' in Spanish society, he had always 'distrusted and disliked their neighbourhood' (Haile 1998:198). Lastly, Wingfield claims that he certainly remembered packing a Bible in his trunk and it must have been 'so embezzled or mislaid' by his servants (Haile 1998:198).

This series of accusations is easily linked to the negative perceptions of Wingfield's alleged Catholicism—his supposed union with, and open admiration of, the Spanish Catholics and his atheism. One of the founding principles of Protestantism was the interpretive power of the Bible, so it naturally became one of their strongest symbols. To not carry, read, or readily be able to produce a copy of the Bible was counter to the Protestant ideal. Thus Wingfield's 'Protestantism', sans Bible, would have been viewed with some scepticism. While there was no specific statute in the Council's rules regarding the embrace of Catholicism in the New World, Wingfield was regarded as socially flawed despite his noble roots.

By combing through the documentary record of James Fort, we may catch a glimpse into the complex religious atmosphere of the developing colony. This brief entre likely does not, however, give us a picture that is by any means complete. An examination of the archaeological remains presented above, in light of the historical context of the Jamestown expedition, can begin to clarify the intricacies of everyday religious observance. As we have stated, this is an inherently difficult process that requires the archaeologist to travel down a series of interpretive paths and switchbacks, always expected to be moving towards some final interpretive road. It is for this reason that we now offer an assortment of interpretations in the hopes that from somewhere amongst the four readings presented, a viable conclusion may be drawn. These interpretive forays should not be considered fixed or mutually exclusive; rather, there is a distinct possibility that an intermingling of these narratives actually occurred. This, nonetheless, is for each individual reader to decide.

Four Interpretations: A Mosaic

Trade Goods

Our first interpretation is anchored by two contentions. First, the Catholic artefacts found at Jamestown are not indicative of a Catholic presence in the fort. Second, non-Catholics recognized the economic value of religious items, such as rosary beads and crucifixes, and utilized them as trade goods with the local indigenous populations (see Rubertone 2000 for a discussion of the archaeology of European/Native American trade goods). The breadth of European-to-Native American bead exchange practices does not need to be recited here; suffice it to say that the bead trade began very early in the European migration across the Atlantic World and in many contexts there are accounts of local indigenous populations actively trading commodities for beads and other means of bodily adornment. The real question is whether or not former religious symbols would have been utilized in such a way. In the case of James Fort, it could be argued that Protestant disdain for Catholic dogma ran so deep that Anglican colonists actively traded away images of Christ and Catholic tokens of worship to non-Christian individuals as a means of rejecting or distancing themselves from the despised iconography.

This sentiment is not without precedent. Rinehart, working at Fort Michilimackinac, uncovered evidence of an active crucifix trade between English soldiers and local native populations (1990). According to Rinehart, the soldiers who settled this former Jesuit fortification had little problem using Catholic iconography as a trade good, casting extensive numbers of identical silver crucifixes. We are left to wonder if perhaps the soldiers were capitalizing on an interest in metal icons planted amongst the surrounding Native American populations by the proselytizing Jesuits. It stands to reason that a similar desire for such tokens existed in the native groups surrounding the Jamestown area. For instance, Jesuit missionaries from Ajacan, the sixteenth-century Spanish outpost located somewhere in the area of the York and James rivers, gifted religious goods to the local Algonquians in an attempt to increase native interest in Christianity (Mallios 2004:137). While their efforts were strictly ministerial in nature, they did inject a supply of Catholic artefacts into the Chesapeake native populations, and thus may have provided an impetus for later English-native exchange systems.

The presence of Catholic small finds as players on an economic stage also makes sense in terms of sheer practicality. As alluded to previously, Catholicism and its associated images were outlawed during this time in England. What better way to rid the English landscape of Catholic images than to bring them to the New World and trade them out of the English marketplace? The seemingly endless bounds of new territory would surely have represented a vast area over which to scatter the unwanted symbols of an illegal religion. While this interpretation might seem plausible at a cursory glance, it does not account for reuse of these items within English society. Religious artefacts tended to be constructed out of recyclable materials, such as the lead and brass used to construct the crucifix and medallion presented above. A simple way to erase the icons' Catholic symbolism would be to melt them down for alternative uses. Naturally, it is difficult to discern whether or not there was some sort of profane status imbued on the forbidden objects that negated their repeated use, even in another form, but this seems unlikely when one considers that the value of Christian religious icons lie not in their materials but in their representative qualities.

Interpreting James Fort's Catholic artefacts as articles of economic exchange may represent a fruitful exercise, but we should be cautious not to employ this line of reasoning in a sweeping manner. Failure to fully scrutinize the contextual circumstances in which English-native exchange occurred can lead to a simplistic, universal reading of otherwise unexplainable objects as trade goods. Much like the Jesuits of the Ajacan mission, perhaps Jamestown's colonists initially offered the religious icons as a means of Christianizing the native populations, but later resorted to exchanging Catholic tokens for supplements to their quickly dwindling food supply. Whatever the case, we merely wish to warn against latching on to one interpretation and applying it across the board. It is much more likely that the Catholic artefacts represent a combination of interpretations and meanings that were dynamic and fluid to those who encountered them.

Personal Adornment

Another possible narrative situates the four artefacts as objects of personal adornment and fashion. This may seem counterintuitive if a strict religious dichotomy is prescribed to this context. We again argue that such an opposition is far too rigid in its attempt to structure not only religious, but colonial ideologies in the post-Reformation era. An atmosphere of religious uncertainty fostered by the newly formed Anglican Church would have been even more palpable for the colonists who were geographically cut-off from the mainstream English culture. This caveat further supports the idea posited here and elsewhere that the colonial moment is a negotiation between what is prescribed and what is practiced. With this in mind, it doesn't seem too implausible to argue that Catholic artefacts could have been worn in a public manner by Protestants who contributed to and were instrumental in the formation of a colonial fashion paradigm.

This concept of counter-hegemonic adornment has been explored by Loren in her investigations of European and Native American interactions in French colonial endeavours in the New World (Loren 2001, 2003, 2007; Fisher and Loren 2003; Loren and Beaudry 2006). Through material gleaned from a variety of Eastern Woodland contexts, she has problematized traditional interpretations that cite European bodily adornment in native contexts as evidence of enculturation, arguing that such artefacts are illustrative of the dialogical relationship that existed in many colonial situations, despite the inherent differences in each group's notions of bodily adornment.

Loren argues that control over the body was central to colonial power and, in the New World context, native nakedness was diametrically opposed to European ideas of civility and modesty (Loren 2001:173). The French colonists therefore often felt obligated to impress their Christian *doxa* on the local populations, both as a moral responsibility and as a desire to exercise control through embodied ideological means. It was never, however, as simple as a mere translation of European standards onto an inert native population. In the face of this established understanding, Loren has produced significant evidence for native influence on European means of dress and adornment. This was often interlaced with social processes of trade interaction and sexual relations between French men and native women due to the lack of women in early colonial contexts (Loren 2003:233). Established rules existed that governed the dress of French citizens based on their social standings, but these were often reinterpreted or spurned as French goods entered colonial trade networks and were adopted by native populations, and vice versa (Loren 2003:234).

As Loren has shown, colonial situations enable novel conceptions of selfhood and personal adornment to be constructed, and this could be the case with the artefacts discovered at James Fort. Perhaps the crucifix and rosary parts shed most of their religious connotations and were appropriated into the colonial fashion scheme. Moreover, this narrative could be coupled with another presented in this discussion, that of trade. Perhaps the colonists who brought these Catholic artefacts for trade with the native populations decided that they were pleasing enough to the eye that they themselves wished to use them as objects of personal adornment. Because the artefacts were intended to be employed as trade goods, they were de-contextualized from any restrictive religious connotations.

This narrative, while absent from the Jamestown documentary record and ethereal enough to elude significant archaeological support, serves as a useful reminder for all researchers when approaching interpretations. Far too often we attempt to discern the 'deep-meaning' of artefacts, and perhaps overlook more simplistic answers. Aesthetics are a powerful category for the human subject. While it might not be the foremost aspect of choice, we generally do not select that which does not appeal to us. Using Catholic artefacts as a way of self-fashioning for aesthetic as opposed to religious reasons would be something that has little or no documentation in either the historical or archaeological record, and thus could represent a newly realized, although difficult to support, colonial fashion fad.

Open Catholicism

The notion that James Fort's religious artefacts represent some sort of anomaly assumes the rigidity of the prescribed martial law doctrine of 1610. One cannot, however, escape the possibility that this idealized prescription was not enacted. As we have attempted to illustrate, Jamestown was a liminal space (liminality, in this case, is defined by the colony's distance from the cultural and ideological centres of England) and as such, provided a stage on which new socio-religious frameworks could be enacted (for a discussion of liminality see Turner 1995). It is also quite evident that despite its royal condemnation, Catholicism was by no means completely eradicated from England's soil. As her monarchs wrestled with Post-Reformation dissention in the homeland, it does not seem too far-fetched to presume that some of that resistance might have made its way across the Atlantic. At that point, would it have been detrimental to the colony if an individual was allowed to practice Catholic rituals whilst no one was around?

This question points to a disconnect between the prescribed and the enacted. The governors of the colony (Gates and Dale) ostensibly wanted to reform the failing colony, but what would have been the effect of forcing individuals to renounce their religion and take up Anglicanism? In the face of the colony's rapid deterioration, could the colonial leaders have afforded the time and energy necessary to condemn religious practices while the walls literally crumbled around them? Could these prescriptions have been overlooked for Catholics in order to elevate morale? Further, one cannot ignore the public declarations of Catholicism present in letters sent back to England. One is reminded of the uncertainty surrounding Wingfield, as it is outlined above. Both archaeological and documentary evidence suggest the possibility of a Catholic presence at James Fort. While some pieces of evidence proclaim the fort was a bastion for Anglicanism in the New World, there is the chance that this was not actually the case.

Of course, the probability that open Catholicism was permitted is not very great. Although we have presented it as possibility, supported by contemporary attitudes in England and the presence of Catholic artefacts in the archaeological record, this does not change the fact that Catholicism was a legally forbidden practice. James Fort was indeed a liminal space, especially during the period of martial law (see below), but even at this time, the superiority of the Church of England was enforced within the colony. In the *Laws Divine, Moral, and Martial*, drawn up by the colony's secretary, William Strachey, colonial ministers were ordered to preach at least twice a week and colonists who refuse to take an 'oath of supremacy' to the monarchy and the Church of England were threatened with death (Haile 1998:27–33). Even the suspicion of Catholicism led to social outcasting, as was the case of Wingfield, who was forcibly removed from office, and Captain George Kendall, a suspected Catholic who was executed for supposedly spying for the Spanish (Haile 1998:48). While we have evidence of extant Catholicism in England at the time, much of the practice was limited to the assumed religiosity of the nobility, who were essentially untouchable, and the private worship of those in the 'dark corners of the land'.

To this point, we have discussed the interpretation of overt Catholicism as an exclusively English phenomenon, but it should also be mentioned that the artefacts could have resulted from the presence of non-English Catholics at James Fort. For example, between 1611 and 1614, the fort held several French and Spanish prisoners.

In 1613, Samuel Argall, the pilot of Virginia, and his men raided the French Jesuit settlement of Saint Sauveur in Maine and carried their Catholic prisoners back to Jamestown (Haile 1998:43). Evidence from James Fort also states that Don Diego de Molina, a Spanish spy, was detained at the site for at least three years during which time he carried on illicit correspondence with the Spanish government (Haile 1998:49). Perhaps these captives carried rosaries and devotional items that eventually made their way into the archaeological record at Jamestown.

'Closet Catholics'

Much like the previous assessment of the religious artefacts as indicative of openly practising Catholics, an interpretation arguing for private Catholicism at James Fort strikes at the heart of issues that question the relation between sociocultural prescription and practised enactment. The crux of this argument is simple. Individuals living within the confines of James Fort practised some form of the Catholic faith outside of the view of their peers and authorities. The objects recovered are material manifestations of this practice. As we outlined above, the precepts of the Society of the Rosary and other individually based Catholic rituals allowed for simple and yet effective worship practices out of the public eye. If these were methods employed by Catholics in England during the same time, it would seem reasonable to suppose that a similar praxis occurred at Jamestown. Separation from Anglican hegemony is another factor that further contributes to this interpretation. In other words, being thousands of miles away from England might have alleviated the paranoia of these clandestine practices. In order to best clarify the conditions in which private Catholicism could have functioned, we must look deeper into the historical and archaeological record of James Fort.

First, one must look to the period of martial law which followed the infamous 'starving time' as an introduction to what was one of the most dictatorial periods in the fort's history. Beginning in 1610, the rule of Gates, Dale, and later De La Warre ushered in a new period for Jamestown. While the fortunes of the colony during the period from 1607–1609 were mediocre, if not god-forsaken, at best, the starving time became the catalyst for a renewed discipline and piety in Virginia. Predicated on the oath of supremacy, the period of martial law established conditions which, if taken at face value, would have created a hostile environment to any detected Catholic presence or practice within the fort. One wonders why Dale required everyone to swear allegiance to the Anglican Church in the first place? Could this act have been set off by Catholic practices during the early months of his arrival? This atmosphere, it seems, would have forced any would-be devotee of the rosary to seek a secluded arena in which to practice his religion. Such spaces of privacy might have been difficult to find. The fort itself was a demarcated place and it is unlikely that one would be so brave as to venture into the wilderness to recite the Lord's Prayer or a Hail Mary. Nonetheless, the archaeology at James Fort points to one possibility for seclusion within the confines of the palisade.

Excavated between 2005 and 2006, Structures 172 and 175 (STR 172 and 175) are the largest continuous buildings to be uncovered at James Fort to date. These structures are a significant departure from earlier architectural forms, which featured rudimentary, earthfast construction (Kelso 2006:106–111). STR 172 and 175 have cobble foundations, brick hearths, and masonry, and were likely half-timbered structures that would have stood approximately two and a half stories high (Kelso 2006:109–110). Their long and narrow form is grounded in the English architectural tradition of row and terrace houses. Spatially, it appears that these buildings were subdivided using the classic post-medieval lobby entrance plan, which is also heavily influenced from East Anglian floor plans (see Johnson 1993). When navigating a structure of this type, one enters into a lobby, partitioned by an H-shaped hearth that heats both rooms using a single chimney flue, and can then go either right or left into adjoining rooms. In this way, it would seem that STR 172 and 175 were segmented into individual rooms that were divided by brick hearths. While this authoritative order presented challenges for the secretive Catholic colonists, it is not out of the realm of possibility that these barrack-like rooms, regardless of their day-to-day functions, could have easily served as stages for rituals in the absence of other inhabitants. Thus the modular nature of the architecture was advantageous in the fact that, for brief moments, it presented a secluded sphere in which one could quickly evoke the Catholic mass.

Concluding Remarks

We have presented an ensemble of possible interpretations selected from the myriad potential understandings of the James Fort religious landscape. While this is an ostensibly clever format, what can it actually do for us? What difference or impact can it provide for archaeological practice and interpretation? This multi-vocal perspective is in many ways an unveiling of the interpretive process (as discussed above). Throughout the archaeological process, the possible understandings of particular contexts are teased out thorough a dialogical set of relations between the researcher and the material culture. By exploring the constellation of possibilities, the readers will be able to choose for themselves the story they find most appropriate.

Taking our own advice, we too have formulated an opinion on this matter. We believe the current body of evidence points to the existence of private Catholicism at James Fort. Given the religious environment in England at the time, which promoted a state religion of Anglicanism while tacitly permitting an underground minority of Catholics to worship, there is little reason to think that such a situation could not have existed within the confines of James Fort. Of course, as the Jamestown Rediscovery Project continues to uncover thousands and thousands of artefacts with each passing year, we will hopefully discover new stories to contribute to the fascinating narrative of James Fort.

Bibliography

Brigden, S. (2000) *New Worlds, Lost Worlds: The Rule of the Tudors, 1485–1603*. New York: Viking.

Coward, B. (1980) *The Stuart Age: A History of England, 1603–1714*. London: Longman.

Dillon, A. (2003) Praying by number: The confraternity of the rosary and the English Catholic community, *c.*1580–1700. *History* 88 (291): 451–71.

Fisher, G. and Loren D.D. (2003) Introduction: Embodying identity in archaeology. *Cambridge Archaeological Journal* 13 (2): 225–230.

Haigh, C. (1998) *Elizabeth I*. London: Longman.

Haile, E.W. (ed.) (1998) *Jamestown Narratives: Eyewitness Accounts of the Virginia Colony, The First Decade: 1607–1617*. Champlain: RoundHouse.

Hill, C. (1975) *Change and Continuity in Seventeenth-Century England*. Cambridge, MA: Harvard University Press.

Johnson, M.H. (1993) *Housing Culture: Traditional Architecture in an English Landscape*. Washington: Smithsonian Press.

Joyce, R.A. (2002) *The Languages of Archaeology: Dialogue, Narrative, and Writing*. Malden: Blackwell.

Kelso, W.M. (2006) *Jamestown: The Buried Truth*. Charlottesville: University of Virginia Press.

Loren, D.D. (2001) Social skins: Orthodoxies and practices of dressing in the early colonial Lower Mississippi Valley. *Journal of Social Archaeology* 1 (2): 172–189.

Loren, D.D. (2003) Refashioning a body politic in colonial Louisiana. *Cambridge Archaeological Journal* 13 (2): 231–237.

Loren, D.D. (2007) *In Contact: Bodies and Space in the Sixteenth- and Seventeenth-Century Eastern Woodlands*. Lanham, MA: AltaMira Press.

Loren, D.D. and Beaudry, M.C. (2006) Becoming American: Small things remembered. In M. Hall and S.W. Silliman (eds.) *Historical Archaeology*, 251–271. Malden: Blackwell.

Luccketti, N. and Straube, B. (1998) *1997 Interim Report on the APVA Excavations at Jamestown Virginia*. Richmond: Association for the Preservation of Virginia Antiquities.

Mallios, S.W. (2004) Exchange and violence at Ajacan, Roanoke, and Jamestown. In D.B. Blanton and J.A. King (eds.) *Indian and European Contact in Context: The Mid-Atlantic Region*, 126–148. Gainesville: University Press of Florida.

Morgan, P. (2011) Religious diversity in colonial Virginia. In P. Rasor and R.E. Bond (eds.) *From Jamestown to Jefferson: The Evolution of Religious Freedom in Virginia*, 74–107. Charlottesville: University of Virginia Press.

Rinehart, C. (1990) *Crucifixes and Medallions: Their Role at Fort Michilimackinac*. Columbia: University of South Carolina Press.

Rubertone, P.E. (2000) The historical archaeology of Native Americans. *Annual Review of Anthropology* 29: 425–446.

Turner, V.W. (1995) *The Ritual Process: Structure and Anti-structure*. 2nd edn. New York: Aldine.

3 Discipline, Churches and Landscape: The Material Culture of Social Hierarchy in Northern Finland from the Seventeenth to the Eighteenth Centuries

Timo Ylimaunu

Introduction

This paper investigates the landscape context of buildings and demonstrates how material culture was used to create cultural and political landscapes in and around the early modern small town of Tornio, in present day Northern Finland (Fig. 3.1). Questions and ideas of power, control and discipline and their relations to built space and material culture are the key issues raised. I will discuss these points through an investigation of the early modern churches in urban and in rural locations, particularly in the area around the Tornionjoki river. I will also indirectly consider the question of imperial colonialism within Europe and some material implications of it (e.g. Johnson 2006).

Analyses of the political and social role of the contemporary church in urban townscapes and the surrounding countryside provides insights into historical processes of modernization, urbanization and colonialism in the European periphery during the seventeenth and eighteenth centuries. I consider the role of the contemporary church in the Tornionjoki river area in Northern Finland, particularly after 1809, when Finland became the autonomous Grand Duchy of Finland within the Russian Empire.

Material culture, like buildings, has different kinds of meanings and values. Architects and planners give their own meanings to built space, while those who use buildings may share these or create new forms of understanding. Therefore biographies of material cultures and built spaces are the result of complex sets of political, social, individual and cultural values and meanings, which are always historically contingent(Saarikangas 2006:38, 41). Built spaces are not only symbols or representations of power, they reproduce political and social meanings and values, which are related to historical events (Foucault 2000; Saarikangas 2006:41). Buildings are not only constructed material pieces but they have a complex social life, which starts at the drawing board: buildings should therefore be interpreted as fluid process (Markus 1993; Saarikangas 2006).

The development of geometric urban space was a significant feature of post-Renaissance modernization both within Europe, and further afield in colonial territories. (Rabinow 1989; Orser 1996; Johnson 1996; Delle *et al.* 1999; Lucas 2006). Contemporary urban maps were created and used in the process of building, but maps themselves may also be seen as providing a mechanism for the control of inhabitants. Names, properties and taxation values, amongst other information, were recorded during their creation. The residents of Tornio were recorded and linked to a map for the first time in 1697. In 1750, the occupations of Tornio's residents were also recorded. Maps and other records of the town's residents functioned as instruments to collect

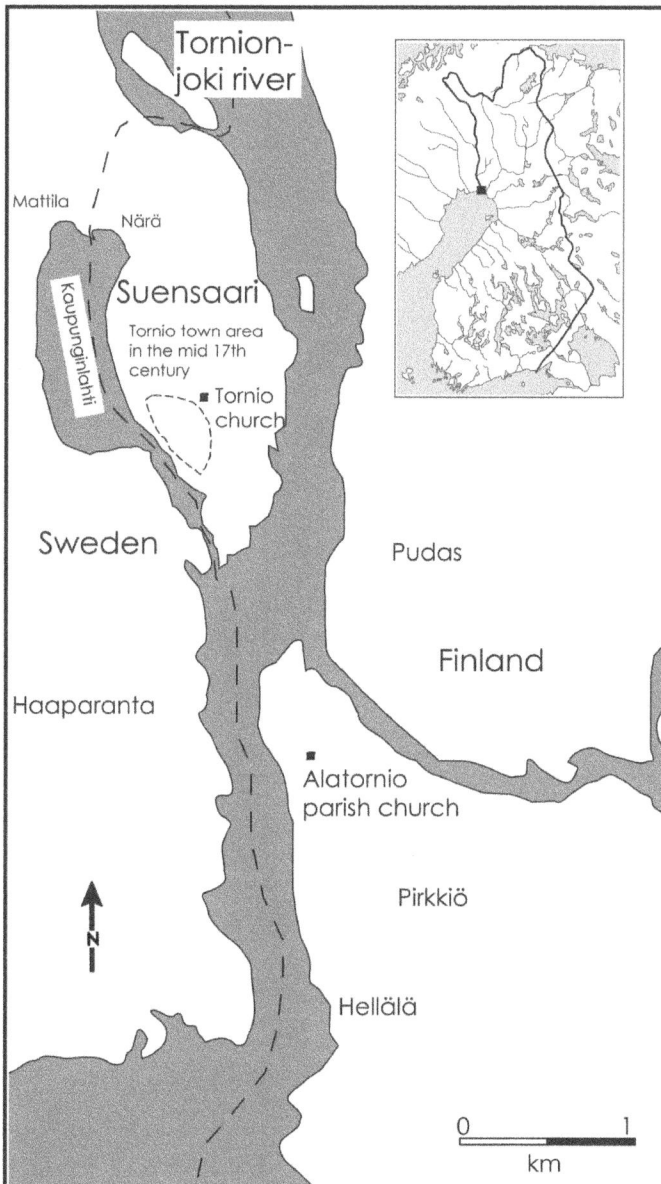

Figure 3.1   Map of Tornio town and its environs (by T. Ylimaunu).

more and more detailed information about the contemporary subjects of the Crown. In so doing they served to create these urban dwellers as unique individuals. Thus contemporary concepts of individualism have to be partly understood as a result of various administrative and bureaucratic acts since the seventeenth century (Foucault 2000; Melkersson 1997; Ylimaunu 2007:108–110), albeit not with present-day implications such as human rights or equality (Pred 1990:149). Indeed, it should be noted that the term 'individual' was used for the first time in the Swedish parliament at the end of eighteenth century (Melkersson 1997:97–98).

Urbanization and the Church

Tornio is located on the northern most coastal area of the Baltic Sea about 70 kilometres below the Arctic Circle. The town was founded on a delta island of the Torniojoki river in 1621 (Figure 3.1). The seventeenth century has been called the great era of urbanization in Sweden, when several towns were founded around the Bothnian Gulf. Tornio was the northernmost of these settlements in Europe until the later half of the eighteenth century. It had some 400 residents by the end of the seventeenth century and some 700 at the end of eighteenth century (Mäntylä 1971; Lilius 1985).

During the seventeenth century, the town had the character of an open village, with a toll fence encircling the built-up area. During the eighteenth century the urban landscape was dominated by three main long streets, which followed the river banks (Figure 3.2). Archaeological evidence shows us that the urban space of the settlement, and particularly the plots by Rantakatu street, started to be enclosed during the last decades of the seventeenth century, and increasingly after the Great Nordic war of 1721 (Ylimaunu 2007:107–113). The process of enclosing plots was the result of the Crown's policy of modernizing and regulating the kingdom's urban space into aesthetic grid plans or baroque radiating street plans (Kirjakka 1982:43; Lilius 1985:14; Kostet 1995:85; Ahlberg 2005:79; Ylimaunu 2006a:167).

Some public buildings were essential for early modern Swedish urban society, such as town halls, warehouses, toll fences, schools and scale houses, where town councils kept official market scales (Mäntylä 1971:30–32; Ylimaunu 2006b, 2007:77–79; Herva and Nurmi 2009). Public buildings were only located in towns, and had importance for administration as well as a symbolic meaning for the urban population. Churches were places of ceremonies and services, but also spaces for maintaining and reproducing social positions, which could be achieved, for example, through the donation of candle crowns (Ylimaunu 2007:74, 93, 96).

Tornio did not have its own church until the year 1644, 23 years after the foundation of the town. Instead, residents had to join services in the parish church, which was located some two kilometres south of the town on another island in the river Tornionjoki. In the early years of 1640, town residents started to plan the church. One reason for this agenda was the general public feeling that the town should not be without a church (Mäntylä 1971:32). The construction of the church dramatically

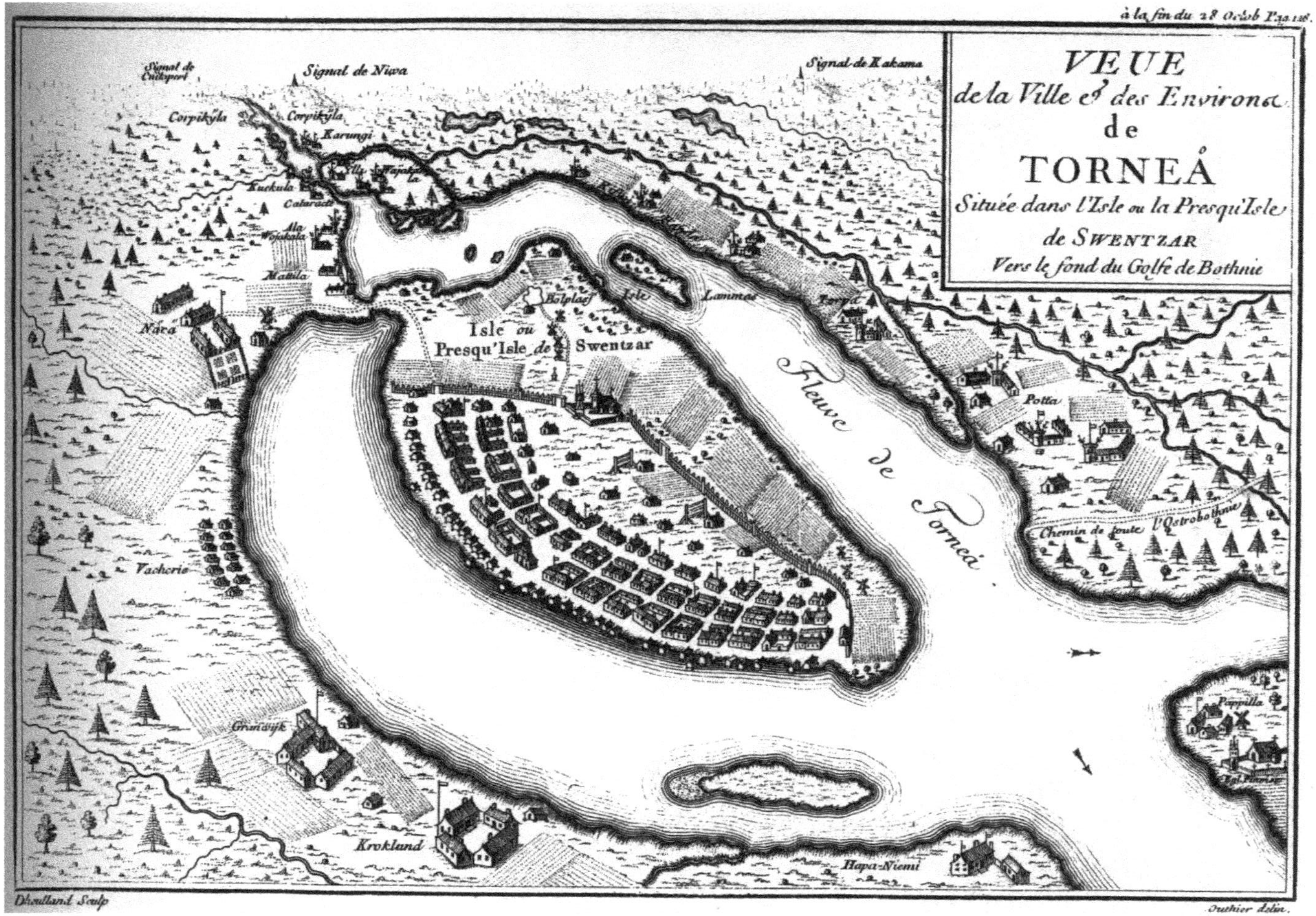

Figure 3.2   Tornio in the early eighteenth century. Drawing made by French expedition to the Tornion River valley in 1736–37. Original in R. Outhier, *Journal d'un voyage au nord en 1736 & 1737* [1738].

Figure 3.3   A view of Tornio at the end of 19th century (photo from the Provincial Museum of Tornio Valley).

changed the urban townscape. At that time, all the urban dwelling houses were single storey buildings, with only some warehouses being of two storeys. However, after 1644 the church with its tower rose above all the other buildings (Figure 3.3). As far as we know, in the seventeenth century the church and town hall were also the only red ochre painted buildings and probably the only ones that stood on a stone foundation. Along with these physical changes, the church changed the mental landscape too, as town residents no longer had to join the ceremonies with the rural peasantry in the parish church outside the town (Ylimaunu 2006b, 2007:32–35, 49–55, 93).

Social Control in the Urban Landscape

Developing mechanisms of control and surveillance was one part of the modernization process in Sweden and other states in the early modern period (Aalto 1996; Foucault 2000; Ylikangas 2000). Early modern society was based on an idea of social inequality (Ylikangas 2000) which was also supported by urban planning. For example, the town administration in Tornio required different annual rental payments for different plots of land; the highest valued plots on Rantakatu street cost 2 copper dalers, Keskikatu plots cost 1 ½ dalers and the poorest and smallest ones in Kolmaskatu cost 1 daler per a year (Mäntylä 1971:243–244). More than just a means of raising funds, the rents served as a social mechanism that controlled where residents lived in the town during the eighteenth century.

The ideology of social control in Swedish urban plans can be traced to Central Europe, for example to the hierarchical street plan of the French town Richelieu. Richelieu was intended to be the residence for the court of the cardinal Richelieu in the first half of seventeenth century (Eimer 1961; Rabinow 1989). These ideas were adapted for Swedish urban planning by French-trained architects shortly thereafter (e.g. Eimer 1961; Ahlberg 2005:266–268).

The changing of urban space into a geometric grid form should be seen as a fundamental change in the power relations between the crown and ordinary subjects. The Crown executed new planned space in both old and new towns, radically altering the urban environment, which had previously grown organically (Matthews *et al.* 2002:112–113). The goal of this regularization process was not only to create a more coherent kingdom through the rationalization of the urban landscape, but also to maintain order and to control its subjects (Foucault 2000; Ylimaunu 2006a, 2007:116–118). As the developing central administration required increasing levels of funding it also required a greater degree of control over the population. From the seventeenth century onwards, therefore, urban maps became an important means of maintaining records of the population and their properties for the purposes of taxation.

The early modern towns along the coastal areas of the Bothnian Gulf were the central points of the crown's administration and power (Lilja 2000:376), but towns were also focal points of Lutheran orthodoxy. So the urbanization process also had a religious dimension. The protestant faith was fundamental to the king's power and his right to the crown, as the king was considered to be only one level below God (Slunga 1993; Melkersson 1997). Material culture was one means of executing this authority. The relationship between Lutheran orthodoxy and urbanization comes to light, for example, in the process by which Tornio's residents obtained their own church. At first, the Archbishop of Sweden was against the plan, but the Chancellor of the King looked kindly on it (Mäntylä 1971:32). It therefore became more essential for the Crown's legitimacy than it was for the church of Sweden's that Tornio received its own church.

Reformed Cruciform Churches

The early period of Christianization began in northern parts of Sweden and Finland during the fourteenth century. First, wooden churches were built at the mouths of rivers that offered good communication routes to the north and east of the European periphery (Wallerström 1983:16–55; Vahtola 1997:56–85; Hiekkanen 2007). The fifteenth century was a period of intensive construction of the first stone churches in mainland Finland; rectangular churches with one to three naves were the main form at this time (Hiekkanen 2007:16–24).

In the early sixteenth century, after the Reformation, timber once again became the preferred construction material, and in the late seventeenth century the first cruciform timber churches were introduced. Inspiration for this type of cruciform church came from Central Europe, via Stockholm. The Catarinas cruciform church in Stockholm was designed to be a model for other Swedish protestant churches. In some cases the altar and pulpit were placed in the central part of the cross, so as to reduce the status of the altar service and to emphasize the importance of the pulpit sermons (Sinisalo 1978:55–56; Gardberg 2002:218). The phenomenon of placing emphasis upon the pulpit sermon is known in other reformed churches, for example in England, and in protestant colonies in America (Johnson 1996; Delle *et al.* 1999).

French-trained architects designed the first Swedish cruciform churches during the seventeenth century. However, in eastern and northern parts of the country local master-builders designed the structures and led the construction process. This group was responsible for building most of the 220 seventeenth- and eighteenth-century churches in these regions. Medieval construction traditions, layouts and styles still influenced the churches during the later centuries, but certain designs were favoured in different regions; rectangular churches were mainly constructed in southwest Finland and in the central parts of Sweden (Gardberg 2002:217–230) whilst timber-made cruciform churches predominated in the northern and eastern parts of Finland and in northern Sweden (Flodin 1993; Gardberg 2002:217–230).

Church Buildings and Social Control

The cruciform church was the most common type in Finland and northern Sweden during the eighteenth century, whilst rectangular churches were predominant in the central parts of the kingdom, where the Crown's administrative control was most intensive. According to Kydén (1998:140, 205) the phenomenon of building cruciform churches in peripheral areas was a direct result of weaker central government control.

This argument may be criticized in several ways. First, the central government in Stockholm redrew and approved all official building plans, including those for churches. After the mid- eighteenth century all new proposals for publicly funded buildings had to be sent to the Överidentendentsämbetet—the Board of Public Works and Buildings— in Stockholm for the approval of the King. After 1776 central administration became even tighter and this led to the redesigning of several buildings (Unnerbäck and Sjöström 1993).

Oversight by the central administration occurred in Finland after the 1809. All church plans were approved by the Bureau of the Superintendent of Public Works and Buildings in the Economic Department of the Imperial Finnish Senate Helsinki, the capital of the new Grand Duchy of Finland. The Bureau of the Superintendent mainly dealt with architectural issues. Thus, the Economic Department took decisions on the construction and function of public buildings, including, for example, where to place the pulpit in a church (Figure 3.4). It was felt that congregations should be able to see and hear the vicar clearly, and vice versa (Kydén 1998:161). So the political members of the Economic Department were directly involved in the maintenance and reproduction of power relationships.

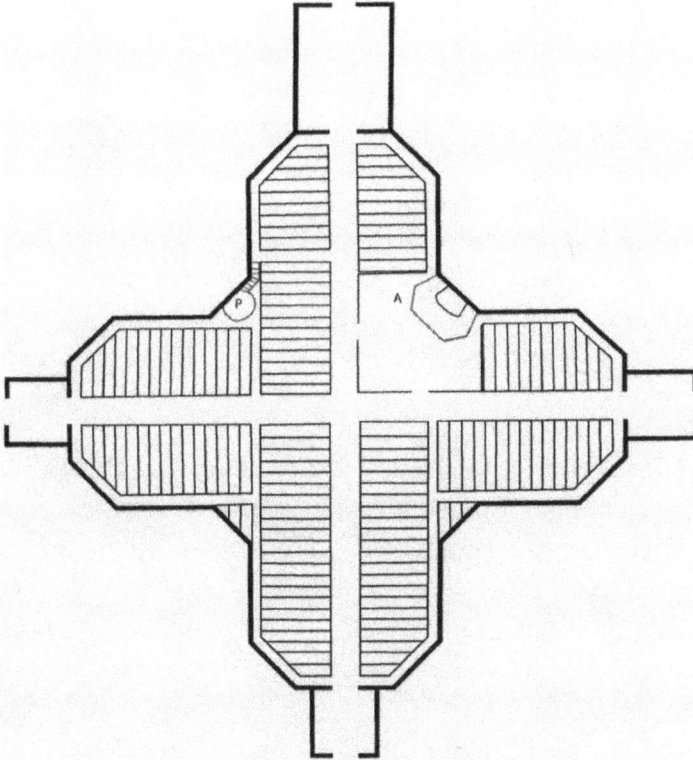

Figure 3.4   The plan of a cruciform church (by T. Ylimaunu).

Second, since the reformation, the church had been under the Crown's direct control and from the end of the seventeenth century the king was the head of the church. The institution of the church became a part of the Crown's administration; from the pulpit matters of obedience and royal edicts and proclamations were directed towards the congregation (Slunga 1993:10–311; Aalto 1996:140; Johnson 1996:104). Attendance at church services was compulsory for parishioners in the seventeenth century and non-attendance punishable by a fine. In northern Sweden and Finland, many areas were without roads, and some people lived more than 50 kilometres from the parish church—here, attendance was required every fifth Sunday, although those who lived nearer had to attend more often. The monitoring of attendance was partly carried out through the use of pew maps, which were based on the socioeconomic status of the parishioners. Every member of the parish had his/her own place in the pew, with the wealthiest sitting on the front rows and poorest at the rear. The orthodoxy of the protestant church gave a solid power-base to the monarch (Slunga 1993; Ylikangas 2000). The compulsory nature of attendance also affected the built environment around the church; parishioners constructed so-called 'cottage village's around parish churches for overnight visits (e.g. Gardberg 2002:95). Parallels can be drawn with England, where pew maps and fines were also used to control parishioners (Johnson 1996:101–108). Thus, pew maps can be compared with urban maps, as a means by which the physical location of worship and dwelling were dictated, according to the socioeconomic position of the parishioners.

The Monarch, as head of the Swedish Church, is referenced in the names of several seventeenth- and eighteenth-century churches. Another way to remind parish members of their ruler was to place the monarch's monogram or name above the main entrance, as at Alatornio and Kemi parish churches. This mirrors the medieval tradition at castles in Finland and in other parts of Europe, where heraldic symbols of lordship were often placed above the main entrance (Johnson 1996:125; Gardberg 2002:133). One purpose of the Swedish church during the seventeenth century was to combat illiteracy. In fact, the ability to read and write was one of the requirements for obtaining a marriage licence (Slunga 1993). When literacy became more widespread in the late eighteenth century, heraldic symbols were commonly replaced by the written names of the lord of the church. Every member of the parish could read the name of the lord, when he/she was entering in to his 'house' (Figure 3.5).

Third, despite the lack of supremacy of the monarchy and rising status of the parliament's power in the eighteenth century, parliament clamped down on social control in nearly all aspects of ordinary life (Melkersson 1997) and the church played

Figure 3.5   The façade of the Alatornio parish church (by T. Ylimaunu).

a crucial role in this process. Extramarital sexual affairs were criminalized; according to the Crown its subjects were expected to get married, build a home, farm the land and pay taxes. Lawbreakers were punished in churches and disgraced publicly within a pillory. The church therefore functioned as a policing body, and the king as the judge (Aalto 1996). This phenomenon was not restricted to the Kingdom of Sweden but was also seen in other parts of Europe (Johnson 1996:104).

Inner spaces of churches can also be compared with the didactic function of lecture theatres. The lecturer had to be seen and heard in the teaching room; similarly the vicar had to be viewed in the pulpit and his sermon had to be audible. This was a central issue in buildings of knowledge production (compare Markus 1993:170). Semicircular, octagonal or oval lecture theatres were built in many universities after the sixteenth century. The audience were separated from the central point, around which tiered benches were arranged. A steep rake minimized obstructions and gave students an unimpeded view. Markus (1993:229–232) has pointed out that semicircular lecture theatres represent asymmetry in the power relations between the audience and the lecturer. Likewise, this kind of power relation was demonstrated in the church, where vicars made a ceremonial entrance to the altar or to the pulpit from the sacristy, as did lecturers from private laboratories into the lecture theatre.

According to Henrik Gabriel Porthan (1739–1804) the best plan for the Lutheran church was round or oval, with the altar and the pulpit placed in the centre of the building and pews around them (H. G. Porthan's lecture from 1801, Porthan 1966:338). Porthan's ideal church was similar to contemporary lecture theatres. Some rounded churches with an altar in the middle encircled by pews were built in Finland during the late eighteenth and early nineteenth century (Figure 3.6), as seen in Hämeenlinna and Nokia (Sinisalo 1978:84–86; Gardberg 2002:231). They represent the centralizing authority in a perfect panoptic form (see Foucault 2000) where material culture symbolizes administration. The vicar was the head of the parish in Finland until the mid-1860s, when the municipal administration was dispossessed from its control over the congregation (Vahtola 2003:261, 324).

Based on the arguments above, the eighteenth-century cruciform churches in northern and eastern parts of Sweden can be interpreted as an instrument that the Crown used to create a landscape of domination. It can be argued that central administration promoted the construction of cruciform churches in peripheral countryside regions where the Crown's administrative power was marginal. The northern and eastern parts of the country were less urbanized than central parts of the kingdom (Lilja 2000:354) and the central administration needed powerful and large buildings that had a strong symbolic relationship to the Crown.

The New Border Area and the Churches after 1809

After the Swedish Russian war of 1808–09 Finland became an autonomous Grand Duchy of Russia. The new borderline was established following the deepest course

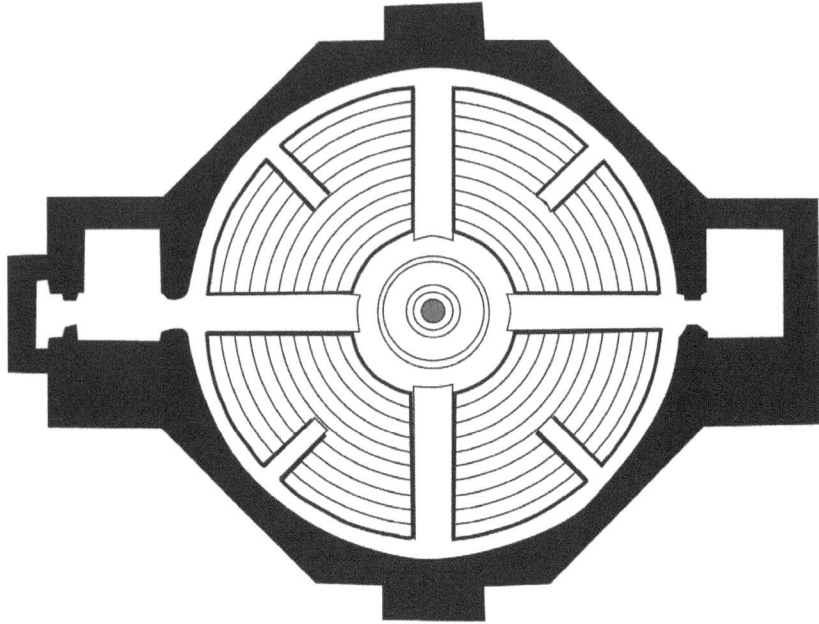

Figure 3.6   The plan of the rounded church of Nokia (drawing by T. Ylimaunu).

of the Tornionjoki and Muonionjoki rivers. The boundary effectively bisected these rivers which had been single cultural and economical areas since prehistoric times (Koivunen 1991). Rivers were also the most important communication channels from south to north before the nineteenth century and the new boundary barred traditional crossings and severed family connections.

North from the town of Tornio the congregations were divided by the new border and only two churches remained on the eastern (Finnish) side of the Tornionjoki river. The problem was the law, which still required parishioners to attend services every Sunday. Members of the congregations wanted to leave the situation as it had been during the Swedish period, meaning that the Finnish community wanted to cross the river to the Swedish side to join the ceremonies in their old churches. The Russian border commissars suggested this too, but the Russian administration refused to allow this; the emperor Alexander understood the social and political role of the Finnish church, and could therefore not allow his loyal subjects to cross the new border to take part in Swedish services. The official policy was to cut in half the old congregations and to create new congregations and this required the construction of new cruciform churches on the Finnish side of the Tornionjoki river. Thus, the tsar Alexander funded new churches in Karunki, Ylitornio, Pello, Muonio and Kolari (Figure 3.7). All the plans were designed by the Bureau of the Superintendent of Public Works and Buildings and they are one of the earliest examples of official imperial architecture of the Grand Duchy. The building process was slow (Kydén 1998:162–166), but the goal was to create a landscape which was colonized by the official imperial architecture on the Finnish side of the Tornionjoki river and to bind the population to the eastern side of the riverbank.

Figure 3.7 The church of Karunki, one of the earliest examples of official imperial architecture of the Grand Duchy (by T. Ylimaunu).

The same also happened in Kemi, some 20 kilometres from the new boundary, where the tsar founded a new church designed in Helsinki (Satokangas 1997:243; Kydén 1998:47, 178, 180). All the new timber-built cruciform churches on the eastern side of the Torniojoki river and one stone church in Kemi were the result of this imperial policy; the Church of Finland was a powerful tool for the Russians to control their new imperial subjects. The new churches stabilized the situation and public opinion near the Swedish border (Kydén 1998).

Creating a new boundary was an imperial project. This was not exceptional during this period. For example, the British Empire was not purely an economic project or the result of economic activity on a global scale: it was as much a cultural project too (Lucas 2006:180). So, for the Russian Empire the new Autonomous Grand Duchy of Finland was also a cultural project; even its ideology was based on an autocratic regime.

From this perspective, the new churches on the eastern side of the boundary can be interpreted as cultural fortifications of the established Russian power in Finland, which looked outward against Sweden. Perhaps it is ironic that the new imperial style was used to build the centres of cities such as like Helsinki and Oulu—as well as churches in western Lapland—and that these buildings are now national monuments within present day Finland.

National consciousness and identity is a social product, which is in constant repro-duction, affected by cultural and political ideas, ideologies and images (e.g. Anderson

2007). From this point of view, the task of the Russian Emperor was to establish his power in the new autonomous Grand Duchy of Finland, and especially in areas around the new boundary. This process can also be seen as the creation of a new national identity for the Finnish population, who had been subjects of the Swedish crown since about 1150, during the early medieval period. It was Russian policy to separate the Finnish and Swedish populations' identity (Teerijoki 2007:24), but in doing so, it perhaps inadvertently created a new identity for the Finnish population (compare Johnson 2006:326–328). So we can argue that Finnish national identity began after 1809, following the separation of Finland from Sweden by Russia.

In conclusion, both churches and urban plans had similar functions for the production and reproduction of social order in different landscapes. Visibility and, by implication, surveillance was one crucial factor in both of these arenas. We can view the Protestant cruciform churches in Sweden and later in the Grand Duchy of Finland as an important instrument of central government coercion.

Acknowledgements

Timo Ylimaunu is a post-doctoral fellow funded by the Emil Aaltonen foundation. This paper is a part of the research project 'Towns, Borders and Material Culture' funded by the Academy of Finland. I wish to thank Anna Badcock, Vesa-Pekka Herva, Risto Nurmi, Jeff Oliver and James Symonds for helping in many ways with the ideas presented here.

Bibliography

Aalto, S. (1996) *Kirkko ja kruunu siveellisyyden vartijoina. Seksuaalirikollisuus, esivalta ja yhteisö Porvoon kihlakunnassa 1621–1700.* Helsinki: Suomen Historiallinen Seura.

Ahlberg, N. (2005) *Stadsgrundningar och planförändringar. Svensk stadsplanering 1521–1721.* Uppsala: Swedish University of Agricultural Sciences.

Anderson, B. (2007) *Kuvitellut yhteisöt.* Tampere: Vastapaino.

Delle, J.A., Leone, M.P. and Mullins, P.R. (1999) Archaeology of the modern state: European colonialism. In G. Barker (ed.) *Companion Encyclopedia of Archaeology.* Vol. 2. London: Routledge.

Eimer, G. (1961) *Die Stadtplanung im Schwedischen Ostseereich 1600–1715.* Stockholm: Scandinavian University Books, Svenska bokförlaget, Bonniers.

Flodin, B. (1993) Överintendentsämbetet och församlingarna. Önskemål, förslag, föreskrifter och förverkligande. In *Kyrkobyggnader 1760–1860. Del 3. Övre Norrland. Finland 1760–1809.* Volym 217 av Sveriges Kyrkor, Konsthistoriskt inventarium. Stockholm: National Board of Antiquities and the Royal Swedish Academy of Letters, History and Antiquities.

Foucault, M. (2000) *Tarkkailla ja rangaista.* Original *Surveiller et punir.* Published in Finnish for the first time in 1980. Helsinki: Otava.

Gardberg, C.J. (2002) *Kivestä ja puusta. Suomen linnoja, kartanoita ja kirkkoja.* Helsinki: Otava.

Herva, V.-P. and Nurmi, R. (2009) Beyond consumption: Functionality, artifact biography, and early modernity in a European periphery. *International Journal of Historical Archaeology* 13 http://springerlink.metapress.com/content/e6010g7374u28275/fulltext.pdf [Accessed: 17.02.2009]

Hiekkanen, M. (2007) *Suomen keskiajan kivikirkot*. Helsinki: SKS.

Johnson, M. (1996) *An Archaeology of Capitalism*. Oxford: Blackwell.

Johnson, M. (2006) The tide reversed: Prospects and potentials for a postcolonial archaeology of Europe. In M. Hall and S.W. Silliman (eds.) *Historical Archaeology*, 313–331. Oxford: Blackwell.

Johnson, M. (2007) *Ideas of Landscape*. Oxford: Blackwell.

Kirjakka, M. (1982) *Kaupunkirakentaminen Suomessa vuoteen 1875. Asemakaavoituksen sekä rakentamista ohjanneiden määräysten ja päätösten vaikutus kaupunkirakenteeseen*. Espoo: Teknillinen korkeakoulu.

Koivunen, P. (1991) Suomen Tornionlaakson esihistoriaa. In O. Hederyd, Y. Alamäki and M. Kenttä (eds.) *Tornionlaakson historia 1. Jääkaudelta 1600-luvulle*. Malung: Tornionlaakson kuntien historiakirjatoimikunta.

Kostet, J. (1995) *Cartographia urbium Finnicarum, Suomen kaupunkien kaupunkikartografia 1600-luvulla ja 1700-luvun alussa*. Monumenta Cartographica Septentrionalia 1. Rovaniemi: Pohjois-Suomen historiallinen yhdistys.

Kydén, T. (1998) Suomen intendentinkonttorin kirkkoarkkitehtuuri 1810–1824. Kustavilainen perinne ja suuriruhtinaskunnan uusi rakennushallinto. *Jyväskylä Studies in the Arts 64*. Jyväskylä: Jyväskylän yliopisto.

Lilius, H. (1985) *Suomalainen puukaupunki*. Helsinki: Anders Nyborg A/S/Akateeminen kirjakauppa.

Lilja, S. (2000) *Tjuvehål och stolta städer. Urbaniseringens kronologi och geografi i Sverige (med Finland) ca 1570-tal till 1810-tal*. Stockholm: Stads- och kommunhistoriska institutet.

Lucas, G. (2006) *An Archaeology of Colonial Identity: Power and Material Culture in the Dwars Valley, South Africa*. New York: Springer.

Mäntylä, I. (1971) *Tornion kaupungin historia, 1. osa 1621–1809*. Tampere: Tornion kaupunki.

Markus, T.A. (1993) *Buildings and Power: Freedom and Control in the Origin of Modern Building Types*. London: Routledge.

Matthews, C.N., Leone, M.P. and Jordan, K.A. (2002) The political economy of archaeological cultures. *Journal of Social Archaeology* 2: 109–134.

Melkersson, M. (1997) *Staten, ordningen och friheten. En studie av den styrande elitens syn på statens roll mellan stormaktstiden och 1800-talet*. Uppsala: Uppsala University.

Orser, C.E. Jr. (1996) *A Historical Archaeology of the Modern World*. New York: Plenum Press.

Outhier, R. (1975) *Matka Pohjan perille 1736–1737*. French original *Journal d'un voyage au nord en 1736 & 1737* [1738], trans. M. Itkonen-Kaila. Otava: Helsinki.

Porthan, H.G. (1966) *Henrici Gabrielis Porthan Opera omnia*. in Porthan-seura (ed.); tertem partem edendam curavit Eero Matinolli. Turku.

Pred, A. (1990) *Making Histories and Constructing Human Geographies: The Local Transformation of Practice, Power Relations, and Consciousness*. Boulder: Westview Press.

Rabinow, P. (1989) 'Kaupunkitilan säätely' In M. Foucault and P. Rabinow *Kaupunki, tila, valta*. Tampere: Tampereen teknillinen korkeakoulu, Arkkitehtuurin osasto.

Saarikangas, K. (2006) *Eletyt tilat ja sukupuoli. Asukkaiden ja ympäristön kulttuurisia kohtaamisia*. Helsinki: SKS.

Satokangas, R. (1997) Nousun aika (1721–1859). In R. Satokangas (ed.) *Keminmaan historia* Keminmaa: Keminmaan kunta.

Sinisalo, A. (1978) Suomalaisen kirkkoarkkitehtuurin vaiheita. In M. Haapio (ed.) *Suomen kirkot ja kirkkotaide* 1. Lieto: Etelä-Suomen Kustannus Oy.

Slunga, N. (1993) Kirkko ja koulu—papisto ja kirkollinen elämä. In O. Hederyd and Y. Alamäki (eds.) *Tornionlaakson historia* II, *1600-luvulta vuoteen 1809*. Jyväskylä: Tornionlaakson kuntien historiakirjatoimikunta.

Teerijoki, I. (2007) *Tornion historia 2*. Tornio: Tornion kaupunki.

Unnerbäck, A. and Sjöström, I. (1993) Inledning. In *Kyrkobyggnader 1760–1860. Del 3. Övre Norrland*.

Finland 1760–1809. Volym 217 av Sveriges Kyrkor, Konsthistoriskt invetarium. Stockholm: National Board of Antiquities and the Royal Swedish Academy of Letters, History and Antiquities.

Vahtola, J. (1997) Keskiaika ja 1500-luku. In R. Satokangas (ed.) *Keminmaan Historia* Keminmaa: Keminmaan kunta.

Vahtola, J. (2003) *Suomen Historia. Jääkaudesta Euroopan Unioniin.* Helsinki: Otava.

Wallerström, T. (1983) Kulturkontakter i Norrbottens kustland under medeltiden. *Norrbotten 82–83:* 16–55.

Ylikangas, H. (2000) *Aikansa rikos—historiallisen kehityksen valaisijana.* Helsinki: WSOY.

Ylimaunu, T. (2006a) Legioonaleireistä ruutuasemakaavaan—varhaismodernien kaupunkien regulointi-ideologiasta. In V.-P. Herva and J. Ikäheimo (eds.) *Klassinen tapaus. Dos. Eero Jarva 60 vuotta.* Oulu: TAIDA.

Ylimaunu, T. (2006b) Ranta-aitat ja kirkko Tornion 17. vuosisadan ensimmäisen puoliskon kaupunkikartoissa. In K. Alenius, S. Jalagin, M. Mäkivuoti and S. Wunsch (eds.) *Mielikuvien maanosat. Olavi K. Fältin juhlakirja.* Oulu: Redactores.

Ylimaunu, T. (2007) *Aittakylästä kaupungiksi—arkeologinen tutkimus Tornion kaupungistumisesta 18. vuosisadan loppuun menessä.* Studia archaeologica Septentrionalia 4. Rovaniemi: Pohjois-Suomen historiallinen yhdistys.

4 'Believe, Hon': Markets, Faith and Archaeology in Twenty-First Century Baltimore

David Gadsby

True faith operates in spite of overwhelming contradictory evidence. The re-development of the 'de-industrialized' city of Baltimore is predicated on a deep and abiding faith in markets, and particularly in the real estate market. As the current economic recession takes hold, mouldering artifacts of the 'past' industrial era serve as reminders of decades of depression and decay, while the city's government urges its citizens to 'believe' in the city's future through a multi-million dollar advertising campaign. Neighbourhoods, such as the historically working-class Hampden, market themselves through heritage; developers demolish historically significant buildings in the name of urban renewal, and indeed, the market. With seemingly boundless optimism, the 'architects' of the city's new, consumption-driven landscape simultaneously celebrate and destroy its industrial past as the public memory of the industrial heritage, embodied in area museums and murals, actively encourages citizens to forget the role of the working class in the construction and subsequent near-destruction of the city.

Throughout the city, pedestrians encounter the signs not only of destruction and decay —industrial ruins, litter piled high, demolished and neglected buildings—but also seemingly endless, unstoppable creation, and rampant consumption of the market-faithful. While its poorest citizens endure (and fail to endure) the relentless danger of a remarkably violent drug market, the richest build monuments to themselves in now-demolished housing projects, factories and working-class neighbourhoods.

These neighbourhoods become sites for encounters between wealthy and working class, material and ideological, new and old. Many such encounters are played out as competitions for control of public resources and spaces. In Hampden, a former textile mill village absorbed into the city in 1889, heritage celebrations, commercial activities —both legal and illicit—and other competitions for the attentions and funds of the neighbourhood's residents feed ongoing class-based competition over the resources, history and character of the place. Developers, merchants and petit-bourgeois free-market acolytes manipulate spaces and discourses in accordance with their faith in the power of markets. At the same time, members of the working class, who have abundant reason to be sceptical, place faith in longstanding institutions, churches, community networks and organizations. Despite their faith, a burgeoning real estate market helps to transform and even to dismantle those institutions.

Within this context, an archaeology of the recent past, called the Hampden Community Archaeology Project, operates on a kind of faith-logic of its own. That faith posits that traditional communities are worth 'saving' and that archaeology can help to preserve them. This archaeology seeks to resuscitate members of the working class as historical agents and foils for the new consumer-driven market faith. Along with discoveries of working-class agency and power come discoveries that point to shame and decay. Along with increasing interest from community members comes increasing apathy, and even antipathy from developers and free-marketeers. I examine how the material world, including the objects recovered during archaeological excavations, informs an understanding of these various faiths as the city and neighbourhood continue to 'develop'.

Sometime in the late 1980s, geographer David Harvey stood on Baltimore's Federal Hill, a promontory with a commanding view of the city's harbour and central business district, and cast a critical geographer's eye upon the city. 'The United States,' he says in the opening passage of the essay describing the view, 'struggled long and hard to get rid of aristocratic privilege, but Baltimore's Downtown skyline says that a financial aristocracy is alive and well. As you look down on the city from Federal Hill, banks and financial institutions tower over everything else, proclaiming in glass, brick, and concrete, that they hold the reins of power' (Harvey 1991:227). In contrast to medieval European cities, whose landscapes evidence the power of church and aristocracy, Baltimore's city centre has no churches: 'God, it seems, has meaning [only] for the working class; mammon is fully in control downtown' (Harvey 1991:227).

Harvey's observation, that there are no impressive churches in downtown Baltimore, is largely correct. Instead those monuments in 'glass, brick and concrete' serve as places of faith. Those who possess true faith 'believe', in spite of overwhelming contradictory evidence. Although the current economic troubles demonstrate some of the profound inadequacies of the free market system, Baltimore's skyline remains an expression of faith in the power of markets not only to correct themselves if anything goes awry, but also, ultimately, to save the world. Baltimore's skyscrapers are cathedrals of the free market, and their erection entails an act of faith (placing at risk of millions of dollars with the expectation of growth) in spite of evidence (the continuing depopulation of the city and the decay of many neighbourhoods outside of the central business district) to the contrary.

At the core of all of this building lies a string of local business groups—the greater Baltimore Committee, the Baltimore Development Corporation, and others. The venerable Greater Baltimore Committee (GBC) has, since 1956, undertaken a number of projects including the now-famous transformation of Baltimore's Inner Harbor from a crumbling port to a tourist site full of museums, hotels, shopping malls and other 'pleasure citadels', to use Harvey's turn of phrase (1991:237). The twin pavilions of Harbor Place lie at its core. The development of the Inner Harbor, credited with 'turning the city around', ushered in a new era in Baltimore. Baltimore not only had to function by paving roads, lighting streets, providing police protection, and performing other municipal duties, but it also had to market itself in order to survive. Suddenly, marketing campaigns could save cities and (perhaps better yet) the city could be remade in the image of the marketing campaign that saved it. In recent years, the GBC has also become an outspoken proponent of free-market capitalism and unfettered growth as the way to save the perpetually suffering city.

Harvey (1991) is quick to point out, however, that the city continued to haemorrhage both people and money after the advent of Harbor Place, losing roughly a fifth of its population and ten per cent of its jobs between 1970 and 1989 (the era of the so-called 'turn around'), and the poorest neighbourhoods in the city remained poor during that period, while the city continued to reduce social services.

Nearly two decades after Harvey's assessment much has changed, but his central point remains valid; radical free market policies, while they may purport to help everyone, tend to leave the poor out of economic progress and increase the gap in income and quality of life between rich and poor. Baltimore's city planning, led by groups like the GBC, continues to operate with boundless optimism in the power of the real estate markets. New buildings are coming up everywhere and despite increasing evidence that the market has been growing unsustainably for some time, developers continue to speculate on residential property values, and build expensive houses and condominiums. All of this development intersects closely with both the notions of heritage, faith, and belief.

At the same time, Baltimore's predominately African-American and working-class neighbourhoods, the ones hidden by the façade of the central business district from the Federal Hill view, are sites of decay, abandonment and murder. The questions that I want to pose in my discussion of Baltimore are central to my own work as an archaeologist in an urban environment, but are also, I think, of broader importance. They stem from my several years' experience conducting community archaeology in Baltimore. In particular, I am concerned with understanding the role that heritage plays in markets and marketing, as well as understanding how heritage can be emancipatory. Tied up in those two questions are questions about how heritage operates discursively, and how heritage monuments and practices can celebrate or memorialize certain pasts even as they actively forget others. I am also concerned with the role of heritage resources in the city—how do cities use the past and how do they protect heritage materials, which are also sometimes called, in the *lingua franca* of the market, 'cultural resources'? Finally, I am concerned with the role of discourse in heritage and particularly in the possibilities for changing discourse through archaeological practice.

First, some background: the city of Baltimore is located along the fall line to the eastern coastal plane at the confluence of two rivers, the Patapsco and the Jones Falls which drain into the Chesapeake Bay. Established in the mid-eighteenth century, Baltimore has long been a centre for both industry and finance. Its situation near the Bay and in close proximity to Maryland's resource-rich hinterland, coupled with an extensive network of turnpikes and later railroad lines, made it a hub of commerce and overseas trade in the nineteenth century (Olson 1997). That trade also fed a large ship-building industry that was joined closely to a series of steel mills on the city's East side as well as a number of cotton duck mills upstream on the Jones Falls. Until well after the Second World War, Baltimore was an industrial town with a thriving working-class culture.

A number of financial interests linked to the shipping and ship-building industries also arose in Baltimore, beginning in the early nineteenth century, when several of the city fathers made fortunes through a variety of schemes—many of which involved slavery and some of which were of dubious legality—and by profiteering in the war of 1812 (Olson 1997:46–47). By the twentieth century, the city's core was home to a number of national and international banks and financial institutions. Many historians of Baltimore consider it to be a financial city first and a manufacturing city second, although in the century between 1850 and 1950, the port supported numerous manufacturing concerns, varying in scale from massive Bethlehem steel yards to small textile and machine shops. The crown cap was first manufactured in Baltimore, as were the over the counter pharmaceuticals Bromo-Seltzer and Noxema (Painter 1899; Kelly 1994; Segal *et al.* 1995).

Since the 1970s, however, Baltimore's major industries, particularly its steel, automobile, and textile industries have moved to cheaper labour markets to the south and overseas. The city's economy has undergone a transition from one based on production to one based on tourism and therefore consumption.

Since Harvey's sojourn to Federal Hill, a number of developments have occurred. The most striking is a real estate boom coupled with the wholesale gentrification of many parts of the city. The former company-town-within-a-city of Canton (Beirne 1976:130–168), an area with a long waterfront, began the redevelopment of its several factories into retail space and condominiums in the mid 1990s. Several other working-class strongholds, notably Fells Point (the oldest part of the city), Federal Hill and most recently Locust Point have undergone similar transformations which have seen the traditional communities outpriced and displaced.

But what of the rest of the city? Despite integration efforts in the second half of the twentieth century, Baltimore remains *de facto* racially segregated (The Goldseker Foundation 2002). The real estate boom of the previous decade took place in a few neighbourhoods near the waterfront or along the main Charles Street thoroughfare. The City's East and West sides have housed much of the city's majority African-American population for the past several decades. These areas have largely missed out on the housing boom. Some areas, despite the best efforts of activists and neighbourhood groups, appear to be war zones, with high rates of vacancy easily detectable by boarded-up windows and doors. Despite the number of abandoned houses in the city, and the housing boom in more affluent parts of the city, the city's public housing authority has cut its occupied holdings by 42 per cent (Jacobson 2007). Poorer areas of the city are plagued by the drug trade and ancillary crime. The city's murder rate, while slightly down from a high in the 1990s, remains well above the national average, especially in poorer areas. The murder rate generates a great deal of public anxiety (Federal Bureau of Investigations 2006). Generally, the public discussion of the issue links drugs and murder, and most of the homicides in the city are widely considered to be gang-related. A recent report commissioned by the Goldseker Foundation assesses the city's situation as a mounting crisis (*The Frog's Lesson: The Baltimore Region* 2002).

Unfortunately, the only tool that the free market possesses to deal with crisis is a marketing campaign and the early years of the new century saw the mounting of several city-sponsored campaigns under Mayor Martin O'Malley to rebrand the city. Most infamous are the adoption of the absurdly optimistic slogan 'The Greatest City in America', an expensive campaign that very recently urged outside investors to 'Get in on' the Baltimore housing boom, and the multi-million dollar 'Believe' campaign. The last example involved plastering the city with billboards and bumper stickers emblazoned with the white-on-black exhortation to Believe. The trouble was that nobody, with the exception of a few schoolkids invited to the kickoff event, knew what we were supposed to believe, although a little research quickly revealed that we were to have faith that Baltimore could kick its drug habit. The ominous Believe billboards, coupled with flashing 'believe' surveillance cameras, made powerful fodder for the city's creative cynics, and it was only a matter of time before people began to experiment with new iterations (Figure 4.1).

Among them are bumper stickers and homemade signs urging us to 'Be Evil', 'Behave', and 'ZOM-Believe'. One popular variant, a meta-marketing ploy from a well-known pseudo-working-class café, plays on a Baltimore working-class turn of phrase that has been adopted into the broader lexicon. It urges the reader to 'B'lieve, Hon'.

Figure 4.1   Surveillance camera mounted on a utility pole decorated with the Baltimore Police Department's logo and the 'Believe' motto (photo by author 2007).

Belief is not the only thing that gets marketed in the new Baltimore. The city also markets its heritage in a variety of ways. Harvey's 'pleasure citadel' at the Inner Harbor boasts a 'Heritage Walk' as well two historic ship museums and two land-based museums of history. Realtors market the heritage-value of the cosy old houses in up-and coming neighbourhoods. Developers boast that they are 'making history' by redeveloping abandoned industrial buildings. Heritage—and particularly the kind that is marketable, the kind is thought to simply reside in monuments and old buildings—is an important way to make money in the new tourism- and consumption-driven Baltimore.

However, Baltimore's heritage is not always the kind that can be consumed. I think it useful to distinguish between two kinds of heritage: that which can be marketed, and that which cannot. The former, notes heritage anthropologist Erve Chambers, involves attempts to preserve fading cultural practices and objects, but often 'become(s) a way to separate the objects...of heritage from their actual heirs, serving to transfer them to the marketplace as commodities' (Chambers 2006:2–3). He calls this type of heritage 'public heritage' and means it to encompass the kinds of heritage traditionally done by government and other heritage professionals, as well as marketers. The latter type, on the other hand, which Chambers labels private heritage, 'encourages us to focus on the ways in which the past is dynamically linked to the present, with heritage values interpreted and identified by community members rather than outsiders' (Chambers 2006:2–3).

John Hartigan (2000) notes that this heritage distinction possesses a class component. He has written about the propensity of working-class whites to regard history in terms of people and events in the past, while middle-class whites tend to regard it as being related to material culture, particularly houses. In the second formulation, houses are of course also imbued with elevated monetary value because of their possession of (any) history. Thus, what was once particular history—the history of working-class struggle, or alternately of neighborhood unity—is transformed into a generic kind of history that is assumed to exist in old houses. Places become worth something not because they are associated with a particular person or event, but because they have 'something about them', 'character' or 'style' that speaks to the aesthetic sensibilities of middle-class gentrifiers.

It is important to note an additional distinction. The first kind of heritage, the marketable kind, is about forgetting. It creates separations between people and places. It sanitizes. It depopulates the past and replaces it with an empty signifier, a 'void' (Žižek 1989:34). Along with the grime of history, it washes away most (though not all) of the human beings, the subjects and agents of history, replacing them with objects that seem to remember the past, but often don't. The second kind—the more authentic kind—is about remembering the details and personages of history. It is a populated past.

In order to be commercially valuable, heritage must be transformed from the first kind of heritage into the second. Indeed, one of the main functions of the city's development process is to transform heritage *sites* into heritage *resources* that can, like all resources, be consumed. If it can't be consumed, then it is eventually doomed to be destroyed and replaced with something that can.

A recent example involves the case of a series of historic rowhouses on St Paul Street in the heart of the central business district, and adjacent to Mercy Hospital (Figure 4.2). The rowhouses were listed as 'significant' buildings on the city's register because they constituted the first integrated block in Baltimore and housed, among other things, the first school in the area to grant higher education degrees to African-Americans. Their status should have afforded them protection for a year after the hospital announced its plans to demolish them as part of a planned expansion.

However, the hospital and its developers were so eager to remove the buildings, and so unwilling to work with preservation professionals and activists, that it was able to convince councilman Keiffer Mitchell[1] to surreptitiously support a bill to remove the building's protection. He was successful, and within days, a crew from the hospital's contracting company, Potts and Callahan, had destroyed them (Hopkins 2007). Similar fates have befallen the historic Rochambeau Hotel, and the 1915 faux-Tudor Odorite building in recent years, and while these events have caused some public controversy, they have done little to bolster the movement to preserve historic landmarks in the city (Adams 2004).

Some heritage resources, however, *can* be turned into sites of consumption without being destroyed. The gentrified working-class neighbourhoods along the Baltimore

Figure 4.2   Ruins of St. Paul Street rowhouses (photo by author 2007).

waterfront provide examples of this, but more striking are the several industrial sites being converted into expensive condominiums and retail spaces. These include the Baltimore and Ohio Grain Elevator which towers over working-class Locust Point, the Baltimore Can Company, and the 1853 Poole and Hunt Foundry, two of which are listed on the National Register of Historic Places (National Register Information System 2007; Environmental Protection Agency 2007). In this case, sites of production are literally being converted to sites of consumption; places where free-market ideology and practice can play themselves out.

One such redevelopment, the Clipper Mill, consists of a series of buildings on the site of the former Poole and Hunt Foundry. Here, they have explicitly used the heritage of a nineteenth-century foundry—partially burned in 1996—as a selling point for new luxury condominiums. A site that had once supported the community's production economy now houses retail, restaurants and houses that working-class people from the nearby neighbourhoods of Hampden and Woodberry cannot even begin to afford (Figure 4.3).

My work in that Hampden neighbourhood began, somewhat naively, as an act of faith of my own. I chose, and still choose, to believe that anthropologists can change the power relations in communities by changing discourse centred on the marketable kind of heritage to discourse that stresses the agency of groups and individuals.

Figure 4.3   The recently re-developed Pool and Hunt Foundry site, now marketed as 'Clipper Mill' (photo by author 2012).

When I moved to the central Baltimore working-class enclave of Hampden in 2002, I noticed two things: first, the place was covered in heritage sites—indeed, it *was* a heritage site—and second, its heritage resources were rapidly being appropriated by middle-class gentrifiers like me who held little regard for the working-class community that still lived there or its traditions. Their heritage was being taken from them, transformed into a marketable good, and then sold to outsiders who came to visit the increasing number of expensive cafés, bars and kitschy shops along its main shopping street, which marketers had re-dubbed 'the Avenue'. 'There's nothing left here for us,' complained one longtime resident, referring to the lack of affordable services along that stretch of road.

An ongoing struggle over public space—the main community-held resource in a neighbourhood like Hampden—is played out annually at the 'Honfest', when Café Hon owner Denise Whiting closes several blocks of the Avenue for a 'public' festival. The culminating event of Honfest is the 'Baltimore's Best Hon' competition, in which women and girls, most of them middle-class visitors to the neighbourhood, dress up in outlandish costumes to lampoon working-class white women.

Just as the only free market response to crisis is to mount a marketing campaign, the archaeologist's only response to crisis is to organize an archaeology project. So in 2004 I began to organize the Hampden Community Archaeology Project (HCAP). The project began with community consultation in the form of a series of public history workshops, public conversations about history at which members of the community voiced their opinions about Hampden's past and present, as well as what they would like to know more about. That consultation allowed HCAP to develop a research programme that addressed community needs in at least two ways. First, by listening to public conversations about the past, we were able to delineate a research programme addressing issues of community interest: race, class, gender and gentrification were of the greatest interest.

These conversations also taught us something about what we needed to be doing as a programme. Hampden's citizens, particularly those who we might consider working-class or 'traditional Hampdenites', are very concerned about their youth. The economic transformations that Baltimore has seen in the last two decades have made it virtually impossible to make a living with a high school degree. Additionally, regionalized (rather than neighbourhood-based) secondary education has meant not only an increasing dropout rate in the neighbourhood, but also a decreasing standard of living for working-class people. Hampden wanted a programme that would work with youth. The second way that we were able to address community needs was by employing local and at-risk youth.

As a result, HCAP began in 2005 to conduct six-week-long summer excavation projects with Baltimore City high school students. We continued to work with them through the 2006 and 2007 field seasons and have worked now with a total of fifteen students from Hampden and surrounding neighbourhoods. Additionally, members of the Hampden community have taken site tours and helped to excavate and screen soils at our several public events. We have conducted archaeological excavations at five sites, generally mill worker tenements and houses dating from the 1840s through the early nineteenth century. In 2008 we extended the programme beyond education to include a student-run oral history project and conducted a public speaker's series through 2009.

The HCAP programme was designed to be intensively participatory and to include members of nearby communities. From the outset we worked, often with mixed results, to involve community members in as many aspects of the project as possible, from research design, to data collection, to interpretation. By 2009 we had performed excavations at five house sites in Hampden belonging to mill managers and workers, a railroad brakeman and a family of grocers. We assembled a collection of over 70,000 objects and performed a series of analyses aimed at better understanding the material dimensions of class and paternalism in nineteenth-century Hampden. We focused on the topics of class consciousness, isolation and alienation

We worked with students at the University of Maryland to transcribe a number of recordings from a 1979 oral history project, conducted oral history and ethnographic research of our own and conducted historical research. The products included two doctoral dissertations—Chidester's (2009) and Gadsby's (2010)—as well as a number of smaller projects and publications.

One of HCAP's key early projects was to organize a series of community history workshops intended to identify interested members of the public, use community input to develop a research design, and present and discuss the results of oral histories and archaeological investigations.

These early outreach efforts helped us to develop themes that would structure our research in the months and years to come, and they allowed us to interpret and discuss the results of our excavations with community members. They also lead us to understand that one important contribution that we could make to the neighbourhood was to provide employment and work experience for its youth. This proved to be fraught territory; simply recruiting youth workers from the neighbourhood was more difficult than we imagined, and anyone who has worked with teenagers knows that, once recruited, they have a profound aptitude for making life difficult. Nonetheless, it demonstrated to us (and perhaps to the neighbourhood) one way that archaeology could have a positive and direct effect on communities in which it is being conducted.

My faith and hope for this project rest in the recognition that archaeologists' power lies in our ability to critically interrogate the past and creatively disseminate information. This has been the project's goal since its inception. Using the tools of archaeology, as well as new century communication tools, we can make heard the silent expressions of the archaeological record.

The project relies on the notion of collective memory—a set of generally agreed upon narratives that people hold about the past (Shackel 2001:655–656). Public memories often serve dominant political groups by eclipsing the sources or even the very presence of inequality. However, they can also be a source of emancipatory power.

By commemorating events that highlight inequality, or by introducing memories that counter the dominant ones, we can counter damaging narratives. In Hampden, this has meant producing historical narratives that decentre mill owners as agents of history, and highlight the working class as an active and self-constituting voice.

In order to change public heritage discourses and memories, HCAP tries to participate in the public sphere in which they are generated. The faith part of this comes in the fact that the deck is stacked against emancipatory narratives. The public sphere is constituted in the middle class and already privileges middle-class voices. While it may be constituted in dialogue and discourse, it is capable of action and its actions intrude into the private lives of its citizens. Planning and policy decisions made in the public sphere rely on the narratives and regulating discourses of the public (Habermas 1994). Governments construct landscapes, build roads and provide services on the basis of those decisions. The appearance of democracy lends them legitimacy, note that the democracy is highly imperfect, often privileging the interests of those with the strongest narrative, or the most money (Harvey 1991). Most decisions about the allocation of public space are not made democratically, but are the product of routine bureaucratic action and everyday municipal decision making. If working-class narratives are left out of planning discourses, then they are left out of the planning. If planners include working-class people, then there is a greater chance that public decisions will reflect their will. If we remember, then, that some of the chief conflicts in Hampden, as in other classed landscapes, are between working- and middle-class people over how public space appears and is used, then we have a compelling reason to try to establish the claim and the voice of working people in Hampden, and to preserve a heritage that *can't* be marketed, but one that serves and commemorates the power of working people in the past.

Harvey has more recently extended his critique of city development by to include 'the right to the city', that is a fundamental right of global city-dwellers to control the shape and destiny of their urban spaces, and thus assert control over their own material and social lives. 'The right to the city,' he says, 'is far more than the individual liberty to access urban resources: it is a right to change ourselves by changing the city' (Harvey 2008:23). Working people, he says, should not be content with the trickle-down 'crumbs' of the wealthy, but should instead assert their right to prosper along with wealthier citizens. Acceptance of such a right would mean a fundamental rethinking of how urban economies run and how power is distributed in cities. It would mean wresting control of the built environment from a few developers and planners, and placing it in the hands of those whose lives and livelihoods are effected by such changes. I suggest that one tool for achieving such change should be material heritage. I have no illusions that Baltimore's problems can be solved only by studying its material past, but I also believe in the power of archaeology to change the way people think, and in turn to change the way they talk to each other about the past.

Note

1. At the time Mitchell served on the board of directors of Preservation Maryland, the state's premier non-profit organization devoted to heritage preservation.

Bibliography

Adams, R. (2004) Today's News Archives: Baltimore's Odorite Comes Down. Vol. 2007.

Beirne, D.R. (1976) Steadfast Americans: Residential stability among workers in Baltimore, 1880–1930. Unpublished PhD Thesis: University of Maryland.

Chambers, E. (2006) *Heritage Matters: Heritage, Culture, History, and Chesapeake Bay*. Maryland Sea Grant: College Park.

Chidester, R. (2009) Class, Community, and Materiality in a Blue-Collar Baltimore Neighborhood: An Archaeology of Hampden-Woodberry. Unpublished PhD Thesis: University of Michigan.

Environmental Protection Agency (2007) *The Can Company, Baltimore, Maryland | Smart Growth Illustrated | Smart Growth | US EPA*. Vol. 2007. United States Environmental Protection Agency. http://www.epa.gov/dced/case/canco.htm. Accessed 4 May 2012.

Federal Bureau of Investigations (2006) *Crime in the United States*. Federal Bureau of Investigations, Washington DC. http://www2.fbi.gov/ucr/cius2006/index.html Accessed 4 May 2012

Gadsby, D. (2010) An Archaeology of Industrial Paternalism, Urbanization, and Class in Hampden, Baltimore, Maryland. Unpublished PhD Thesis: American University.

Hartigan, J. (2000) Remembering white Detroit: Whiteness in the mix of history and memory. *City and Society* 7 (2): 11–34.

Habermas, J. (1994) *The Structural Transformation of the Public Sphere: An Inquiry into a Category of Bourgeois Life*. Cambridge, MA: MIT Press.

Harvey, D. (1991) A view from Federal Hill. In E. Fee, L. Shopes and L. Zeidman (eds.) *The Baltimore Book: New Views in Local History*, 227–249. Philadelphia: Temple University Press.

Harvey, D. (2008) The right to the city. *New Left Review* 53: 23–27

Hopkins, J. (2007) *Demolish List*. Vol. 2007. Baltimore: Baltimore Heritage.

Jacobson, J. (2007) The dismantling of Baltimore's public housing: Housing Authority cutting 2400 homes for the poor from its depleted inventory. *The Abell Report* 20 (4): 1–9.

Kelly, J. (1994) Noxzema put on top shelf in museum show. *The Baltimore Sun*. http://articles.baltimoresun.com/1994-11-28/news/1994332134_1_noxzema-baltimore-museum-pharmacy. Accessed 4 May 2012

National Register Information System (2007) Poole and Hunt Company Buildings. National Park Service.

Olson, S.H. (1997) *Baltimore: The Building of an American City*. Revised and expanded bicentennial edition. Baltimore, MD: Johns Hopkins University Press.

Painter, W. (1899) *Closure for Sealing Bottles* U.S. Patent No. 625055 Patented May 16, 1899. United States Patent Office, Washington, DC.

Shackel, P.A. (2001) Public memory and the search for power in American historical archaeology. *American Anthropologist* 103 (3): 655–670.

Segal, D., Trimarchi, M. and Corcoran, E. (1995) Gimme A Bromo [Final Edition]. *The Washington Post*. Washington, DC: Sep 4, 1995. p. F.03 http://proquest.umi.com/pqdweb?did=19403588&Fmt=3&clientId=11430&RQT=309&VName=PQD. Accessed 4 May 4, 2012

The Goldseker Foundation (ed.) (2002) *The Frog's Lesson: The Baltimore Region*. The Goldseker Foundation, Baltimore. http://www.goldsekerfoundation.org/uploaded_files/0000/0016/frogstory.pdf Accessed 4 May 2012

Žižek, S. (1989) Looking awry. *October* 50 (Autumn): 30–55.

Part II

Faith in Fashion

5 Trans-Atlantic Perspectives on Eighteenth-Century Clothing

Carolyn L. White

Introduction

Historical archaeology took root in the investigation of colonial encounters, focusing on English, Dutch, French, Spanish and Portuguese colonial engagements around the globe. Early definitions of historical archaeology centred the discipline on the study of the spread of colonization around the globe; Deetz described historical archaeology as 'the archaeology of the spread of European culture throughout the world since the fifteenth century and its impact on indigenous peoples' (Deetz 1977: 5). Whilst the scope of historical archaeology has diversified significantly in the last two decades, the study of colonialism is still an important strand within the discipline. Archaeologists increasingly have turned their attention to other areas of the world, employing techniques and approaches developed first in western colonial contexts. In taking up more wide-ranging colonial relationships, archaeologists have honed their skills in trying to reach an understanding of the impacts on and the relationships between the colonizer and the colonized in the new colonial environment. In this chapter, I am interested in exploring the relationship *between* the both sides in the colonizing relationships, examining connections between originating country and colonized place through the objects people used to clothe and adorn themselves.

Residents of the British colony of New Hampshire, USA and residents of London, England, were connected through many cultural threads. Like people throughout the world and throughout time, residents of both places communicated ideas about themselves as individuals and as members of various groups through the clothing they wore and the physical appearance they created (White 2008, 2005). In New Hampshire, the objects people used to construct this appearance were imported from England, almost exclusively, through the eighteenth century and into the nineteenth century. In the pages that follow I explore the connection between England and the New England colonies through trading practices and by comparing the choices individuals made in personal appearance as suggested by archaeological evidence in America and England.

The materials discussed here are drawn from household sites in Portsmouth, New Hampshire, USA and London, England. In comparing these assemblages, I have turned to look at the originating country, England, as an equal player in the trading practice, and have begun to explore the role of Britain as a supplier of personal adornment goods to America in the eighteenth and nineteenth centuries. This paper reflects on the manipulation of physical appearance through clothing in eighteenth-century England and America, with a perspective that encompasses *both* sides of the Atlantic. The comparison between these contemporary societies reveals many similarities and differences in the material world of each community. It also raises issues around the comparability of sites from vastly different contexts.

This trans-Atlantic evaluation of England and her colonies takes clothing as a class of material culture and compares it across a divide. How are the clothing and accessories worn by men, women and children the same? How are they different? What do these similarities and differences mean? This paper engages three research tracks. First, I present a summary of the materials relating to personal adornment research conducted in America, to examine the kinds of materials worn by Americans. Second, I present preliminary analysis of the use of personal adornment on domestic sites in England in order to look at the ways that people expressed individual identity and social groupings through clothing and personal appearance. Third, I compare the assemblages to highlight and interpret the parallels and variations in the construction of physical appearance in cross-national perspective.

Clothing and Individuality

Clothing provides one of many avenues through which people express individual and group identity (White 2005, 2008, 2010; Fisher and Loren 2003; Loren 2001). The physical appearance of a person is the result of a series of restricted and unrestricted choices that an individual makes based on a host of economic, social, cultural, temporal and locational factors.

Access to clothing and personal appearance of people in the past can be elusive (White 2005:7). Visual evidence is restricted to portraits of wealthy individuals and written documentation is fragmented and sparse as people very rarely comment on their own views of clothing (see White 2005 for a discussion of sources for identifying artefacts of personal adornment). In the nineteenth century the development of photography provides important evidence for understanding clothing across wide-ranging demographic groups (see Severa 1995; Mrozowski *et al.* 1996). The best evidence for the clothing and adornment of marginalized groups of people in the seventeenth and eighteenth centuries is archaeological (see also Egan and Pritchard 1991).

Archaeological data provides excellent evidence for understanding what people were wearing, but personal adornment artefacts make up a very small percentage of a given archaeological assemblage. This fact is owing to a variety of factors ranging from preservation conditions, long-term curation by individuals and families, relative rarity as a subset of personal possessions, and social, legal and religious restrictions (White 2008:20). Despite the restrictive nature of the material data, personal adornment as a class of material culture provides important clues to understanding the relationship between the colonizer and the colonized, and the disparate character of life in two distant places.

American Personal Adornment

Six archaeological sites on the grounds of Strawbery Banke Museum (Marshall Site, Wheelwright Site, Follett Site, Sherburne Site, Rider Wood Site, Shapiro Site) and four located elsewhere in Portsmouth (Richard Hart Site, Hart-Shortridge Site, Richard Shortridge Site, Warner Site) provide the American data for this study. These sites are domestic households and the individual episodes of occupation and deed transfer are known for each house. As a result, the artefacts recovered from these households can be linked to the wide range of demographic groups represented across the city (White 2002).

Nearly 200 personal adornment artefacts dating to the eighteenth and early nineteenth centuries were identified in Portsmouth, New Hampshire, in excavations undertaken between 1976 and 2002; these artefacts are categorized as clothing fasteners, jewelry, hair accessories, and miscellaneous accessories (White 2002). In this section I summarize the personal adornment materials recovered from these sites (see White 2004, 2008 for detailed analysis of two of these sites).

Clothing

Clothing fasteners, in the forms of aglets, buckles, buttons, and hooks and eyes were identified across the Portsmouth sites. These artefacts indicate that Portsmouth's residents wore stylish, if somewhat modestly embellished, clothing in a wide variety of styles throughout the eighteenth century. In this section I present the sorts of garments suggested by the clothing fasteners working from outer garments to inner garments, top to bottom.

Coats were worn by men throughout the late seventeenth to early nineteenth centuries, and the recovery of large coat buttons confirm that this was a common, though varied, garment among Portsmouth men. Most of the coat buttons are simple, undecorated buttons made of either pewter or copper alloy (Figure 5.1). Pewter, white metal, gilded copper alloy, silver, bone and shell coat buttons were identified across the sites, indicating the choices of these clothing details across the economic spectrum. Undecorated pewter or copper alloy stand at one end of the spectrum, and large gilded copper alloy buttons stand at the other (White 2005:58–59).

Waistcoat buttons were recovered across the Portsmouth sites. Indications of fashionability, status and expense are restricted to the material and decoration on the waistcoat button (White 2005:59). Brass button covers for stamped brass waistcoat buttons of various designs illustrate the range of choices that an individual could have when deciding which buttons to use on his garments. Waistcoat buttons of leather,

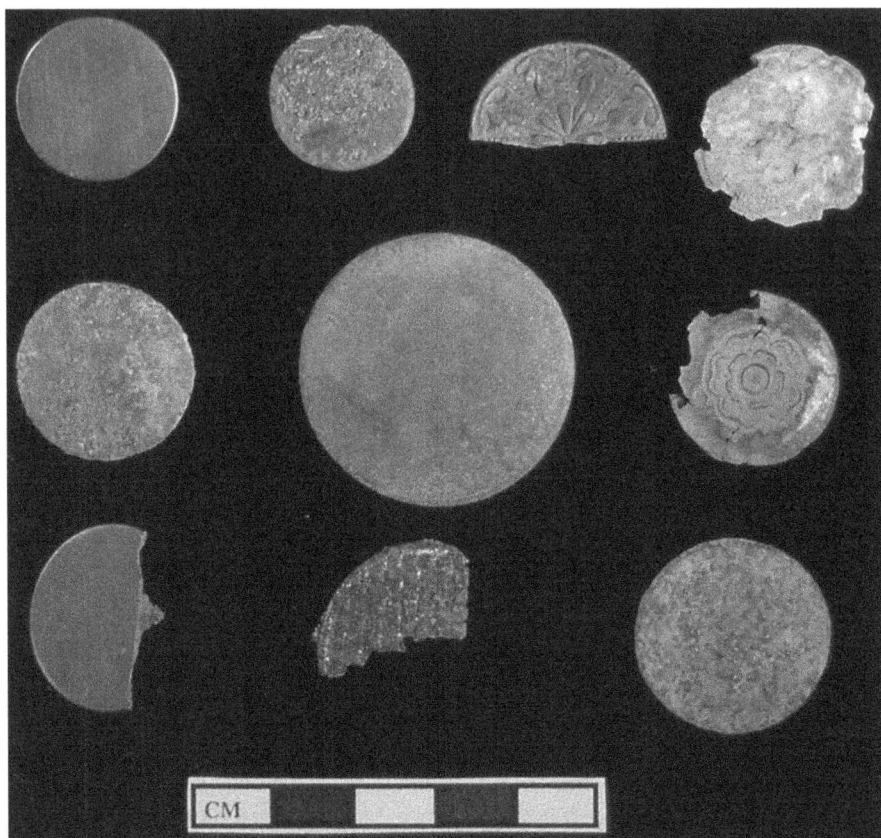

Figure 5.1   Examples of coat buttons from Portsmouth, New Hampshire.

bone, shell, lead, copper alloy, but mostly pewter were identified. Waistcoat buttons were decorated less frequently than coat buttons, which is not surprising, as waistcoat buttons were smaller, less expensive, and less prominently displayed on the body.

One girdle buckle was recovered at the Sherburne Site, and is one of a very few artefacts that provides insight into women's garments in Portsmouth. The buckle would have been part of a girdle, which was a belt that wrapped around the waist of the gown.

In the late seventeenth through the eighteenth century shirts were fastened at the wrist by sleeve buttons. The Portsmouth sleeve buttons are mainly common octagonal pewter buttons with crude engraved designs and others are round with more elaborate floral designs. Interestingly, the assemblage lacks sleeve buttons set with crystals or pastes, which were very fashionable in the eighteenth century.

A variety of undecorated buttons in the assemblages may have been used to fasten shirts at the neck. Horn and bone button moulds would have been covered with a fabric that would complement the shirt and allow the button to be sewn onto the shirt. Sew-through horn and shell shirt buttons were also used in Portsmouth. Metal shirt buttons, both decorated and undecorated, were also worn. Neckwear was an essential component of both male and female clothing, and buckles were used to fasten clothing elements such as stocks and collars (Cunnington and Cunnington 1972; White

2005:45). A simple stock buckle with modest cut designs was recovered from the Richard Hart Site; this buckle is the only example of such a buckle in the assemblage. Other buttons recovered at the sites were also used to fasten neckwear—an elaborate gilt button from the Richard Hart Site with a zigzag design is probably a stock button.

Trousers and breeches are represented in several ways in the Portsmouth sites. Some of the undecorated buttons in the assemblage likely fastened trousers or breeches at the waist and at the knees. Some of the trouser and breeches buttons are metal, and some of these are decorated, suggesting that there was choice in regard to the level of elaboration that might be used in something as functional as a trouser button. These buttons further suggest that visual differentiation between people operated on very mundane levels. Knee buckles were also used to fasten breeches at the knees, and a number of these were identified in Portsmouth. Oval and square shapes were used, though in general, this form of breeches fastener was not popular in Portsmouth with buttons being favoured.

Footwear

Shoes buckles are one of the most prominent and easily identifiable elements of personal appearance in the archaeological assemblage from Portsmouth. Made of copper alloy, pewter, and silver, the buckles range from small square buckles that were fashionable in the early to mid-eighteenth century to very large Artois-style buckles fashionable in the last quarter of the eighteenth century (Figure 5.2; White 2005:41). The decoration on the buckles runs from dramatic openwork, floral and rococo motifs, to more restrained decorations of simple lines, grooves and beading. The myriad forms and designs point to the level of individuation that corresponded to the shoe buckle. In fact, there are no two decorated shoe buckles that are alike, although there are a few undecorated shoe buckles that are the same. The decoration was a means that people had of visually setting themselves apart, marking themselves as part of a social grouping through the choices made in the selection of the shoe buckle decoration. Those who could not afford expensive decorated shoe buckles had a more narrow range of buckle forms from which they could select, and the fact that their shoe buckles might match someone of their own socioeconomic background would be a visual cue as to their class and status. Boots are suggested by two artefact types. Two garter buckles used to hold up top boots with a strap were recovered; this type of boot was fashionable in the last quarter of the eighteenth century. Spurs are suggested by a spur buckle and a spur rowel, which would have been worn with boots.

Other Clothing

Some of the other clothing suggested by the artefactual assemblage is more difficult to pinpoint, since the artefacts are parts of what could be many different kinds of individual garments. A fragment of metallic braid from the Richard Shortridge Site is a clothing component that is impossible to link to a particular garment. It is an expensive elaboration, used by a man to decorate a coat, glove or gauntlet, or by a woman to trim a gown. Aglets, used to prevent the ends of lacing from unravelling,

Figure 5.2   Examples of shoe buckles from Portsmouth, New Hampshire.

were recovered, although it is impossible to know specifically what kind of lacing was being used. It is also difficult to connect the numerous hooks and eyes found across the sites to particular garments of clothing since they had broad use on many clothing items. Both men's and women's clothing was fastened with hooks and eyes whenever edge-to-edge closure was desired (Cunnington and Cunnington 1972:114, 228).

Jewelry

Portsmouth residents wore very little jewelry. The general absence of this type of personal adornment is demonstrated in portraiture, wills, probates and newspaper advertisements, which reinforce both the relative rarity and high value placed on these items (Andresen 1982:127). The rarity of jewelry meant that it carried a high visual impact when worn. The Portsmouth sites yielded a small number of jewelry artefacts of both the expensive and less expensive sorts; a single gold earring recovered at the Richard Hart Site would have been a dramatic fashion statement when worn, and at the Sherburne Site a cut crystal bears a cypher of two interlocking Cs surrounded by a chain border that would have been filled with gold wire and set in a ring or brooch. On the less expensive end of the scale are two crude brooches that could be pinned to a garment, and are likely to have had a primary function as fasteners.

The group of beads found across Portsmouth suggests an array of jewelry but are not clearly diagnostic. The beads can be divided into standard beads and seed beads. The standard beads are likely to have been parts of jewelry items such as necklaces, bracelets and earrings. The single gold bead recovered at the Sherburne Site affirms that Portsmouth women occasionally wore gold bead necklaces as they did throughout eighteenth-century America (Wright 1990:19; Fales 1995; White 2005:82–83). Only eight seed beads were recovered in the Portsmouth excavations. Two beads are yellow coloured, but they are also found in dark and light blue, red, green, pink and white. The seed beads were probably sewn onto textiles, forming designs on clothing or accessories such as purses or moccasins, although they could also have been employed in earrings (White 2005:82).

Hair Accessories

Documentary sources suggest that Portsmouth residents were concerned with hair fashions. For example, an advertisement by Isaac Williams, 'Periwig-Maker, Hair-Cutter, and Dresser from Boston' in the *New Hampshire Gazette*, promises:

> an Assortment of HAIRS as can be imported from London, Also a Collection of the best that can be had in this Country for Wigs. He hopes that Gentlemen both in Town and Country will oblige him with their Custom, where they may have Wiggs of the neatest Fashion, and of any Colour both for Sea or Land. N.B. As the Fashion of Hair is so much extinguished it is needless to mention any Thing in regard to the Dressing of Hair; a new Fashion is come over for Wiggs in imitation of Hair. (February 1, 1765)

Although the interest in hair styling is not reflected in large numbers of accessories, most likely due to their fragile and ephemeral nature, several hair accessories were recovered. One side comb and four double-sided dressing combs with fine teeth were identified. As suggested by Williams' advertisement, wig curlers were used to maintain and dress wigs that were worn by men and women; two sites (the Rider-Wood site and the Sherburne site) yielded wig curlers.

Miscellaneous Accessories

The category of miscellaneous accessories incorporates a variety of artefacts from the Portsmouth excavations. A cosmetic tool, fans and several watch accessories and components were recovered. The cosmetic tool had multiple uses: a cosmetic spoon for measuring or applying ointments and powders; a manicuring tool used to clean the fingernails; and an ear scoop used for drawing wax from the ear for use in sewing. As a manicuring tool, the object would be used to clean and maintain the fingernails. Well-groomed hands were a sign of gentility and were powdered to improve their appearance. The use of a special tool such as this implies a concern for maintaining the hands in a particular manner—more than standard hygiene and care. This is a specialized tool that was probably a luxury item (White 2005:121). Fan sticks provided support for the fan leaves and would have been visible even when the fan was closed; two examples of carved bone fan sticks were recovered, one with intricate carvings and one with a more simple carved design. Several items related to watches were also found. A watch case fragment is probably a *fausse montre* (false watch), a stylish accessory in the late eighteenth century (White 2005:130, 132). Such watches were high-status items, although they were less expensive than a working watch. A watch seal engraved with a rather crudely rendered anchor would have been worn on a chain, potentially with other watch accessories. Three lengths of chain may have formed parts of watch chains.

The Assemblage

What does the Portsmouth assemblage of personal adornment artefacts reveal about what people wore? As a whole, the assemblage portrays a society that matches expectations of eighteenth-century appearance and, in keeping with eighteenth-century social structures, the assemblage is as broadly modest and unassuming as it is fashionable, expensive and stylish. The assemblage reflects the cross-section of residents in Portsmouth, ranging from wealthy merchants to artisans, to widows, workers, indentured servants and enslaved peoples. An ensemble of expected attire—coats, waistcoats, shirts, buckled shoes and buckled breeches—are some of the main garments suggested by the artefacts. Men's clothing resonates most clearly in the assemblage. Clothing fasteners dominate the collection and plain buttons form the majority of the subassemblage of buttons (Figure 5.1). The sites produced very few expensive items, reflecting the modest garb worn by most people in daily life.

At the same time, it is clear from the assemblage that some Portsmouth residents were aware of current fashions and strove to keep up with them. While the assemblage may not contain examples of what would have been the most costly items, such as paste shoe buckles or high-priced jewelry and watches, there are many examples of items that are still expensive and stylish (Figure 5.2). For example, there is immense variety in the form and decoration of shoe buckles. Large Artois-style buckles were recovered in contexts that date to the 1760s–1780s, the time period in which large shoe buckles were at the height of fashion. Likewise, large buttons were also very fashionable and these were also recovered in contexts dating to the 1760s–1780s. Buckles and buttons were highly visible on the body and were the main ways that men displayed their status and fashionability in the period. The assemblage demonstrates that Portsmouth residents were attentive to their grooming habits, along with a penchant for the fan and watch and chain or equipage as decorative accessories.

The source for almost all of the personal adornment artefacts recovered in Portsmouth was England. Eighteenth-century Americans obtained almost all of their clothing from British sources; in the late eighteenth and early nineteenth century production of textiles and clothing accessories (particularly buttons) began in America in large enough quantities to supply the inhabitants.

English Personal Adornment

Turning to the eastern side of the Atlantic, two archaeological sites excavated by the Museum of London Archaeological Services and curated at the London Archaeological Archive Research Centre provide the material for an examination of British personal adornment and identity construction: Bishopsgate and Fleet Valley. The sites are massive and the scale of the excavations and the sorts of materials recovered highlight some of the issues involved with cross-Atlantic comparison.

Bishopsgate

The excavations at 250 Bishopsgate took place in 1995 and 1996. The site was occupied from the Roman period to the 20th century. In the eighteenth century residential structures were located on the site, following its use as an artillery ground in the seventeenth century. The post-medieval materials comprised only a small portion of the recovered artefacts and features, and were not the focus of the excavations. In fact, the final report states, 'the seventeenth and eighteenth century finds are unremarkable' (Thomas and Dunwoodie 1997:48). Despite this assessment and the small size of the assemblage, the artefacts show a range of clothing and aspects of personal appearance.

Clothing is represented by the fasteners found at the site. Metal and bone buttons used to fasten men's coats are plain, with the exception of one textured example. Two strap buckles were found, one rectangular and one double framed, and while these were used on men's clothing, their use is unknown. These are fragments of adult men's clothing, made of common sorts of materials. One ivory and one tortoiseshell double-sided dressing comb was recovered representing the category of hair accessories. Jewelry is present in an assortment of standard beads made of amber, jet and glass.

Each of the artefacts noted above was recovered in a unique context, unrelated to the rest of the assemblage. Each artefact may reflect the garb of a number of people, as they were distributed across the site's seventeenth- and eighteenth-century contexts. The small size of the assemblage means that it cannot provide a comprehensive view of the garb of the people of the neighbourhood, except in the sense of a potentially misleading Spartan aesthetic. The Bishopsgate materials, by and large, are less elaborate than the Portsmouth materials, though they parallel them in the distribution across a variety of categories.

Fleet Valley Project

The Fleet Valley Project took place between 1988 and 1992 and offers a compelling contrast to Bishopsgate as well as to the Portsmouth assemblages. Fleet Valley was an immense excavation, with prehistoric, Roman, Saxon, Medieval and Post-Medieval artefacts recovered from many sites within a project area of more than 50,000 square metres and 100 different areas of excavation (McCann 1993:1). The personal adornment artefacts total over 300 artefacts. The large number of artefacts provides an excellent opportunity to study the range of materials worn by people in post-medieval

London. Nonetheless, the scale of the site means that few artefacts were recovered in the same context, so they are representative of a broad range of time and space.

Clothing

Clothing fasteners dominate the assemblage, as is typically the case in eighteenth-century assemblages and is certainly shown in New England (see White 2004, 2008). The buttons recovered at the site are mostly coat and waistcoat buttons, with small numbers of shirt and breeches buttons (Figure 5.3). Since the assemblage falls largely in the middle of the eighteenth century, it is difficult to distinguish between coat and waistcoat buttons, since it was late in the eighteenth century that the difference in size became dramatic (White 2005:57). Nonetheless, there are several decorated buttons in the assemblage indicating the variety of coats and waistcoats worn by adult men in eighteenth-century London.

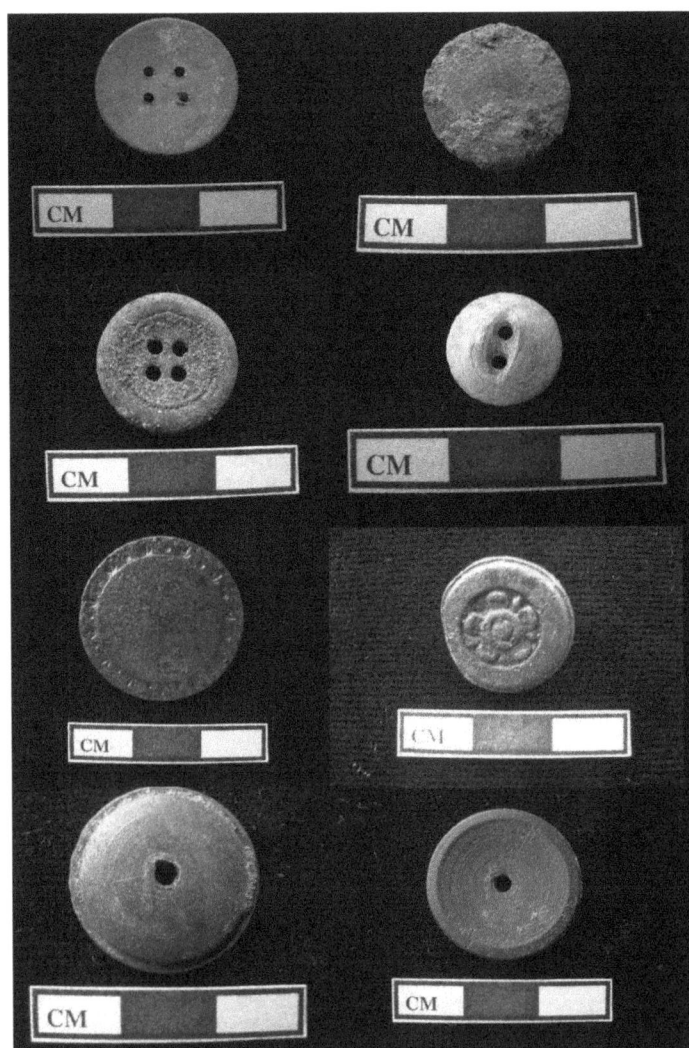

Figure 5.3   Examples of buttons from the Fleet Valley Project, London.

The buttons are made of a range of materials including copper alloy, iron, bone and shell. A wide series of manufacturing methods are also present, from hollow cast to die stamped copper alloy crimped over bone cores, to solid cast buttons (see White 2005:63–72 for further information on identification of such forms). The bone buttons are single and four-hole variety cores, all of which would have been covered by metal or cloth material. Two small shell buttons were also identified. The range of materials is representative of the diversity of materials from which people could select to adorn their clothing.

There is evidence of button manufacturing from two different loci within this large site in the form of waste from making bone and shell buttons. A recovered oyster shell demonstrates just how low the ratio of raw material to usable material was, making shell buttons among the most expensive in the eighteenth century, as a single button was punched from the shell. The low density of waste also demonstrates the small scale of production of these materials, typically occurring on a cottage industry level.

Edge to edge closure is also well-represented across the site and shows a less visible mode of garment closure; the form and detail of the textiles were far more important than the adorning elements of the garments. While it is not possible to assess the particular piece of clothing on which these artefacts were worn, at least some of them were probably used on stays or to fasten dresses. Rather than being exclusively plain, there are some hooks that possess decorative motifs.

A large Artois-style shoe buckle and sword buckles indicate the presence of these clothing items on the site. The rest of the buckles are double-sided strap buckles with no specific associated garment, though they do have a known association with men's clothing generally. The site, however, lacks a broad range of buckles, contrasting with the popularity of this form of shoe closure at the Portsmouth sites.

Jewelry

Jewelry is represented in several different forms. Standard and seed beads in a variety of size, colours and forms were found in large numbers, spread across many contexts. This could represent manufacturing on site rather than the discard or loss of personal jewelry items. The range of sizes and narrow array of colour on a given site underscores this possibility. Two table-cut colourless gems were also recovered, suggesting a pair of earrings, or the preparation of gems for setting in jewelry. In addition, two gold-plated plain finger rings were identified (Figure 5.4). The rings are unusual finds and may have been betrothal rings, memorial rings or simply modest decorative adornment (White 2005:93–97).

Hair Accessories

Hair accessories in the form of combs, wig curlers and wire ornaments were found across the Fleet Valley sites. Fourteen fragmentary and relatively intact dressing combs made of bone and ivory were found. The presence of wig curlers attests to the care of wigs, worn more typically, but not exclusively, by wealthy individuals. A broad range of delicate wire

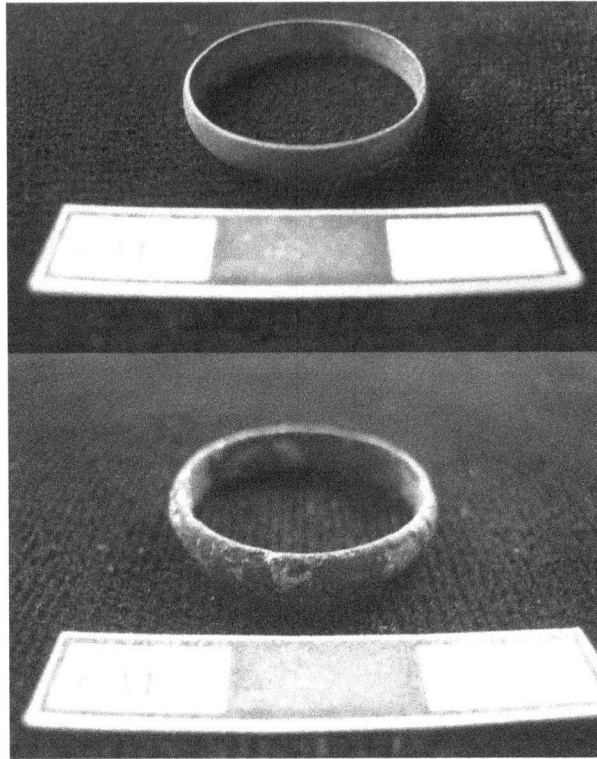

Figure 5.4   Examples of finger rings from the Fleet Valley Project, London.

artefacts also suggest the presence of additional hair ornaments. These would have been used in the very elaborate hair styles of the eighteenth century, when women's hair was piled high on the head, and frizzed and built up with false hair (White 2005:111–114). Decorative elements such as feathers, ribbons, gems and more sculptural elements were used to adorn the hair, making it a focal point of women's fashion.

Miscellaneous Accessories
The category of miscellaneous accessories offers few materials. Three fan sticks were recovered on the sites, attesting to the use of the fan as a popular accessory in the eighteenth century (Figure 5.5). Of course, these are specifically gendered artefacts, used by women, possessing a language all their own (Armstrong 1974:180–184). One of the sticks suggests a late eighteenth-century date as it possesses the 'narrow attenuated style calculated to give a cartwheel effect when the fan was opened' (Marschner 1983:1).

The Fleet Valley materials exhibit a very broad range of clothing worn in seventeenth- and eighteenth-century London. The scale of the excavation and the way that it cut across many different areas of the city means that a cross section of the community is represented in the assemblage. It is not surprising, then, to see the broad range of materials and examples of artefacts in a variety of categories. What is surprising is the overall ordinary character of most of the artefacts. The assemblage consists mainly of

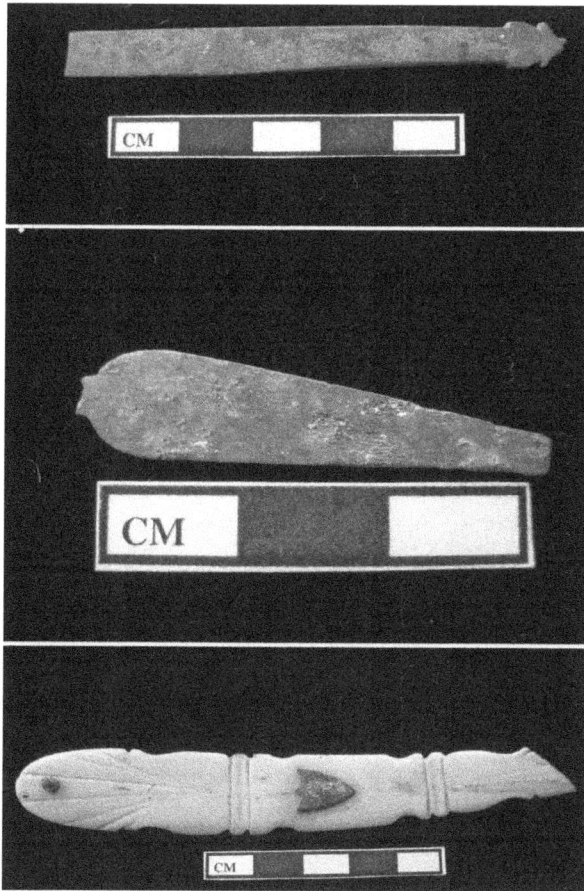

Figure 5.5   Examples of fan sticks from the Fleet Valley Project, London.

very common materials punctuated by a few unusual examples of fine or rare items, such as the rings, gems and fans. There is very little reflection of current fashions or even of a common style, which might be expected in such an assemblage.

Clothing Across a Divide

Comparing sites on either side of the Atlantic allows a perspective on the ways that the inhabitants of the colony and the country of origin clothed their bodies, and within those actions lies an array of issues regarding personal choice, identity construction and consumer behaviour. This trans-Atlantic comparison also raises a host of interpretive issues in terms of scale, excavation strategies and treatment of assemblages.

The greatest interpretive challenge is presented by scale; the British sites were large-scale excavations undertaken for major construction projects in the city of London as compared to the individual households excavated in Portsmouth. The scale and excavation priorities may also have affected the sorts of materials recovered. The Richard Hart Site in Portsmouth measured 891 square metres of which 118 square metres were excavated. Fleet Valley, by contrast was over fifty times larger than that area (50,000 square metres).

One aspect of dress that is revealing in terms of the similarity and difference between dress in England and America is the trajectory of dress in America before and after independence. In the years approaching and following the revolutionary war, the archaeological record does not provide a clear distinction between the two eras; there is little evidence that Americans took up the nationalistic movement to reduce reliance on imported British goods in terms of fashion and personal appearance in any significant way. The archaeological record shows that people continued to pay very close attention to trends in clothing and adornment, set and spread by British fashion and production (see White 2010). The assemblage of personal adornment artefacts provides evidence that Portsmouth's residents complied with and took up patriotic ideology only selectively, maintaining a link to English visual identity via an affinity for English fashions while forging a new national American identity. Although these people were displaced and were establishing themselves in new environments, new landscapes and new communities, they retained a link to the place they had left through their garments and personal adornment.

Bibliography

Andresen, K. (1982) The Layered Society: Material Life in Portsmouth, N.H., 1680–1740. PhD Dissertation, University of New Hampshire. Ann Arbor, MI, University Microfilms International: Ann Arbor Dissertation Services.

Armstrong, N. (1974) *A Collector's History of Fans*. London: Studio Vista.

Cunnington, C.W. and Cunnington, P. (1972) *Handbook of English Costume in the Eighteenth Century*. London: Faber and Faber.

Deetz, J. (1977) *In Small Things Forgotten: The Archaeology of Early American Life*. New York: Anchor Books.

Egan, G. (n.d). Assessment of Non-Ceramic Finds (Medieval and Post-Medieval) from the Fleet Valley Project. Manuscript on file at the London Archaeological Archive and Research Center.

Egan, G. and Pritchard, F. (1991) *Dress Accessories c. 1150–1450. Medieval Finds from Excavations in London*: 3. London: HMSO.

Fales, M.G. (1995) *Jewelry in America 1600–1900*. Woodbridge, Suffolk: Antique Collectors Club.

Fisher, G. and Loren, D. (2003) Embodying identity in archaeology. *Cambridge Archaeological Journal* 13: 225–230.

Loren, D. (2001) Social skins: Orthodoxies and practices of dressing in the Early Colonial Lower Mississippi Valley. *Journal of Social Archaeology* 1 (2): 172–189.

Loren, D. (2010) *The Archaeology of Clothing and Bodily Adornment in Colonial America*. Gainesville: University Press of Florida.

Marschner, J. (1983) Five Fragments of Bone/Ivory Fan Sticks. Manuscript on file at the London Archaeological Archive and Research Center.

McCann, B. (ed.) (1993) *Fleet Valley Project: Interim Report*. London: Museum of London Archaeology Service.

Mrozowski, S.A., Ziesing, G.H. and Beaudry, M.C. (1996) *Living on the Boot: Historical Archaeology at the Boott Mills Boardinghouses, Lowell, Massachusetts*. Amherst: University of Massachusetts Press.

Severa, J. (1995) *Dressed for the Photographer: Ordinary Americans and Fashion, 1840–1900*. Ohio: Kent State University Press.

Thomas, C. and Dunwoodie, L. (1997) *250 Bishopsgate London, E1: London Borough of Tower Hamlets, A Post Excavation Assessment*. London: Museum of London Archaeology Service.

White, C.L. (2002) *Constructing Identities: Personal Adornment from Portsmouth, New Hampshire, 1680–1820*. PhD Dissertation, Boston University, Proquest, UMI Dissertations Publishing.

White, C.L. (2004) What the Warners wore: An archaeological investigation of visual appearance. *Northeast Historical Archaeology* 33: 39–66.

White, C.L. (2005) *American Artifacts of Personal Adornment, 1680–1820: A Guide to Identification and Interpretation*. Lanham, MD: AltaMira Press.

White, C.L. (2008) Personal adornment and interlaced identities at the Sherburne Site, Portsmouth, New Hampshire. *Historical Archaeology* 42 (2): 17–37.

White, C.L. (2010) 'Beholden to foreign countries': Trade and clothing in Portsmouth, New Hampshire In C.D. Dillian and C.L. White (eds.) *Trade and Exchange: Archaeological Studies from Prehistory and History*, 113–128. New York: Springer Press.

Wright, M. (1990) *Put on Thy Beautiful Garments: Rural New England Clothing, 1783–1800*. East Montpelier, VT: The Clothes Press.

6 Articles of Faith and Decency: The Huguenot Refugees

Greig Parker

Introduction

During the mid-sixteenth to the early-eighteenth centuries, several hundred thousand Protestant refugees fled religious persecution in France and the Low Countries. The refugees migrated primarily to neighbouring Protestant territories where they established their own churches and communities. These churches subsequently provided a vital support network for the second wave of Protestant refugees who arrived in the late-seventeenth century following the Revocation of the Edict of Nantes, which had effectively banned Protestant worship in France. Despite the risk of imprisonment and extreme hardships, hundreds of thousands of Protestants chose to leave France rather than abjure their faith. Many of the refugees were destitute upon their arrival and relied upon the charity and support of both the French churches and the host community. The refugees were composed primarily of artisans, professionals and the nobility. They brought with them skills, techniques and fashions that have been credited with playing an important role in the economic and cultural transformation of their host countries.

This paper discusses how an analysis of material culture can help us understand Huguenot beliefs and social practices. In particular, it examines how, by popularizing and disseminating elements of French culture within their host societies, the Huguenot refugees contributed towards to the erosion of the very values that they were trying to uphold. Huguenot artisans involved in the production of luxury items popularized the extravagant and ornate designs created by the court of the Catholic king Louis XIV. They increased the availability and affordability of fine cloths, ornate furniture and personal adornments. In so doing, they promoted and spread the ownership of styles of material culture that were disapproved of by their faith. This can be seen to have been a cause of friction within congregations, and to have also led to disputes between different Reformed churches. In addition, these changes in the fashions and standards of decency of the wider society resulted in the modification of understandings of decency within the refugee communities themselves. This can, perhaps, be seen as a contributory factor in explaining the relatively rapid integration of the refugees into their host societies.

In exploring these issues, this paper aims to show how material culture played a significant role in shaping the social practices of the Huguenot community, and how these changes in social practices produced unintended consequences due to the recursive nature of the inter-relationships between material culture, social practice and identity. The main argument of this paper is that the contribution of the Huguenot refugees to the production and spread of luxury goods resulted in a modification of standards of decency in both the host society and amongst the Huguenots themselves. Disagreements over standards of decency became a source of conflict within the Huguenot communities and led to a decline in group cohesion, resulting in increased integration.

Theoretical Perspective

One of the primary concerns of this discussion is the relationship between the material environment (landscape, architecture and material culture) and social identity (e.g. age, gender, class, ethnicity and status). It seeks to explore how identity is created, maintained and modified, and the role played by the material environment in this process. The approach taken to understanding this relationship is one that is based on practice theory, particularly that proposed by Bourdieu (1977) and Giddens (1984), and subsequently developed by authors such as Barrett (1988, 2000), Dietler and Herbich (1998), Lightfoot, Wake and Schiff (1998), and Silliman (2001). Social identity is seen as being created, maintained and modified through practice. The material environment helps shape practice, and is itself modified through practice. The material environment can therefore be used to make inferences about practice and, as a result, identity.

Three key concepts of practice theory are of particular relevance to this paper: the habitus, social fields and body hexis. Bourdieu describes the habitus as being a set of durable dispositions that structures social practice (Bourdieu 1977:72). Here, it is used to refer to the range of 'ways of doing' considered appropriate in any given situation, and which are often performed in a routine or habitual manner. The habitus varies between individuals, groups and fields of social practice due to differences in circumstances. Importantly, the relationship between the habitus and social practice is recursive: habitus shapes, and is itself shaped by, practice. The concept of fields of social practice holds that social practices can be seen as taking place within different domains, each with their own logic or 'ways of doing' (a habitus). Individuals strategically perform different social practices in order to gain capital, which may be cultural, economic, social or symbolic in form. Each social practice often takes place within multiple fields simultaneously and, as a result, fields are inter-related and may share structural similarities. In particular, dispositions that originate in one field may be transferred to another field, while changes in capital or social practices in one field may cause changes in another field. Body hexis is used to refer to the embodiment of the habitus through bodily comportment (Bourdieu 1977:87). Each individual has only one body and yet it operates within multiple fields. It can therefore be seen how dispositions may be transferred from one field to another through body hexis.

The Huguenots Refugees

The Huguenots were French Protestants during the sixteenth to eighteenth centuries. The rapid growth of the Protestant movement in France in the mid-sixteenth century resulted in the French Wars of Religion (1562–1598). A fragile peace was agreed with the Edict of Nantes that provided some degree of protection for Protestants, albeit with numerous restrictions upon their activities. At the turn of the century, it has been estimated that France contained one million Protestants (Benedict 2001:93). New civil wars broke out in 1621 culminating in the siege of La Rochelle in 1628/9. Although the defeat of the Huguenot forces ended the religious warfare, the Catholic authorities continued in their attempts to convert Protestant worshipers and prevent the practice of their faith.

The full accession to the throne of Louis XIV in 1661 led to renewed persecution of the Huguenots. Louis enacted a number of oppressive laws that included the exclusion of Protestants from a variety of professions and the prohibition of inter-faith marriages. Huguenot refugees had migrated in small numbers to neighbouring countries since the middle of the sixteenth century. The renewed levels of persecution that began in the 1660s increased this migration to perhaps a few hundred per year (Benedict 2001:69). The Revocation of the Edict of Nantes in 1685 effectively prohibited Protestant worship and required Protestants to convert to Catholicism. Ministers who refused to convert were banished, while Huguenot lay-people were prohibited from attempting to leave the country (Gwynn 2001:28).

Following the Revocation, and despite the restrictions on emigration, approximately 200-250,000 refugees fled to neighbouring Protestant territories (Murdoch 1985:51). The majority of Huguenots, however, remained in France. Increased toleration of Protestantism did not arrive until the late eighteenth century and its recognition as a state religion was not achieved until the nineteenth century.

The largest numbers of refugees fled to the Netherlands, England and Germany. Relying on the charity of their host societies and the support networks of previous generations of refugees, they formed close-knit urban communities in many large towns and cities. The refugees were composed primarily of artisans, professionals and the nobility. They have been credited with having had an important cultural and economic effect on the development of western societies by bringing with them new skills and designs in areas such as luxury goods and the textile industry (Gwynn 2001).

However, by the mid-eighteenth century, most members of the Huguenot communities appear to have become socially, economically and ideologically integrated into their host societies, with only a minority perceiving their Huguenot descent as being a primary aspect of their identity (Gwynn 1998:17; van Ruymbeke 2001:332). Several authors have suggested various reasons to explain this pattern, such the size of the communities, their distance from France, their success at establishing a well-organized church, and the assimilationist tendencies of the host society (van Ruymbeke 2003:2). This paper suggests an additional cause that may have influenced the process of integration: the role of the refugees in the production and popularization of luxury goods.

Huguenots and Luxury Goods

There is a substantial body of research that demonstrates a rapid growth in the luxury goods market in Western Europe at the end of the seventeenth century (Beier 1986; Berg and Clifford 1999; Earle 1989; Weatherill 1996). This included both the spread of once-rare items and the introduction of new forms and styles. Increasingly, luxury goods became available to a wider section of society (Lemire 2000:394).

The Huguenot refugees have been credited with having played a significant role in the manufacture and popularization of luxury goods in a number of countries (Gwynn 2001:81–95; Frijhoff 2003:147). This was due, in part, to the popularity of French fashions during the period, and the difficulty and expense in obtaining them. The Huguenots brought with them new manufacturing skills and techniques that enabled them to produce luxury items that often approached the quality of French imports (Figures 6.1 and 6.2). This was because many of the refugees were the same individuals who had produced these goods prior to their migration. They continued to follow changes in French fashions after their migration and were themselves significant consumers of luxury goods (Riding 2001:136).

Figure 6.1   Two-handled covered silver cup (1736–37) by Paul de Lamerie, London (copyright Victoria and Albert Museum, London).

Figure 6.2   Waistcoat (1734), Spitalfields, London (copyright Victoria and Albert Museum, London).

Huguenots and Decency

The Huguenots were members of the Reformed Church (Calvinists). Based upon the writings of John Calvin, they believed in an omnipotent, omniscient and omnipresent God. A key, and controversial, tenet was that of double predestination. This held that all of humanity was depraved and salvation was only by God's grace. Being omniscient, God had foreseen who would be saved (the elect) and who would be damned. A person could not know the mind of God, could not earn salvation and could not be absolved of their sins. Instead, they were required to simply live as good a Christian life as possible and trust in having been granted salvation. As a result, all of one's actions mattered as they demonstrated whether one was to be damned or saved.

As Rublack (2005:61) has argued, Calvinism was seen by many of its members as a form of social renewal. There was an emphasis on civility and decency in order to rid society of what was seen as the corruption and moral decay that had gone before. She suggests that all aspects of behaviour (a habitus) were used to demonstrate this godly lifestyle, from the trimming of beards to the way in which beer was drunk.

Calvinist principles of civility and decency emphasized simplicity and self-discipline in all aspects of life. Members were expected to display neither frugality nor excess, and act in a manner appropriate to one's rank and status (Roelker 1972:409). As this was a relative standard, there were disagreements between Calvinist churches and congregations; Dutch Calvinists, for example, appear to have been more conservative than French Calvinists. There also seem to have been differences between different French-speaking groups, perhaps even reflecting regional differences in attitudes (Gwynn 2001:214–15). It is important to note that the majority of Huguenots did not conform to the conservative and austere Puritan stereotype that is often assigned to Calvinists (Frijohff 2003:159; Richardson 2006:503).

Luxury Goods and Decency

The involvement of the Huguenots in the luxury goods industry and their standards of decency suggests an apparent contradiction. The Huguenot refugees were instrumental in the production and popularization of the very items commonly used to portray the values that they opposed: excess and the gratuitous display of wealth.

This was, in fact, a cause of tension both within and between communities. Calvin argued that the accumulation of wealth was positive as it demonstrated God's blessing of the Reformed way of life, and enabled this wealth to be used for good works. The wasteful use of wealth, however, was sinful and he condemned luxurious clothing, vain decoration of the body, luxurious décor and sumptuous living. Luxuries were seen as being a distraction from religious contemplation (Murdock 2006). Weber (1930) has argued that this translated into a Protestant work ethic, in which economic activity was perceived to be good, while idleness was considered sinful.

The doctrine of double predestination also supported the positive aspects of wealth accumulation. For those Huguenots working in the luxury goods trade, customers who bought excessive or unnecessary items were damned. However, good could be produced from this sinful activity by the use of the profit for good works. The elect could also purchase luxury items, such as gold watches or porcelain vessels, provided that they did so in order to display civility and decency appropriate to their rank and status. This demonstrated God's blessing of the Reformed lifestyle and enabled consumption itself to be seen as a godly activity by using profit for good ends.

Others, most notably those labelled as Puritans, took a harsher line over the luxury goods trade and wealth accumulation more generally. Baxter, for example, warned of its dangers, although his position seems to have been largely motivated by his belief that wealth accumulation promoted idleness and wastefulness, rather than anything inherently sinful about wealth itself (Weber 1930:56).

Luxury Goods, Decency and Assimilation

It is clear that Huguenot attitudes to luxury goods were tied to their attitudes to decency, both in the use of the goods themselves and the use of the profit from their sale and manufacture. However, each of these attitudes had positive and negative consequences, and each changed over time.

Amongst the positive aspects were that it provided economic opportunities for the refugees who were trying to adapt to their displacement to a foreign society. Beyond simply enabling them to provide for their basic survival needs, their skills and knowledge in luxury goods design and manufacturing meant that their host societies, in particular the upper ranks, were more sympathetic to their plight. Additionally, their success and profit allowed them to fund good works such as supporting the church and the provision of charity to other refugees. Their ability to display civility and decency demonstrated God's blessing on them and reinforced their belief in being amongst the 'elect'. In all these ways, Huguenot production of luxury goods served to strengthen their group identity.

However, it can be argued that there were also negative consequences to Huguenot involvement in the luxury goods trade and in their attitudes towards decency. In many ways, they were promoting a Catholic version of French culture that was characterized by opulence, extravagance and excess. This was directly contrary to their expressed beliefs about decency. It also supported the regime of Louis XIV, who had been responsible for their persecution, by promoting the import of French goods and fashions, such as luxury textiles and jewellery (Riding 2001:134).

Attitudes to decency varied over time in both England and other European countries. Broadly speaking, the mid-seventeenth century in England was a period of austerity, reaching its height during the Interregnum. The Restoration brought a period of extravagance and opulence. This was, in part, a reaction to the preceding period, but it was also promoted by the monarchy, which admired the grandeur of the French court. By the early eighteenth-century, opinion had begun to change and there were an increasing number of calls for modesty and less extravagance. Throughout these periods, there was a steady increase in the availability of luxury goods throughout English society. Once-rare items became commonplace and the diversity of luxury items dramatically increased. These included artefacts associated with hot beverage consumption, upholstered furniture and personal adornments (Weatherill 1996:25). Huguenot involvement in the luxury goods trade played a significant role in increasing the range and availability of luxury items, and in helping spread the consumption of such items to the lower ranks. This resulted in a change in fashions and attitudes to decency amongst the host society, in a direction that ran counter to the values traditionally held by the Huguenots.

Consequently, Huguenot standards of decency also began to change. Huguenot standards were relative to that of the host society and were negotiated by members of the community: neither frugal nor excessive, and appropriate to one's status. Therefore, as the fashions and standards of the host society accepted increasing amounts of personal adornments, the use of fine cloths, and the display of wealth amongst the upper and middle ranks, similar changes were taking place to Huguenot standards of decency. There was a movement away from the simplicity and self-discipline that had once been a key element of their group identity. Although the standards of decency amongst the Huguenots were still conservative in relation to their host society, they were less conservative in comparison to previous generations of Huguenots.

However, with the change in wider society back towards more modesty and restraint during the early eighteenth century, the distinction between Huguenot standards and those of the host society became less apparent. Members of the Huguenot community amongst the middle and upper ranks were held up by social commentators, such as Hogarth, as exemplars of good standards of decency and something to be emulated. This weakened one of the most important processes for the maintenance of group identity: the identification of difference (Jenkins 2004:4).

Evidence for the changes in Huguenot standards can be found in the consistory, or church court, records from a number of Huguenot communities. In the late sixteenth century the consistories enforced sanctions against a wide range of indecent and criminal behaviour, including dancing, the selling of rouge by apothecaries, and extravagant hairstyles (Benedict 2002:471). However, by the late seventeenth and early eighteenth centuries only the most serious offences were being punished, such as violence, sexual misconduct and heresy (Gwynn 1994). This may have been due to the sheer volume of offences being committed or the fear of losing members to the Anglican Church. Disputes resulting in members leaving the Church are also documented, as are attempts by the Elders to prevent intermarriage with the host population or attendance at Anglican services.

The concern over the changes in decency taking place within the community was expressed in an entry in a Huguenot church register (West Street Register 1699): 'Vanity, luxury and scandal nearly hold sway over us. Everyone submits to their inducement, and proud ambition creeps in the midst of our misfortunes' (Cottrett 1991:199).

These changes in Huguenot standards of decency had further consequences. They became a source of tension within the Huguenot community. The standards of the older and more conservative members increasingly were at odds with those of the younger and more liberal members due to the profound differences in the social context in which they had been formed. English-born members of the French community, who had not directly experienced persecution or migration, gradually came to feel that their values were closer to the host society than to those of the more conservative sections of the Huguenot community. As a result, understandings of similarity and difference became blurred and Huguenot identity was transformed from one founded on religion or ethnicity to one that was primarily based on kinship.

In the mid-eighteenth century, the liberal more integrated members of the community increasingly came to identify themselves as Huguenot descendants rather than as Huguenots. These individuals maintained links with the community and provided financial support to the church, but attended Anglican services and often lived and worked outside of the community. The conservative, often older, members of the community whose primary identity was Huguenot continued into the late eighteenth century, but their numbers rapidly declined. By the nineteenth century the Huguenot descendant identity was all that remained.

Support for this argument perhaps comes from Gwynn's suggestion that those Huguenots most closely associated with the luxury goods trades became assimilated more quickly than others (Gwynn 1998:17; 2001:210; cf. Parker 2011). The west London Huguenot community was primarily involved in luxury goods production and retail, whereas the community in east London was largely focused upon textile manufacture. Gwynn proposes that the closer interaction with the upper and middle ranks, such as the aristocracy and gentry, by the western community led to their earlier assimilation. Gwynn's argument is given weight by Berry (2002) who has emphasized the importance of 'polite consumption'. She argues that shopping in the eighteenth century should be understood as a social practice in which vendors were required to be aware of the correct forms of etiquette in order to sell their goods to the upper and middle ranks. It would follow, therefore, that successful Huguenot vendors would need to be much more familiar with, and take part in, English social practices as compared with those in the east who had much less direct contact with these consumers.

Archaeological evidence for differences between Huguenot and non-Huguenot households in London during this period is fairly limited. Jeffries (2001) has been unable to identify any clear patterns between the two groups in his analysis of the material obtained during the recent excavations in Spitalfields. Probate inventories offer an alternative source of evidence for the analysis of the ownership of household items. Richardson (2006) has compared the wills and probate inventories of Huguenots and non-Huguenots from late sixteenth century Canterbury. She has identified that Huguenots owned relatively fewer domestic textiles and other items associated with the display of wealth, as well as having differences in clothing. She suggests that this can be seen as an expression of identity based upon the values of the community.

The current paper forms part of a research project that builds upon Richardson's work by examining probate inventories from London during the late seventeenth and early eighteenth centuries. It uses a far larger sample of household inventories and compares the ownership of items such as luxury textiles and religious artefacts between Huguenots and non-Huguenots, and their change over time. It also examines Gwynn's contention that the Huguenot community in west London assimilated before the eastern community, by comparing items considered likely to be indicators of increasing integration.

Theoretical Model

Translating this argument into the conceptual framework of practice theory perhaps offers further insights into the issues discussed so far. Luxury goods production, luxury goods consumption, decency and civility, and group identity could all be defined as separate social fields. Each possessed a habitus that structured, and was structured by, the practices of individuals attempting to gain the specific capital associated with that field. Although separate, these social fields were closely interrelated and transpositions commonly occurred between each habitus.

Thus far, I have argued that changes in the field of luxury goods production, due to the Huguenot contribution, meant an increase in the number of luxury goods that were of higher quality and which were more affordable. This altered the field of luxury goods consumption, in which demand increased and the goods were purchased by a greater proportion of the population. This caused a change in the field of decency and civility that shifted the norms of appropriate display of wealth and luxury. This produced transformations in the field of group identity, as standards of decency and civility were held as a key element in defining Huguenot group identity. This can be summarized as in Figure 6.3.

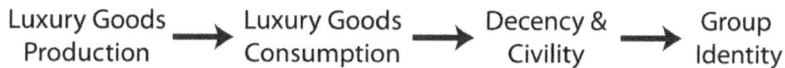

Luxury Goods Production → Luxury Goods Consumption → Decency & Civility → Group Identity

Figure 6.3   Diagram of linear transformations occurring between fields.

The theoretical model suggests a mechanism through which these changes occurred: the recursive relationship between the habitus and practice. Modifications in the habitus of one field caused changes in practices that produced changes in the habitus of another field. The concept of body hexis also helps to explain why this would have created intracommunity conflict. Body hexis, in many ways, refers to the embodiment of the values of the community. The importance of bodily comportment, dress and personal adornments were explicitly recognized by both theologians and the wider community during this period. This meant that changes in clothing fashions and the use of personal adornments could become highly contested. Changes in dress and accessories, as well as the use of new forms and styles of artefacts, implied a change in body hexis, and therefore a change in the habitus. The acceptance or rejection of these changes defined the group's habitus and thus its values and identity. The wearing of clothes or jewellery previously considered to be exclusive luxuries of the upper ranks was not just simply confined to the fields of consumption or fashion because the body was also operating in other social fields such as decency and civility. To a community such as the Huguenot refugees, this quickly became transposed into the fields of religion, morality and group identity, and as a result, they became important and highly contested issues.

However, the theoretical model also makes it apparent that this argument, at least in its current form, is likely to be far too linear and simplistic. It fails to describe the complex, multi-dimensional and recursive nature of the interactions between these fields. Figure 6.4 illustrates a more realistic representation of field interaction and yet this too ignores the role of a range of other fields relating to politics, economics and religion, which seem likely to have been important in providing a comprehensive explanation of the integration of the Huguenot communities.

The model itself can also be criticized either on theoretical grounds or on its accessibility to non-specialists. For example, both the terminology and the concepts themselves may appear confusing and their definitions difficult to understand without

Luxury Goods Production ⟷ Luxury Goods Consumption

Decency & Civility ⟷ Group Identity

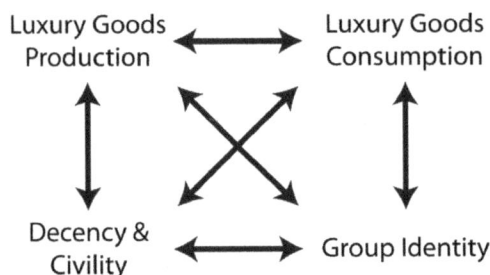

Figure 6.4   Diagram of complex and recursive transformations occurring between fields.

substantial background reading (e.g. social fields and the habitus). An advantage of using a linear argument is that it offers greater accessibility to a wider audience. This paper has attempted to combine both approaches by setting a linear narrative structure within the context of an explicit theoretical model. This provides a framework for specific areas of investigation to be placed within a wider context, allows for alternative interpretations of the data and offers new directions for future research.

Conclusions

This paper argues that the role of the Huguenot refugees in the production and spread of luxury goods was a causal factor in their integration into the host society and, further, that the material environment, in the form of luxury goods, played a significant role. This is not to suggest that this was the sole cause, or that the role of the material environment was dominant, merely that it may have made a significant contribution to the process of integration.

This paper also argues for the importance of linking research questions into a more comprehensive theoretical framework. This is important for understanding the context of the specific issues under analysis, offers alternative directions for future research, and increases accessibility for non-specialists in this field.

Acknowledgements

I would like to thank Michael Mair, Hugh Willmott, Jim Symonds, Anna Badcock and Clare McVeigh for their help and support in writing this paper.

Bibliography

Barrett, J. C. (1988) Fields of discourse: Reconstituting a social archaeology. *Critique of Anthropology* 7 (3): 5–16.
Barrett, J. C. (2000) A thesis on agency. In M. Dobres and J. Robb (eds.) *Agency in Archaeology*, 61–68. London: Routledge.

Beier, A. L. (1986) Engine of manufacture: The trades of London. In A. L. Beier and R. Finlay (eds.) *London, 1500–1700: The Making of the Metropolis*, 141–167. London: Longman.

Benedict, P. (2001) *The Faith and Fortunes of France's Huguenots, 1600–85*, Aldershot: Ashgate.

Benedict, P. (2002) *Christ's Churches Purely Reformed: A Social History of Calvinism.* New Haven & London: Yale University Press.

Berg, M. and Clifford, H. (eds.) (1999) *Consumers and Luxury: Consumer Culture in Europe 1650–1850.* Manchester: Manchester University Press.

Berry, H. (2002) Polite consumption: Shopping in eighteenth-century England. *Transactions of the Royal Historical Society* 12: 375–94.

Bourdieu, P. (1977) *Outline of a Theory of Practice.* Trans. R. Nice. Cambridge: Cambridge University Press.

Cottret, B. (1991) *The Huguenots in England: Immigration and Settlement c.1550–1700.* Cambridge: Cambridge University Press.

Dietler, M. and Herbich, I. (1998) Habitus, techniques, style: An integrated approach to the social understanding of material culture and boundaries. In M. T. Stark (ed.) *The Archaeology of Social Boundaries*, 232–63. Washington DC: Smithsonian Institution Press.

Earle, P. (1989) *The Making of the English Middle Class: Business, Society and Family Life in London 1660–1730.* London: Methuen.

Frijhoff, W. (2003) Uncertain brotherhood: the Huguenots in the Dutch Republic. In B. Van Ruymbeke and R. J. Sparks (eds.) *Memory and Identity: The Huguenots in France and the Atlantic Diaspora*, 128–71. Columbia SC: University of Southern Carolina Press.

Giddens, A. (1984) *The Constitution of Society: Outline of the Theory of Structuration.* Cambridge: Polity Press.

Gwynn, R. (1994) *Minutes of the Consistory of the French Church of London, Threadneedle Street 1679–1692.* London: Huguenot Society of Great Britain and Ireland.

Gwynn, R. (1998) *The Huguenots of London.* Brighton: The Alpha Press.

Gwynn, R. (2001) *Huguenot Heritage: The History and Contribution of the Huguenots in Britain.* 2nd edn. Brighton: Sussex Academic Press.

Jeffries, N. (2001) Historically visible but archaeologically invisible? The Huguenots in 17th-Century Spitalfields. *Medieval Ceramics* 25: 4–64.

Jenkins, R. (2004) *Social identity.* 2nd edn. London: Routledge.

Lemire, B. (2000) 'Second-Hand Beaux and Red-Armed Belles': Conflict and the creation of fashions in England, c. 1660–1800. *Continuity and Change* 151 (3): 391–417.

Lightfoot, K.G., Wake, T.A. and Schiff, A.M. (1998) 'Daily practice and material culture in pluralistic social settings: Archaeological study of culture change and persistence from Fort Ross, California. *American Antiquity* 63 (2): 199–222.

Murdoch, T. (1985) *The Quiet Conquest: The Huguenots 1685 to 1985.* Rugby: Alec Jolly.

Murdock, G. (2006) Calvin, Clothing and the Body. *Proceedings of the Huguenot Society of Great Britain and Ireland* 28 (4): 481–494.

Parker, G. (2011) Expressions of conformity: Identifying Huguenot religious beliefs in the landscape. In C. King and D. Sayer (eds) *The Archaeology of Post-Medieval Religion*, 107–20. Woodbridge: Boydell & Brewer.

Richardson, C. (2006) The material culture of stranger life. *Proceedings of the Huguenot Society of Great Britain and Ireland* 28 (4): 495–508.

Riding, C. (2001) Foreign artists and craftsmen and the introduction of the Rococo style in England. In R. Vigne and C. Littleton (eds) *From Strangers to Citizens: The Integration of Immigrant Communities in Britain, Ireland, and Colonial America, 1550–1750*, 133–43. Brighton: Sussex Academic Press.

Roelker, N. (1972) The appeal of Calvinism to French noblewomen in the sixteenth century. *Journal of Interdisciplinary History* 2: 391–418.

Rublack, U. (2005) *Reformation Europe*. Cambridge: Cambridge University Press.

Silliman, S. (2001) Agency, practical politics and the archaeology of culture contact. *Journal of Social Archaeology* 1 (2): 190–209.

van Ruymbeke, B. (2001) From ethnicity to assimilation: The Huguenots and the American immigration history paradigm. In R. L. Vigne (ed.) *From Strangers To Citizens: The Integration Of Immigrant Communities in Britain, Ireland, and Colonial America, 1550–1750*, 332–41. Brighton: Sussex Academic Press.

van Ruymbeke, B. (2003) Minority survival: The Huguenot paradigm in France and the diaspora. In B. van Ruymbeke and R. J. Sparks (eds.) *Memory and Identity: The Huguenots in France and the Atlantic Diaspora*, 1–25. Columbia, SC: University of Southern Carolina Press.

Weatherill, L. (1996) *Consumer Behaviour and Material Culture in Britain 1660–1760*. London: Routledge.

Weber, M. (1930) *The Protestant Ethic and the Spirit of Capitalism*. London: Allen & Unwin.

Part III

Colonial Entanglements

7 Assuming the Aspect of a Civilized Place: Methodists in Paradise

Jonathan Prangnell and Kate Quirk

Australia was as far from the centre of Empire as it was possible to get and it became the focus of much evangelical interest. In 1809 the Wesleyan Missionary Committee claimed that their Gospel was heard throughout 'three-quarters of the globe' (Bollen 1973:227) and it made sense to the men of the Wesleyan Methodist Conference to approve, in July 1814, a request from New South Wales Methodists for a missionary to be sent to the colony (Wright and Clancy 1993:4). Consequently, 29-year-old Staffordshire missionary Samuel Leigh arrived in Australia in 1815 to undertake evangelistic work amongst the 'bound, the fallen and the faint' (Bollen 1973:228) of Sydney Town. This was very much the era of Evangelical Revival (Turner 2003) when the Anglican and non-conformist churches sent missionaries to the ends of the earth (Johnston 2003:15), although the arrival of a dissenting missionary within the colony caused initial concerns for the (Anglican) authorities (Wright and Clancy 1993:4). In 1822, Sydney itself became the base for Methodist missionaries moving out into the Pacific Islands (Wright and Clancy 1993:12) although the London Missionary Society had been operating in the Pacific since 1797 (Grimshaw and Nelson 2001:297; Horne 1894:27; Johnston 2003:116).

Due to Australia's convict origins the civilizing mission was not seen initially as an effort to convert indigenous Australians to Christianity, commerce and Western ways of life—concerted efforts to achieve that were to come later (e.g. Grimshaw and Nelson 2001; Thompson and Johnson 1899)—but it was primarily seen as a mission to 'the most godless [White] people ... lost to all sense of virtue, and abandoned to every species of wickedness' (Johnson 1798:22). With all this missionary work happening, the churches within colonies of the major European powers established 'home' missions to preach to the non-indigenous working classes, 'native' missions to preach to, and to care for, the indigenous populations and the higher prestige 'foreign' missions sent to even more exotic places, such as Tahiti or Africa (Piggin 1996:66). The Methodists of Sydney did not even consider establishing a 'native' mission until 1820 and then nothing further was done until 1824 when the missionary William Walker took over the Native Institution at Parramatta. The Methodist running of the Institution proved a complete failure with the subsequent expulsion of Walker from the ministry and the Church (Wright and Clancy 1993:11–12).

The Methodist Church in Australia came into its own in the gold rushes of the 1850s and 1860s (Croggon 2001:69), where its highly flexible style of mission lay preaching was uniquely adapted to the ephemeral nature of the goldfields (Quirk 2007:159; Townend 1869:142–143; Wright and Clancy 1993:30). The lay preachers would move into a new area as demand required, setting up their own tent amongst the miners and holding services and Sunday schools wherever they could. Partly as a result of this flexibility Methodist congregations grew dramatically, outstripping growth in both Anglican and Catholic numbers (Croggon 2001:69). The presence of Methodist laity, preaching God, temperance and respectability, is seen as one of the reasons that the Australian goldfields never reached the reported levels of chaos and lawlessness seen in the earlier Californian rushes (Piggin 1996:25).

Since the eighteenth century, evangelical religions have argued that people could save themselves through self improvement (Fitts 2001:115–116) and that they were not predestined for salvation or damnation. The newly emergent middle classes were greatly influenced by these new Protestant religions (Davidoff and Hall 2002), particularly the idea of self improvement. As Fitts tells us, 'Victorian writers were adamant that respectability was not based on birth or wealth but could be learned by anyone who accepted the ideology of domesticity and genteel behaviour' with its associated temperance, hard work and thriftiness (2001:116). During the nineteenth century, the middle class, who were always the backbone of evangelical congregations, began to not so subtly influence the style of the religion. This was particularly so in the United States, which is defined, even to this day, by its extreme religiosity, but also in Australia and the United Kingdom. Middle-class morals with their concern with work, with decency and gentility started to feed back into evangelical religion (Fitts 2001), and it became, as Piggin notes of the Australian context 'unrelentingly and mercilessly moralising' (1996:33).

In 1855 an Australasian Conference, independent from London, was finally established to control Wesleyan Methodist activities in all the Australian colonies and the New Zealand and Pacific island missions (Wright and Clancy 1993:38). Although the first minister was sent to Brisbane in 1847 (Dingle 1947:21) and despite the political separation of Queensland from New South Wales in 1859, the administration of Queensland Methodism did not separate from New South Wales until 1893. This was mainly brought about in response to vast numbers of people moving northward and westward throughout the Australian colonies (Smith 1965:1), in search of gold and other resources. As the *Queensland Christian Witness and Methodist Journal* (July 1893) reported 'were it not for our missionar[ies], a sermon or prayer would never be heard in some of those faraway, solitary, bush homes, and we rejoice that something is being done to meet the spiritual needs of scattered populations'. To coordinate the work of the Church in reaching these disparate populations the Australasian Conference established the Home Mission Service (originally entitled the Church Sustentation and Extension Society) in 1865 (Wright and Clancy 1993: 44–45) but it was not, however, until the early 1890s that the society moved to set up its first Home Mission

Station in Queensland, at the goldmining town of Paradise. The fact that the first home mission station was established at Paradise caused amusement for Methodists at the time and ever since. In 1965 the Rev G. D. Smith, the General Superintendent of the Home Mission Department, wrote that 'one of the most delightful functions organised during the centenary year of the Home Missions was held in Paradise. In case there should be any misunderstanding let me hasten to say that I am referring to the Church Militant not the Church Triumphant!' (Smith 1965:1).

It was primarily the aim of home mission stations to preach to, and save, the white settler population from itself, following the call of the secretary of the Queensland Home Mission Society that 'every duty they owed to the foreign race they owed still more to their own people' (*Queensland Christian Witness and Methodist Journal,* March 1895). Home missionaries were exhorted to 'boldly march in step with the advancing tide of population; …follow them into the primeval forest of our coastlands; onto the broad savannahs of pastoralia; [and] into the sterile regions where the adventurer hazards his life in the quest for gold' (*Queensland Christian Witness and Methodist Journal,* June 1895). This quest for gold was driven by the colonial government and at the London Colonial and Indian Exhibition of 1886 Queensland mounted a massive promotional exercise aimed at gaining capital for the mining industry (McKay 2001:153, 2004:39). This resulted in the listing of Queensland gold mines on the London Stock Exchange and the 'colony's gold mining boom became the speculation event of the year' (McKay 2004:40). Between 1886 and 1890, 54 companies were established in Britain to invest in Queensland gold mining, with a combined capital of £7,495,428 (Murray 1995, appendix 3). Queensland goldrushes, however, tended to be short lived and many speculators lost money.

In an effort to bring about the 'evangelicalisation' of the colony, Methodist ministers visited the newly founded mining township of Paradise a number of times in early 1891 (Quirk 2007:208) and reported that 'these 600 people are without minister, church or means of grace of any description' (*Queensland Christian Witness and Methodist Journal,* July 1891). By the middle of the year they had set up a permanent base in the township. Paradise was located on the eastern bank of the Burnett River in southeast central Queensland, inland from Maryborough and 260km north of Brisbane, the capital of Queensland. It was founded in the last years of the 1880s, upon the discovery of gold-bearing reefs in the region by the Allen brothers. At the time, it was heralded as 'the coming field' (*The Wide Bay and Burnett News,* 22 February 1889:3) and significant efforts, but much less capital, were invested in the town. Accordingly, the population rose from less than 40 in 1890, to more than 600 in 1891. Like most of Queensland's gold towns, Paradise did not develop in an organized manner but boomed suddenly through the rapid influx of working men who were hoping to strike it lucky. Many of the miners had been working at nearby mines, such as Mount Shamrock, but were enticed to Paradise by its promised riches. The first mine to be sunk was the Homeward Bound shortly followed by the Lady Margaret and the Patterson. By December 1889, six separate lines of reefs were being worked and the gold was reported to be visible to the naked eye (Prangnell *et al.* 2005:7). Most of the work occurred in a narrow band two miles long and half a mile wide along the alluvial flats and terraces of the Burnett River between Finney's Creek and Scrubby Creek (also known as Paradise Creek).

By the time Paradise was officially proclaimed a goldfield in December 1890, more than 100 people were already living on the field. It was described as 'rather prettily situated' (*The Wide Bay and Burnett News*, 20 August 1891:3), 'picturesque' (*The Queenslander*, 23 May 1891:983), and 'assuming the aspect of a civilized place' (Queensland Department of Mines 1891:74). Once established, Paradise was the largest town in the district, boasting a police station and courthouse, seven hotels, a lemonade factory and numerous retail stores and trade workshops, including a tobacconist, at least two butchers, a chemist, sawmill, bootmaker, four bakers, three drapers, two blacksmiths, three grocers and a dressmaker. The Paradise boom, however, was to be very short-lived. As early as 1892 it was realized that the mines would never produce enough payable gold, and the inhabitants of the town gradually left, driven out by poverty and hopelessness as one by one the hard-rock mining enterprises ground to a halt. Paradise struggled on until 1904 when it was finally abandoned.

Archaeological, historical and populist conceptions have tended to portray the Australian goldfields as rough, masculine places, devoid of community connections and family life. However, this was seldom the case. Rather, the population of the Australian goldfields, like those of North America, can be conceived of, in Douglass'(1998) terms, as a 'community without a locus'—a collection of families and individuals who move together from one strike to the next, bonded by social and kin ties and by shared history. Many of the people who moved to Paradise came from existing nearby fields and they brought their community ties and networks with them (Quirk 2007:137). At Paradise, women and children quickly came to make up the greater part of this community. At Christmas of 1889, for example, the township was described as having 'plenty of Adams but no Eve' (*The Wide Bay and Burnett News*, 9 January 1890) but just two years later women and children accounted for almost half of the town's inhabitants, and would later constitute over 90% of the population (Prangnell *et al.* 2005:25).

The day after the Home Mission Society sanctioned his appointment in July 1891, the first missionary, John Gardener, left Brisbane for Paradise, undoubtedly filled with an evangelical zeal to save the town from itself. Even the mission horse 'Tom' was pressed into service as an exemplar of Methodist respectability and restraint (Prangnell *et al.* 2005:45). Tom accompanied Gardener on the steamer trip from Brisbane to Maryborough. The horse apparently became upset by the motion of the steamer and the sailors jestingly offered him a beer to calm his nerves. Missionary Gardener declined on Tom's behalf, stating that 'he is a staunch teetotaller, and would not take it if offered to him as he is going about the country setting a good example' (*Queensland Christian Witness and Methodist Journal*, August 1891).

On his arrival Gardener noted that 'the reason for sending a home missionary to Paradise, incongruous as it may seem, can easily be conjectured when our friends are told, there are about 700 people there, five hotels, with three more almost in the course of erection, and not one church or mission hall' (*Queensland Christian Witness and Methodist Journal*, August 1891). Gardener worked hard rectifying this situation, and using volunteer labour from the township had, by October, erected a small Residence for himself, organized a Sunday School for the children, a 'Band of Hope Society' for concerned teetotallers, a 'Mutual Improvement Society' which aimed to teach social graces to the young men of Paradise and began fundraising for the construction of a Mission Hall (Prangnell *et al.* 2005:43). He also initiated regular church services for people in Paradise and surrounding townships (Quirk 2007:209).

Despite this rapid and impressive progress Gardener resigned from his position as missionary after only five months, claiming ill health as the reason for his sudden departure. It appears, though, that the townsfolk of Paradise were not sorry to see him leave as his popularity had declined quickly when he refused to allow a black and white minstrel show, organized to raise funds for the much-needed schoolhouse in the town, to take place in the Mission Hall as he was opposed to the blackening of their faces (Prangnell *et al.* 2005:44). Community displeasure was summarized by a newspaper correspondent who wrote that 'The expressions of the people here are rather derogatory to the action. They ask if church bazaars, gifts, sales, etc., with their lotteries, raffles by dice throwing, lucky bags, fishponds, and other petty swindling trifles are not more dangerous to the religious morals of youth than a well-conducted minstrel concert, in which only songs and choruses of a high moral character are introduced' (*The Wide Bay and Burnett News*, 12 December 1891). Gardener was obviously successful in spreading the Methodist's anti-gambling message but overestimated his influence within the community.

The concert was held to much acclaim in one of the local hotels, but Gardener resigned and was replaced by missionary Albert Taylor who only remained at Paradise until April 1892. The first two missionaries were at Paradise a total of nine months but this period had seen the construction of the Mission Hall and the Residence and they had laid the foundation for the 'straightforward evangelical program' (Wright 1984:31) of Methodist missionary activities on this and neighbouring goldfields. Paradise was the centre of a 260 mile circuit that saw the missionary preach at numerous scattered and small mining towns including Mount Shamrock, Mount Perry and Gin Gin.

Taylor was replaced by missionary James Kirke. Kirke, the son of a schoolmaster, was born in Scotland in 1858, and was working as a clerk at a stone quarry in Lancashire when he met Jane Buckley, a weaver (Quirk 2007:211). They married in 1882 at a Wesleyan Chapel in Lancashire, and their first child, Agnes, was born there two years later. The young family immigrated to Australia in late 1884 and settled in Armidale where James Jnr was born in 1886, and his sister Gertrude in 1890 (Quirk 2007:211). Once at Paradise two more boys, Gilbert Shuttleworth Kirke and Malcolm Kinloch Kirke, were born in 1894 and 1895 respectively (Quirk 2007:211). Gilbert's middle name is after the Shuttleworth family, the richest permanently resident at Paradise. The Shuttleworths were the largest land owners in Paradise and patriarch Digby was a mine manager as well as secretary of the School Committee, secretary of the International

Order of Good Templars and committee member and journal editor of the Mutual Improvement Society (Quirk 2007:193–194). In all these positions he would have worked closely with Kirke and it seems certain that fictive kin ties existed between the families.

James Kirke enjoyed a successful start to his Paradise career: Sunday School attendance reached 74 while church membership grew to 12 and up to 500 people attended weekly services at the various townships and fields in the circuit. Meanwhile the Band of Hope continued its temperance push and James described the Mutual Improvement Society as coming on in 'leaps and bounds', expressing the hope that 'this class will tend to the social elevation of the young men of Paradise' (*Queensland Christian Witness and Methodist Journal*, July 1892). The Society was to prove even more popular later that year when its membership was extended to include women. James also established a library for the Sunday School, a 40-person church choir, and held numerous fundraising events including for a church organ and for a number of improvements to the Mission Hall including the installation of doors and windows and the replacement of benches with forms (Prangnell *et al.* 2005:44–45).

The efforts of James Kirke are reasonably well documented in the official Methodist records, but the documents are silent on the role Jane Kirke played at the Mission, as neither she nor the children are ever directly referred to in Methodist records (Quirk 2007:212). Carey (1995:229) notes 'in the contemporary official record, missionary wives are virtually invisible' and attributes this to the 'screening' tendencies of missionary husbands and church bodies, all of whom wanted to downplay women's involvement in mission activities. Towards the end of the nineteenth-century women's participation in evangelical religions grew and they began to take a direct role in missionary activities (see Tennant 1999; Walls 2002:179). This created dissonance within the Protestant churches as such involvement was seen as an affront to genteel ideals of women's behaviour and as a threat to the patriarchal order of the churches. The expectation was that the missionary's wife would lead by example and be a faultless representation of the ideals of Christianized domesticity (Carey 1999:236; Quirk 2007:213). As an 1899 account recorded it is

> through the presence of missionaries' wives [that] Protestant missions have been able to show the great object-lesson of a Christian home. The mutual trust of husband and wife, their helpful companionship, the brightness of their children's lives, and all the other elements that make the sweetness and charm of a Christian home have been, and are still, among the most potent influences for good in heathen lands. (Thompson and Johnson 1899:188–189)

Earlier in the century, though, the condemnation of any women's involvement in mission activities can clearly be seen in Dickens' creation of Mrs Jellyby (in *Bleak House*) who was utterly devoted to her missionary duties to the natives of Borrioboola-Gha whilst completely indifferent to her personal appearance, family and home (Plotkin 1997:23–25).

The Kirkes remained at Paradise until May 1896, by which time the decision was made to move the Mission to nearby Gin Gin, an agricultural community, which seemed to be waxing as Paradise waned (*Queensland Christian Witness and Methodist Journal,* May 1896). The parsonage was dismantled and moved with the family to the new Mission site, but the Mission Hall remained at Paradise, continuing to be used by visiting missionaries officiating at services, weddings and other religious ceremonies (Quirk 2007:213). Although there is some evidence to suggest that the hall was eventually sold and removed to a nearby town, where it served as a house (Prangnell *et al.* 2002:37), the archaeological evidence points to it having remained in place and subsequently been quarried for timber by locals.

During 2002 and 2003, the site of the Paradise township was archaeologically surveyed and the Home Mission Station was excavated, along with 17 other sites throughout the township. Over 2500 individual artefacts were recovered from the mission, of which 1045 were ceramic sherds. These were highly fragmented and yielded a minimum vessel count of only 48. Table and teawares predominate with at least 14 teacups and saucers in many different patterns. Approximately a third of the ceramics were porcelain, which is highly unusual for Australian mining sites, and there were eight sherds from a Wedgewood-style jasperware bowl that is the most expensive ceramic object identified in the Paradise assemblage. Sherds from two 'motto' mugs were also found.

There is no evidence of alcohol consumption at the mission itself, which is not surprising given the sense of triumph conveyed when the first missionary, Gardener, recorded that three men were so moved by one of his sermons that they immediately repaired to the parsonage to sign temperance pledges. Abstinence, if not teetotalism (Harrison 1971:179–180), was an important part of Methodist teaching. There was also a generally low level of alcohol consumption across the entire township and this may indicate the effectiveness of the missionaries in spreading the temperance word, despite the presence of the seven hotels. It may also, though, reflect the economic situation of Paradise and the Australian colonies more generally. Dingle's (1980) exploration of drinking patterns in Australian history has shown that alcohol consumption was tied to cycles of boom and bust. The 1890s, which saw an Australia- wide depression, marked a low point in drinking, and Paradise, where times were repeatedly described as 'dull', would have been particularly hard hit by this.

Smoking, on the other hand, was fairly widespread throughout Paradise, with only three residential sites not offering any archaeological evidence of tobacco consumption. Smoking paraphernalia ranged from clay tobacco pipes to cigarette holders complete with sterling silver ferrules. Methodists abhorred smoking with the official line that 'use of tobacco makes it more difficult to be a Christian—hinders a Christian mightily in being a true witness to his Lord' (*Queensland Christian Witness and Methodist Journal,* February 1890) yet, sherds of clay pipe stem were found at the Mission Hall. Given the fact that no tobacco-related remains were recovered from the Mission Residence itself, it seems likely that these pipes belonged to parishioners and it conjures up an image of a group of bearded men quickly throwing their pipes to the ground behind their backs when the missionary appeared.

Unlike the standard picture of goldfields' life, that has single men eating from cheap tin plates and drinking from tin mugs, the missionaries ate from ceramic plates, drank from ceramic teacups, and prepared their food in ceramic bowls. They, like many other people at Paradise, evidently considered ceramics significant enough to the creation of a home that they were willing to transport them over many miles—it took at least a full day of horse-drawn cart travel to reach Paradise from the district hub of Maryborough. It is clear that the Kirkes brought some of their ceramics assemblage with them, because they owned items which were almost certainly not for sale at Paradise. Their table setting included the highest quality items of any recovered from the town. This suggests that they were not content to 'make do' with the blue-banded or cable-patterned ware that proliferated throughout Paradise and the Queensland historical archaeological record generally. Their ceramics assemblage was more complex, more decorative, more expansive and more expensive than was strictly necessary and included porcelain tea sets, items of New Wharf pottery and Wedgwood-style jasperwares. The missionaries were evidently taking some pains to make their home 'cozy', as the Ladies of New York's Five Points Mission might have said (Fitts 2001:127). As Little explains 'nearly everyone within the European global market owned ceramic tableware and teaware because it was nearly always appropriate to do so. One alternative, that of owning no appropriate equipment, would result in being defined as culturally 'other': uncivilised' (1997:236).

The archaeological evidence also indicates connections between the missionaries and other families at Paradise. Two hundred and eighty metres from the Mission, over the hill on a different drainage line, lived the family of George Buzza, a Cornish-born carpenter. The Buzzas lived on a block of land on the eastern edge of town high on an east/west ridgeline that runs perpendicular to the main alignment of the township. The block has archaeological remnants of a small house and fireplace with an extensive surface scatter of artefacts, including the largest ceramics assemblage in Paradise (Quirk 2007:269). The ceramics assemblages from the Kirkes' and the Buzzas' contain eight patterns in common, five of which do not occur at any other place in Paradise. The unparalleled correlation in the ceramics from the houses suggests a commonality of behaviour and/or some special bond between the two families. It is possible that the Buzzas donated items to the mission or that the Buzzas were somehow partly responsible for the suite of material culture items used in the mission residence.

Other relationships existed between the Mission and other inhabitants of Paradise. Mr Turk, a stamper battery owner, was involved with raising money for the Sunday School library. Just like *Anna of the Five Towns* (Bennett 1906), Miss McGhie, daughter of James McGhie, magistrate and the biggest mine owner and entrepreneur in town, taught singing to the Sunday School class. Mr Walker, proprietor of a grocery and drapery store, helped organize a choir to greet visiting Methodist ministers and aided the first missionary when he arrived. Finally there was the Shuttleworth family, two of whose daughters were married in the Methodist Hall, and after whom missionary Kirke named his first Paradise-born son. All of these families were from the upper echelons of Paradise society and it can be assumed that all of these people were active in the church, and that as a result, the genteel concerns of the Methodists may be reflected in the assemblages from their homes.

The first thing that unites the archaeology of these five places, the Mission, and the Turk, McGhie, Walker and Shuttleworth houses, is the method of rubbish removal. Almost all of the 97 houses identified during the archaeological surveys had obvious rubbish middens to the rear of their houses, while all of the known Methodist-related sites, with the exception of the Buzza family, either removed their rubbish to the town dump, or used pits to dispose of rubbish through burning and burial. This treatment of refuse suggests a concern with order, neatness, cleanliness and outward appearance that matches the ideology of the missionary world.

These sites are also notable because, with the exception of the Walkers, they all lack evidence of alcohol consumption, suggesting that they shared the strong temperance ethic of the Methodists. This stands in direct opposition to the popular conception of the Australian goldfields as wild, lawless and Godless places. This long-standing idea has been reinforced by historical and archaeological studies that have concentrated on the dramatic aspects of life rather than the mundane, everyday existence of the people. Lawrence (1998, 2000) has suggested that this 'traditional characterisation of rollicking masculine goldfields culture' (2000:17) played an important part in the creation of the idealized Australian identity (Greenwood 1978:46–47) but now needs to be reconsidered. The archaeological evidence from Paradise supports Lawrence's contention that historic constructions of goldfields' life have more to do with modern identity that past reality. For instance, there is very little evidence for the use of firearms and there is far more evidence for the consumption of aerated waters at Paradise than there is for alcohol consumption.

One area in which the Methodist congregation clearly did not follow their Church's ideas however, was in their attitude to tobacco consumption. All Methodist-related sites, except of course the Mission Residence itself, included items of tobacco-smoking paraphernalia. Most notable among these was a risqué pipe depicting a reclining nude from James McGhie's house. This, needless to say, was very un-Methodist for a number of reasons. Taken together, the presence of smoking artefacts at the homes of these ostensibly upright Christian folk, suggests that for some reason, they did not see smoking as immoral. One reason for this can be found in their shared class allegiances. All of these families were as middle class as anyone got at Paradise. While the middle class saw smoking and drinking as reprehensible in the working class, they tolerated it amongst themselves, as long as it was done in private by men and not to excess. As Lady Bracknell remarks in *The Importance of Being Earnest* (Wilde 2000:308), she approves of smoking because 'A man should always have an occupation of some kind'. The presence of tobacco pipes at all of these sites suggests that this attitude was shared by the middle class of Paradise, and possibly demonstrates the range of simultaneous and conflicting beliefs it is possible for one to hold.

The assemblages from the Mission and the known Methodist related homes demonstrate leanings towards respectability and gentility. The rubbish removal practices are suggestive of genteel concern with order and cleanliness. The paucity of alcohol-related items reflects religious objections to such practices, and the ceramics assemblage shows some of the elaboration associated with genteel dining and home furnishing. The artefact assemblages are humble in comparison with those from middle-class London or New York, but they stand out among the material culture of the townsfolk of Paradise. The items reflect the best efforts of the inhabitants of Paradise to assume as civilized an aspect as was possible when located between the unashamed demands of evangelical Methodism and the reality of life in an isolated frontier gold-mining town.

Bibliography

Bennett, A. (1906) *Anna of the Five Towns*. London: Chatto and Windus.

Bollen, J.D. (1973) A time of small things: The Methodist Mission in New South Wales, 1815–1836. *The Journal of Religious History* 7: 225–247.

Carey, H.M. (1995) Companions in the wilderness? Missionary wives in Colonial Australia, 1788–1900. *The Journal of Religious History* 19 (2): 227–243.

Croggon, J. (2001) Methodists and miners: The Cornish in Ballarat 1851–1901. In K. Cardell and C. Cumming (eds.) *A World Turned Upside Down: Cultural Change in Australia's Goldfields 1851–2001*. Canberra: Humanities Research Centre, The Australian National University.

Davidoff, L. and Hall, C. (2002) *Family Fortunes: Men and Women of the English Middle Class, 1780–1850*. London: Routledge.

Dingle, A.E. (1980) 'The truly magnificent thirst': An historical survey of Australian drinking habits. *Historical Studies* 19 (75): 227–249.

Dingle, R.S.C. (1947) *Annals of Achievement: A Review of Queensland Methodism 1847–1947*. Brisbane: Queensland Book Depot.

Douglass, W.A. (1998) The mining camp as community. In A. B. Knapp, V. C. Pigott and E. W. Herbert (eds.) *Social Approaches to an Industrial Past: The Archaeology and Anthropology of Mining*. London: Routledge.

Fitts, R.F. (2001) The rhetoric of reform: The Five Points Missions and the cult of domesticity. *Historical Archaeology* 35 (3): 115–132.

Greenwood, G. (1978) *Australia: A Social and Political History*. London: Angus and Robertson.

Grimshaw, P. and Nelson, E. (2001) Empire, 'the civilising mission' and indigenous Christian women in Colonial Victoria. *Australian Feminist Studies* 16 (36): 295–309.

Harrison, B. (1971) *Drink and the Victorians: The Temperance Question in England 1815–1872*. London: Faber and Faber.

Horne, C.S. (1894) *The Story of the L.M.S.* London: London Missionary Society.

Johnson, R. (1798) [1978] Letter from Reverend Richard Johnson to Governor John Hunter. In G. Mackaness (ed.) Some letters of Rev. Richard Johnson, B.A. First Chaplain of New South Wales Part II. *Australian Historical Monographs* 21 (New Series).

Johnston, A. (2003) *Missionary Writing and Empire, 1800–1860*. Cambridge: Cambridge University Press.

Lawrence, S. (1998) Approaches to gender in the archaeology of mining. In M. Casey, D. Donlon, J. Hope and S. Wellfare (eds.) *Redefining Archaeology: Feminist Perspectives*. Canberra: Research Papers in Archaeology and Natural History.

Lawrence, S. (2000) *Dolly's Creek: An Archaeology of a Victorian Goldfields Community*. Melbourne: Melbourne University Press.

Little, B. (1997) Expressing ideology with a voice, or obfuscation and the Enlightenment. *International Journal of Historical Archaeology* 1 (3): 225–241.

McKay, J. (2001) 'Only a gilded show': Australian gold at international exhibitions 1851–1901. In K. Cardell and C. Cumming (eds.) *A World Turned Upside Down: Cultural Change in Australia's Goldfields 1851–2001*. Canberra: Humanities Research Centre, The Australian National University.

McKay, J. (2004) *Showing Off: Queensland at World Exhibitions, 1862–1988*. Rockhampton: Central Queensland University Press.

Murray, A. (1995) Pennies from Heaven: The Queensland Government Mining Journal, 1900–1929. The University of Queensland: Unpublished MA Thesis, Department of History.

Piggin, S. (1996) *Evangelical Christianity in Australia: Spirit, Word and World*. Oxford: Oxford University Press.

Plotkin, D. (1997) Home-made savages: Cultivating English children in 'Bleak House'. *Pacific Coast Philology* 32 (1): 17–31.

Prangnell, J., Cheshire, L. and Quirk, K. (2005) *Paradise: Life on a Queensland Goldfield*. Brisbane: UQASU and Burnett Water.

Prangnell, J., Reid, J., Herbert-Cheshire, L. and Rains, K. (2002) Archaeological Survey of Paradise: Stage 1. Survey and Historical Research. University of Queensland Archaeological Services Unit: Unpublished report.

Queensland Department of Mines (1891) *Department of Mines Annual Return 1891*. Brisbane: Queensland Government.

Quirk, K. (2007) The Victorians in 'Paradise': Gentility as Social Strategy in the Archaeology of Colonial Australia. The University of Queensland: Unpublished PhD thesis, School of Social Science.

Smith, G. D. (1965) Methodists in Paradise. *The Methodist Times* 39 (4): 1.

Tennant, M. (1999) Pakeha deaconesses and the New Zealand Methodist Mission to Maori, 1893–1940. *The Journal of Religious History* 23 (3): 309–326.

Thompson, R.W. and Johnson, A.N. (1899) *British Foreign Missions 1837–1897*. London: Blackie and Son.

Townend, J. (1869) *Autobiography of the Rev. Joseph Townend with Reminiscences of his Missionary Labours in Australia:* London: W. Reed.

Turner, W.J. (2003) *John Wesley: The Evangelical Revival and the Rise of Methodism in England*. London: Epworth Press.

Walls, A.F. (2002) The missionary movement: A lay fiefdom? In D.W. Lovegrove (ed.) *The Rise of the Laity in Evangelical Protestantism*. London: Routledge.

Wilde, O. (2000) *The Importance of Being Earnest and Other Plays*. London: Penguin.

Wright, D. (1984) *Mantle of Christ: A History of the Sydney Central Methodist Mission*. St Lucia, Qld: University of Queensland Press.

Wright, D. and Clancy, E. (1993) *The Methodists: A History of Methodism in New South Wales*. St Leonards, NSW: Allen and Unwin.

8 Reflections on Resistance: Agency, Identity and Being Indigenous in Colonial British Columbia

Jeff Oliver

Introduction

This chapter sets out to briefly trace some of the more salient contours of archaeological research into the consequences of nineteenth- and early twentieth-century colonialism. Recent work on indigenous cultural entanglements within expanding networks of European influence has clocked a significant theoretical shift. Early research took its cues from colonialist forms of thought, which assumed that native exposure to the outside world would inevitably result in the acculturation of European value systems. A more recent position, this time framed by developments in postcolonial theory, sees colonialism feeding the creation of hybridized, fragmented and shifting realities, but ultimately realities characterized by a healthy dose of indigenous *resistance*. A sizeable literature on resistance has provided our accounts with an important degree of ambiguity; namely it has encouraged an awareness of native agency in the contact zone. However, a narrow emphasis on the confrontational aspects of indigenous inhabitation, particularly where it implies a defence of certain cultural imperatives in the face of colonial 'progress', can blunt our understanding of what were incredibly complicated reactions. Because this period witnessed dramatic but asymmetric social, political and economic changes, the consequences of colonialism are far too varied, across time and space, to be neatly framed within the inherent antagonism of the colonizer/colonized coupling. By looking at how native people became entwined in the colonial landscape and participated in consuming its 'culture', I argue that questions of identity and agency can only be really appreciated by understanding how different lines of tension played out in different social arenas and at different scales of analysis.

It is not my intention to pursue this concept across the world of former European colonies. That task would be more daunting. Rather, I shall limit my comments largely to that part of the world I know best: the northwest coast of North America. I therefore intend to do three things: first, to outline the historiographical shift that has occurred in our thinking on the consequences of indigenous interactions with colonial cultures;

second, to reconsider the theoretical armatures that inform such analyses; and finally, by drawing on a case study from southwestern British Columbia, to demonstrate the complexity of the *experience* of colonialism and how it gave meaning to the many social arenas of everyday life.

Colonialism and Northwest Coast Peoples: From Acculturation to Resistance

It is difficult to point a time or place where the effects of expanding networks of colonial influence on the indigenous peoples of the Northwest Coast became the object of sustained academic research. For those disciplines concerned with their study, more traditional concerns held sway. Rather than documenting the 'inevitable' decline of Northwest Coast cultures, the late nineteenth- and early twentieth-century salvage ethnography of Boasian anthropology was almost entirely focused on preserving a semblance of 'Indian life' at an imaginary point in time *before* 'contact'. Likewise, archaeology, a discipline that came into its own by the middle of the last century on the coast, regarded itself best suited to unravel the big questions of prehistory. It is perhaps therefore not surprising that 'tainted' excavation layers and material culture from 'the post-contact period' has more often than not been regarded in spoil heaps than in academic discussion, at best relegated to excavation appendices.

Nevertheless, the considerable changes occurring among indigenous cultures did not go unnoticed. The increasing penetration of 'foreign' material culture and its associated practices into 'traditional' indigenous life was not uncommonly observed by late nineteenth-century European colonial officials, missionaries and journalists. While there is inconsistency within these accounts to be sure, such changes were generally considered to confirm the enduring belief that native cultures would soon dissipate in a context of increasing European acculturation (e.g. Gosnell 1897). Stimulated in part by a growing sense of paternalism for native welfare, academic interests too began to document and discuss these transformations. The historiography of this research as it evolved over the course of the twentieth century is unsurprisingly complex, too complex to be treated in any detail here. Nonetheless, it is worth picking out some of its more salient contours.

Broadly speaking, the history of intercultural relations on the Northwest Coast is commonly divided between the late eighteenth- to mid nineteenth-century fur trade and the subsequent colonial period. Cultural exchanges during the fur trade resulted in items such as iron tools, glass beads and wool blankets being quickly incorporated within the prestige and subsistence economies of Northwest Coast peoples. Local exchange networks ensured that trade goods such as these were relatively common up and down the coast. While evidence from the archaeological and historic records suggest important degrees of alteration to indigenous cultural practices at this time (see Acheson 1995; Acheson and Delgado 2004; Fisher 1977; Marshall and Mass

1997), compared with the later colonial period, such changes are often seen as relatively superficial to indigenous institutions (e.g. Fisher 1977; Martindale 2006).

It was the annexation of the coast by Britain (and later Canada) and the expansionist United States that ratcheted up the pressure to change on local groups. In this context the evidence of 'contact' has been seen to represent a sharp tipping point, after which indigenous peoples experienced a demise of the 'old ways', followed by stages of acculturation, though the visibility of certain hybridized and composite forms of material culture (e.g. Howay 1941; Smith 1955) and religious syncretism (e.g. Amoss 1978; Barnett 1957) did raise certain incongruities. The establishment of new colonial centres such as New Westminster and Seattle provided important nodal points from which the transmission of ideas and objects emanated outward, to the effect that early efforts in salvage ethnography tended to favour more remote corners of the coast, less impacted by immigrant settlement and therefore less culturally 'diluted'(e.g. Boas 1894). And yet, even at native settlements isolated from major centres, the arrival of missionaries in the last quarter of the nineteenth century has been described as having had a 'civilizing' effect that 'was dramatic and nearly instantaneous' (Hobler 1986: 16; see also Duff 1997).

Historical and archaeological evidence has been used to sum up the rapid changes seen among natives during the colonial period. For example, late nineteenth-century photographs document the effects of colonizing efforts on indigenous habitations extremely well, with traditional post-and-beam structures being quickly replaced by gabled-roof and milled-timber constructions intended to house nuclear families. Excavated materials also confirm this picture. Hobler's (1986) comparison of the ratio of 'European' and 'indigenous' artefacts at eight former village sites on the central coast of British Columbia indicated to him that archaeologists could assess the degree of European acculturation according to time period (see also Fladmark 1970). Thus, early contact sites with a few iron tools, trade beads and other 'trinkets' could be said to have been operating largely according to a pre-contact cultural logic, whereas those with a clear penetration of objects, from cut nails and ceramic sherds to medicine bottles and rifle cartridges, were seen to be climbing the ladder of European civilization (see also Carlson 2006:202; Lightfoot 1995:207; 2006:278).

If scholarly enquiry over much of the twentieth century has assumed native cultural decline, the last two or three decades, conversely, has seen a cross-disciplinary shift in the way the evidence of colonialism is viewed. Influenced by processes of global decolonization and indigenous revitalization movements, more recent strands of thinking have begun to seriously question older expectations about the capitulation of native cultures as well as their general invisibility within colonial scholarship. As part of a growing postcolonial critique, a good deal of research has rightly pointed out that indigenous peoples were not passive receptors of colonial culture but agents in their own right who integrated or rejected outside influences according to certain cultural parameters (Gosden 2001; Lightfoot *et al.* 1998; Silliman 2001). Such observations were already beginning to impact the work of some Northwest Coast anthropologists in the 1970s, partly as a result of the incredibly rich ethnographic record of the region (e.g. Blackman 1976). By the 1990s, these views were becoming commonplace among scholars working in the area of cultural studies. Consequently, interpretations have increasingly found that Northwest Coast peoples were able to take charge of circumstances in a variety of social arenas, maintaining a degree of cultural coherency and control over certain kinds of decision-making and cultural exchanges, despite distinct power asymmetries and socio-economic realignments in the colonial landscape. Significantly, the study of what Ferris (2009) has called 'Native-lived colonialism' is moving away from generalizations of acculturation towards variable patterns of cultural survival, revitalization and resistance.

Voices of resistance may take many forms, from organized acts of defiance to more improvised forms of dissent. For example, acts of defiance sometimes took the form of political rallies in opposition to unjust colonial policies, such as the institution of the Indian reserves, which appropriated the vast majority of land for newcomers, while leaving the Coast Salish with what was left (Carlson 2001d; Harris 2002; Lutz 1999). At other times, resistance was an impulsive and opportunistic act to register defiance in the face of colonial power, such as by wrecking survey monuments (Stadfeld 1999) or even intimidating colonial survey parties charged with outlining property cadastres (e.g. Taylor 1975:36).

Archaeologists, too, have begun to investigate the ways in which the politics of resistance infused different social settings. Attention to the spatial contexts of use and the form that historic objects took has begun to reveal patterns that imply novel kinds of decision-making. Rather than taking items of European manufacture at face value, as indexes of acculturation, a focus on how artefacts were consumed suggests that native peoples manipulated incoming European materials in ways that fitted or expanded upon the underlying cultural logic of their peoples. In other words, they commonly took objects of mass production and other colonial influences and slotted them neatly into their own cultural framework. Such observations are more commonly associated with the earlier contact period, for example, in the way that European iron was adapted within existing native technology templates, with iron axe heads becoming the working blades of traditional adze forms. However, similar kinds of observations are now becoming central to the study of the later colonial period as well. Perhaps one of the most commonly recognized, but less studied, areas of intercultural admixture was in the context of indigenous architecture (but see Blackman 1976; Perry 2003; Lepofsky *et al.* 2009). A particularly notable example of changes to the built environment has been studied by Prince (2002), who has shown how the Kimsquit of the central coast of British Columbia adapted European materials and design features into the building of grave house architecture, a pattern also observable from other parts of the central and north coast. Milled timber and Victorian gabled roofs and windows were integrated into an earlier traditional type of burial, itself influenced by older kerfed-box and 'tented' burial forms common along the north coast (McIlwraith 1948:453; Vastokas 1966:120). Other popular commercially available items such as kettles, wash basins and even sewing machines, which were found inside and associated with these structures, were used to mark the social status of the deceased in accordance with long-standing practices of conspicuous consumption. Significantly, for Prince (2002:52) the refusal to abandon traditional funerary practices suggests an important element of coherence with the past.

Hybrid engagements with the material world were not restricted to conspicuous acts of display, but also filtered down into the very mundane corners of everyday life. Archaeologists have long known that local groups refashioned a variety of mass-produced objects such as ceramic, glass and metal into pre-contact tool forms (Hobler 1986:24, fig. 4; Marshall and Mass 1997; Prince 2002:52). Perhaps one of the most novel, and risky, was the knapping of glass telegraph insulators into 'stone' tools. Still, knowledge of these kinds of activities tended to remain peripheral to archaeological interpretation, the subject of campfire anecdote; less often were they viewed as being able to shed light on actual cultural politics. Their potential in providing a commentary on the connected concepts of identity, tradition and resistance has been explored only more recently. It has been suggested from evidence excavated at turn-of-the-century Tsimshian sites on the Skeena River that the reuse of fragments of glass as knives, scrapers, burins, awls and spokeshaves, when metal tools were common, may have represented a tacit acknowledgement of their difference, of 'Tsimshian-ness', at a time when the colonial state was becoming increasingly draconian. Indeed, for Martindale (2009:78), these patterns indicate that they 'were likely aware of the symbolism of their actions', an argument that puts resistance as a foremost concern within native mindsets.

Progress in the archaeology of colonialism has produced two significant outcomes, reflecting a major turn in the historiography of this period. First, the acknowledgement that an indigenous archaeology is a vital part of the archaeology of more recent history, which speaks volumes about the way we are fast leaving behind the contrived boundary between prehistory and documentary history (Lightfoot 1995). Second, the recognition that processes of colonialism were not unidirectional and characterized primarily by a loss of indigenous identity at the expense of western cultural values. On the contrary, it is now more commonly understood that exposure to the outside world implied a series of complex cultural decisions about what was appropriate and socially efficacious given indigenous cultural values, which continued to shape the rules of engagement with the outside world (Martindale 2009:77; Prince 2002).

Reflections and Reconsiderations

Still, there are also reasons why we should pause and reflect on these arguments in the interest of continuing to move understanding forward. In a context animated by the opposition of colonizer and colonized, it is perhaps easy to assume that indigenous agency, whether breaking farmer's fences down to reach the old fishing rocks or building houses to the dead that satisfy time-honoured conventions, was consistent with an active attachment to the past, to tradition and identity. While natives may, from time to time, have associated such meanings with objects and practices, it is highly doubtful that they informed the kind of persistent cultural flag waving and identity appraisals which are so often implied. Recent examinations of colonial history indicate that indigenous peoples were not necessarily interested in making themselves stand out as the 'anthropologist's other' (Oliver 2010). Indeed, it is becoming clearer that many actively and whole-heartedly participated not only in some of the advantages brought about by immigrant settler societies, but even occasionally acted to implement colonialist policies on other indigenous peoples (e.g. Loo 1996). Given such ambiguities, why does archaeology often find it difficult to move beyond the wooden double-act of colonizer and colonized?

Two significant problems would appear to continue to hamper our work in this area. The first is an impoverished view of indigenous agency which assumes that the freedom to act must necessarily be consistent with resisting efforts of colonization (Oliver forthcoming). While we cannot ignore the possibility of this kind of individual or collective action, we should not forget that agency is also about forms of action which serve to maintain and even rework important social norms and institutions, which are viewed as being central to the coherence of any given social practice (Ortner 2001; Robb 2010). Agency should therefore not be viewed simply as a reaction or break against colonization because it is instrumental to the very alteration of social structures and desires, given the reworking of value systems in a context of relatively rapid change. In other words, agency is about the possibilities afforded within any given social landscape, though such possibilities are themselves shaped by local power structures and senses of appropriateness. A second problem is connected to the often unquestioned belief in the idea that indigenous identities are somehow natural categories. While it is understandable, in fact justifiable, that present day indigenous communities should wish to assert ties with cultural forbearers, as is common with a range of social organizations, from nation states to ethnic groups the world over, much more troubling is marshalling the meaning and content of contemporary identities as a means of interpreting the past. In archaeology, the idea of naturalized native identities has been most strongly linked with the documentation of what Jordan (2009) refers to as 'indigenisms', artefacts and features that retain a supposed element of cultural or ethnic distinctiveness. However, in the same way that western mass-produced objects cannot be isolated as evidence of European identities, 'native' artefacts that are seen to retain traditional design elements or objects used in 'traditional' ways cannot be said to be necessarily evidence of faithfulness to cultural tradition. Indeed, given that contemporary indigenous communities are also known to have selectively reinvented themselves in an unstable and ever-shifting world (Clifford 2001), we should only expect that practices and objects that serve to define people in any one historical setting do not necessarily serve to define them in others. In another way, the values that define identities in the present should not be assumed to be coterminous with those in the past. Indeed, as Silliman (2009) puts it, for social agents, communities or households to move on in the world they must in fact change to remain the same.

The implications of not taking these issues seriously assumes a ready-made world, one devoid of the variable historical processes that go into world-making (Barrett 2000:62; Barrett 2001:153; see also Dornan 2002:324). Ironically, when we take a step back to view the postcolonial counter-narratives we are creating, they can appear at times as monolithic as the colonialist histories we are so quick to criticise. Understanding the incredibly complex social arenas of the colonial world, with its often contradictory desire lines and ambiguous outcomes, requires us to be critical of normative understandings of indigenous agency and identity.

In the argument I develop below, I want to suggest that it may be more productive to start from the notion that intercultural relations must also be considered a creative phenomenon, enabling issues that go beyond the fault-lines of modernization/ tradition. This is not to throw a positive spin on the experience of colonialism, but rather to show how entanglements between the human and material world can give voice to identities and traditions which cross cut more polarized viewpoints. Such a standpoint requires us to engage critically with a variety of influences, which served to rework the social and cultural fabric of this period, often in ways hard to anticipate. It includes paying attention to colonial power structures and how these were materialized in the landscape; and demands that we get to grips with how such impositions acted on native agency in terms of both the conditions and affordances that this realignment provided. Finally, a nuanced analysis of the responses to colonialism must also engage with an investigation of the different social arenas and different scales of social life that colonial influences altered and transformed. A comparative approach provides a degree of analytical purchase not afforded by studies that concentrate on single contexts of interaction. Those who wish for more detail about this theoretical outline are referred to work I have published elsewhere (Oliver forthcoming). The remainder of the chapter attempts to shed light on some of the complex outcomes of the intertwining of indigenous institutions within the geography and introduced value systems of colonialism through two comparative case studies. In particular, it shows how changing historical conditions are implicated in the creation of new social and cultural categories, including new impetuses for resistance, which are part and parcel of the colonial process, not abstracted from it.

Agency and Identity Politics in Colonial British Columbia

The Fraser Valley in southwestern British Columbia provides an interesting picture of the effects of colonialism on Halkomelem-speaking Coast Salish populations as it witnessed change on a scale incomparable with many other parts of the Northwest Coast. Indeed, over less than a single lifetime between 1858 and the turn of the twentieth century the valley passed through remarkable transformations, changes which took Europe itself millennia to develop (Harris 1997:68). Prior to the colonial period, the human geography of the valley was characterized by a constellation of native residential groups connected by dense webs of bilaterial kinship relations (Duff 1997:25; Harris 1997:71), which commonly linked people living both inside the valley with others residing outside. By the beginning of the new century native connections with the land and with kin had been seriously disrupted through the foundation of a property grid and the establishment of Euro-Canadian agriculturally based communities. The colonial state was quick to appropriate land leaving indigenous peoples with little means to appeal. Perhaps most insidious was the introduction of the Indian reserve system. One of its principal aims was to socially engineer the development of a 'civilized' agrarian society, in other words one that aped European values (Carlson 1996). The consequences of the new apparatus of control however, were much more ambiguous and reveal interesting shifts within the social and cultural logic of native groups, providing for new ways of living and thinking that served to rework older notions of appropriateness as well as helping to pioneer completely new ones. On the one hand, the colonial landscape created conditions ripe for the ethnogenesis of a 'virtual' (Jenkins 2005) form of indigenous (national) identity centred on the central and upper valley. This transformation served to transcend and deemphasize older more localized lines of decent and cooperation—relations that were selective and sinuous and did not take in all groups in equal ways (Thom 2009). On the other hand, while these tensions helped to draw the lines of difference at the level of ethnicity (principally in relation to settler society), the new colonial order was also creative of other kinds of social distinctions that hinged on certain shared experiences, which greatly complicate the black and white categories of colonizers and colonized. A significant impetus for these changes developed around new routines in an increasingly agrarian landscape.

The Hop Yards and the Ethnogenesis of the Stó:lō Nation

By the 1870's white-owned hop yards became important centres of economic production in the upper valley. However, because farm labour was almost non-existent due to the fact that the settler population was still quite small, farmers turned to the local Coast Salish population for wage labour. The picking of hops for beer was quite different from other forms of native wage labour, such as logging or road building (see Knight 1978), which took men away from the family unit for long periods of time and had potentially corrosive effects on a variety of cultural institutions. Significantly the farms were situated in close proximity to native village sites, which clustered along the banks of the Fraser River and its tributaries, providing a focus for local employment. In addition, the work was not physically demanding so family members could work together for about a month during the late summer, harvesting, sorting and baling hops. In fact, so lucrative were the prospects that hop picking became an important part of the annual round along with fishing and gathering activities and began to attract people from different parts of the coast and interior as well (Carlson and Lutz 1996:119; Hancock 2001:70).

Examining how indigenous groups engaged with the spatial conditions of hop yards is crucial for understanding their role in creating new social categories. Because the picking season endured for around a month, families chose to situate themselves right in the hop fields, living side by side in temporary camps. These settlements were situated within a new landscape of fenced fields, ditches and rows of crops; a capitalist landscape of relative neutrality that failed to respect older lines in the land and visual cues of the past. Later residential camps were laid out within fenced spaces adjacent to the hop fields. Here family units occupied undifferentiated wooden bunkhouses ordered by the principle of the grid. These were places physically disconnected from the aboriginal landscape and devoid of connections, mythological, historical or otherwise, that gave the different kin groups who came to work the fields their different formulations of power and identity. Instead, the geography of the hop yard afforded a measure of equality and common experience which downplayed older social distinctions (Figure 8.1). As a result, hop yards became centres of negotiation where the meeting of more disparate groups had the opportunity to create new common ground. This did not mean that all involved got along equally and there was a degree of segregation along lines of culture and language (Hancock 2001:70). The implication, however, was the encouragement of forms of interaction that cut across the traditional smaller-scale residential and kinship networks, particularly at the scale of common languages, opening up the possibility of broader ties between a

ROAD

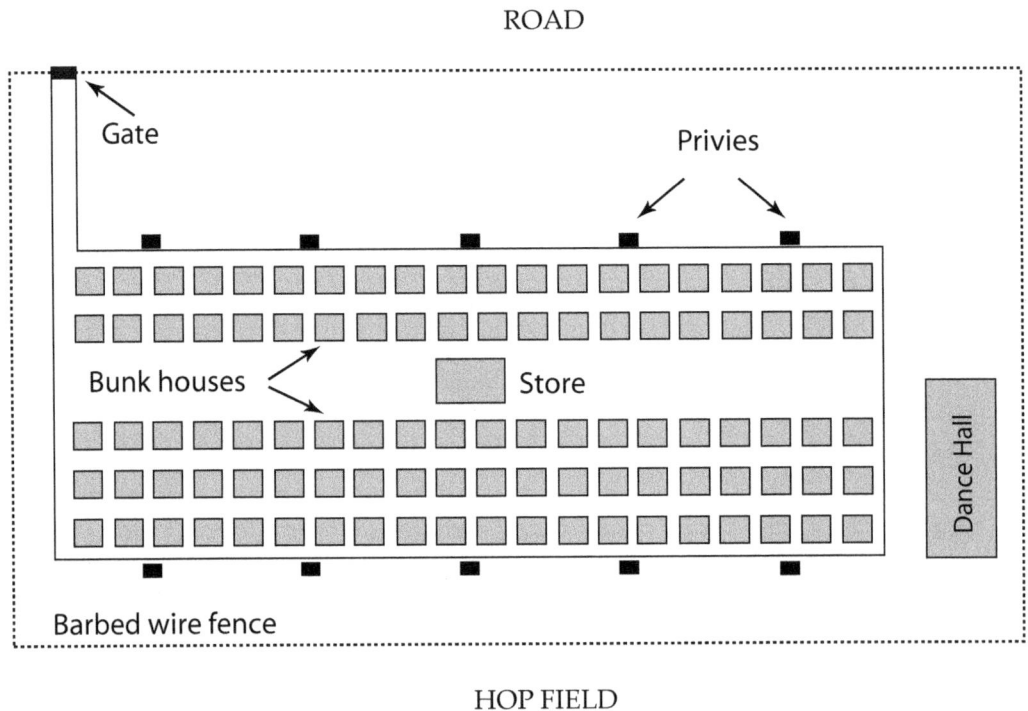

Figure 8.1   Typical plan of a hop yard residential camp (adapted and redrawn from Hancock (2001:70) by Ana Jorge).

range of people that would not ordinarily have engaged in regular contact. Moreover, considering that normal outlets for inter-community exchange, such as potlatches and winter dances, were no longer easy options for social interaction because they were banned or seriously discouraged (Tennant 1990:51), then it is much easier to see how the hop yards became one of the few places where large groups could routinely exchange information and express opinions, particularly after the turn of the century when native peoples required passes to leave their reserves. Most importantly, these places enabled new forms of self-determination.

Above all, the hop yards appear to coincide with the creation of a new 'Stó:lō' ('river people') identity, a social category that many indigenous people living across the valley continue to identify with today. While the word 'Stó:lō', literally translated from the Halkomelem word 'river' (Galloway 1993), is certainly more ancient than the colony of British Columbia, prior to the twentieth-century ethnographic accounts as well as oral traditions persistently document much more local-scale terms of communal identification hinging on kinship relations or very loosely conceived 'tribal' groupings (Barnett 1975; Carlson 2007; Duff 1952; Suttles 1990). Indeed, earlier acts of protest often took the form of petitions on the behalf of named local groups (Carlson 2001b; Harris 1997:133), rather than the cross-valley, emerging-nationalist forms of unity seen in later periods. It was well after the establishment of the colonial landscape and its geographies of exclusion, but in particular the establishment of hop yards, that historical records begin to document the existence of the 'Stalo Indians' as a new unified voice of dissent (e.g. BCLA PCILQ 1914; see also Carlson 2007:173). As John and Jean Comeroff (1992:57) argue in the context of ethnic minorities, 'the substance of their identities, as contrived from both within and outside, is inevitably a bricolage fashioned in the very historical process which underwrites their subordination'. This does not mean that social identifiers used today were invented out of thin air, but it does suggest that words, which may have had older roots, came to take on new meanings.

The hardening of the Stó:lō as a self-identified, valley-wide, inclusive 'nation' (see Carlson 2001c) should not be seen as a simple matter of resistance against the loss of tradition. That logic had changed irrevocably from the early history of contact. More appropriately, their interests arose from the experience of new institutions, new material conditions and new ways of getting ahead, which had been influencing life in the valley for half a century. As native petitions from this period demonstrate, colonial policies had unjustly taken much of the good agricultural land, meaning it was difficult to share in the opportunities afforded by the capitalist landscape. Of emerging native desires, historian John Lutz (2001:64) suggests that when the white capitalist economy expanded into the valley, 'the Stó:lō lost no time in taking full advantage of the opportunities it presented'. In the main this represented a fairer distribution of resources, namely good farm land, which would provide them with an equitable existence within this still-developing colonial space. As a means of accomplishing this goal, early twentieth-century petitions begin to show how the power of numbers served to affect change for the 'grievance of the Stalo Indian' (BCLA PCILQ 1914). We cannot discount the role of other industrial spaces, such as salmon canneries, in helping to unite broader communities of dissent based on common forms of subjugation. However, within the Fraser Valley the long-standing role of the hop yards provided important nodal points for the reworking of pre-contact value systems within the emerging framework that colonialism permitted.

The formulation of the Stó:lō Nation as a distinct 'ethnic' community, founded on a perceived history predating the colonial period (e.g. Carlson 2001a), is an example of what Clifford (2001) terms an 'indigenous articulation'; that is the selective mobilization of ideas and practices, both old and new, which serve to redefine indigeneity in an ever-shifting world. My point about the renegotiation of community-based identity, from an emphasis on many localized genealogical networks to a singular territorially defined cultural formation, is not born out of a desire to demonstrate some kind of inauthenticity on behalf of present-day indigenous peoples. Rather, it is to argue the point that such formulations are not natural categories but are the product of specific historical processes (see also Carlson 2007:174–175).

Billy Sepass (K'hhalserten): Native Chief, Respected Farmer

Cultural entanglements work at a variety of scales of social life and their consequences affect people in different ways. One social arena in particular that brought a broad cross-section of people together was in the context of establishing an agrarian-based lifestyle. It was not only settlers who sought to improve their social positions through establishing farms, as I have alluded to above, indigenous peoples also saw the social and economic efficacy of an agricultural production. In some regards, native and settler lifestyles were not all that different in the late nineteenth and early twentieth century. Both struggled to clear stands of old growth forests and to deal with the instability of an undeveloped market (Kostuchenko 2000:11–13). In this respect, activities that draw people together in the undertaking of certain practices can result in 'shared histories', which can involve a good deal of mutual respect (Harrison 2004; Byrne 2003). These kinds of activities were not usually raised at the broader scale of race relations. However, in a number of instances native prosperity helped to create other forms of social identification that were far more ambiguous than the labels 'settler' and 'native' tend to imply.

One of the most successful 'Indian' farmers in this context, regarded highly by natives and settlers alike was 'Billy' Sepass, Chief of the Scowkale Indian reserve in the upper Fraser Valley (Wells 1987:35). Traditionally, high status and respect among the Coast Salish was mediated through the control of resource sites, such as favoured fishing places, the ownership of ancestral names and stories—also connected to conspicuous places in the landscape—as well as various kinds of cultural and environmental knowledge (Duff 1952:80–87). But by the late nineteenth century this became much more complicated. The rolling out of a new colonial order over almost half a century meant that access to these resources became much more restricted. Moreover, other socially efficacious knowledge systems and cultural categories, ones introduced by immigrant settler society, began to compete, interact and shape more 'traditional' forms. In fact, it is worth pointing out that the office of 'Chief' was given a new sense of undue pre-eminence by colonial authorities in a culture which had formerly been guided by a range of leaders valued for different forms of specialist knowledge. In this context a number of high ranked natives, like Sepass, began to draw upon the symbols of improvement traded upon by white society, particularly agricultural improvement and the material trapping of the successful farmer, in order to help reassert and cultivate their positions of authority. This does not mean a simple abandonment of 'indigenous' values; rather Sepass used his knowledge as an arbiter of power within native circles, helping to reinforce his elevated position, while at the same time gaining respectability within white society.

This is aptly demonstrated by certain improvements Sepass made to his land within the Scowkale reserve, which seem to embrace aspects of European culture. For example, he constructed a frame-built house with steep gable ends and dormer windows. Around the house was a white picket fence that created a zone of exclusion between the domestic space of the house and the working space of the farm. Social respectability was achieved not merely through adopting certain aspects of European housing styles, but by actively participating in the improvement of one's land which meant harnessing it for agriculture. According to historical sources, it was through previously working as a farm labourer that he gained a deep knowledge of agriculture practice, particularly how it brought social and economic advantage—an ability that he became much regarded for by his own people as it brought the Scowkale reserve a modest amount of financial returns (Wells 1987:35–37). By taking a leading role in the social changes advocated by settler society, Sepass was lauded by his white neighbours. At the same time, he reified and institutionalized his position of esteemed rank within native social structure in a distinctly innovative way.

Perhaps one the most compelling artefacts which attests to this ambiguity is found in a map drawn by Sepass in 1918 assisted by his past employer A.E. Wells (Wells 1987:75) (Figure 8.2). Apparently drawn out of historic interest, the map depicts a highly stylized and exaggerated view of the rivers and sloughs of the upper valley, suggesting a more phenomenological engagement with landscape that somewhat subverts the idea of the Cartesian principles of mapping. It also depicts English and Halkomelem place names, farmsteads, local churches, roads, bridges and the Scowkale Indian reserve, even the location of the 'Luckukuk falls first picnic in 1871'. In its juxtaposition of toponyms important to both natives and newcomers it has been argued that the map reveals the ongoing conflict that continued to draw the line between the two groups (Schaepe 2001:126). To be sure, conflict was an important theme of this period, but I want to suggest that for Sepass the map represented something quite different, namely that colonialism was also about moving on, accepting conditions and making something with what you had. Of particular interest is his selective portrayal of his own farm in terms that are conspicuously similar to established white settlers, but that also, at the same time, differentiate him from other members of the Scowkale Reserve. The homes of non-natives such as 'W. Higginson's', 'A.C. Wells', and 'J. Fletchers House', among others, are represented by individual solid rectangles, in the manner of Sepass's own property, located within the boundaries of the Scowkale reserve. Interestingly, his own farm, however, is readily distinguished across the river from the reserve proper, which is represented as single homogeneous rectangle, despite there being at least seven other family dwellings as early as 1877 (Canada, Department of Indian Affairs 1877). It is only by the inclusion of his farm within the boundary line demarcating reserve lands that any association with that community is made.

It is probably pushing my argument too far to suggest that Sepass' biographical mapping of the upper valley reflected the complexity of social relations during this period. What it does suggest, however, given our knowledge of Sepass and how he appropriated his surroundings, is a new hybridized existence—one that drew influences from different backgrounds but which was equally conversant in the expectations of social decorum demanded by each. Such an interpretation satisfyingly rids us of having to choose between colonizer and colonized and allows us to recognize that social

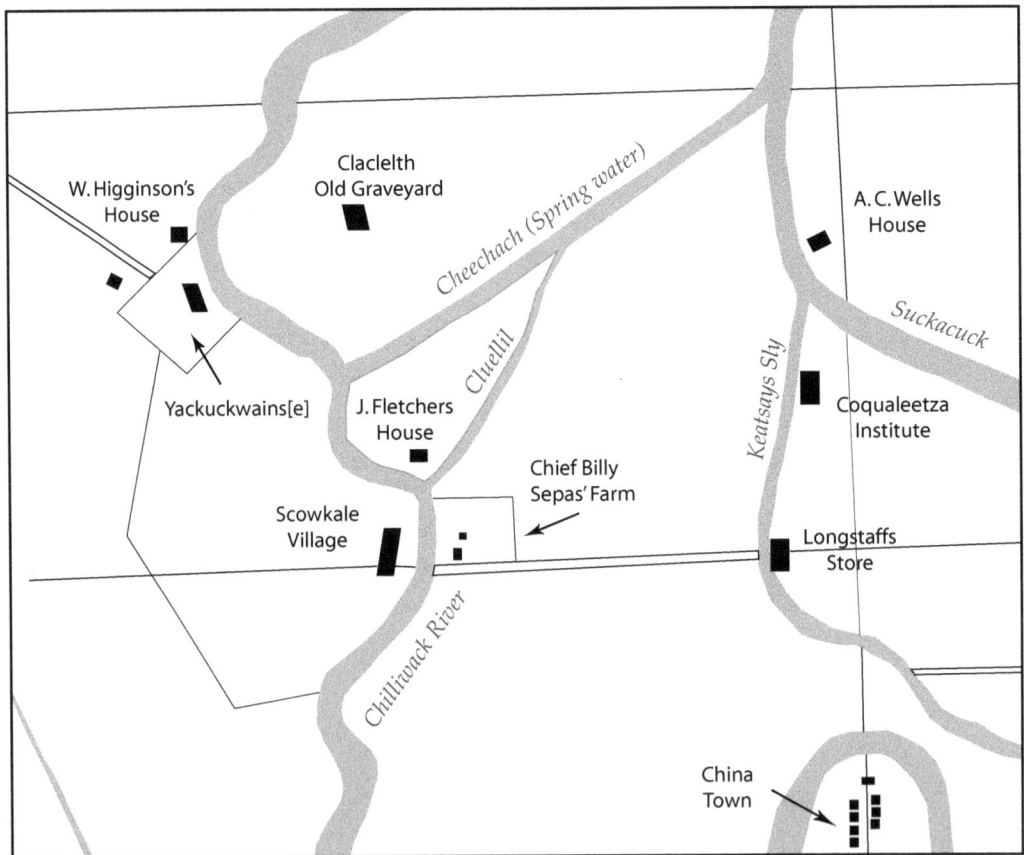

Figure 8.2   Detail of map of the lower Chilliwack River (adapted and redrawn from Wells (1987:78–79) by Ana Jorge).

identities—whether native chief or respected farmer—come into focus when certain issues are at stake. Perhaps most remarkably, however, it seems to embody the agenda of an individual who was actually less concerned about the past and more interested in carving out a stable future given existing realities.

Conclusion

I began this chapter by reviewing how theories of acculturation and resistance in Pacific Northwest Coast archaeology often depend upon making value judgements about whether material assemblages can be said to be more like mass-produced western objects or whether they seem to obey more traditional design templates. Recent approaches that consider resistant forms of behaviour are important as they highlight the fact that colonialism was not a one-way process in the way that new forms of material culture and new ways of living became integrated into native communities. However, the issue of resistance is far more complicated than this as it goes to the heart of how indigenous peoples saw themselves and how different institutions were formed within the framework of the colonial state. I have argued that equating agency very narrowly with the defence of tradition chains indigenous history to the role of the subverted underdog within the colonizer/colonized coupling. Such a formulation is arguably pernicious to a rounded sense of the colonial past, as it pays little attention to local historical processes and how these helped to encourage different conceptions of desire and identity depending on what lines of tension were important in any given moment. I have attempted to show that indigenous desires were already very much part and parcel of entanglements within the colonial landscape, which encouraged social and cultural recombination according to certain parameters. While colonialism could be devastating to older ways of living, and limited the extent to which people could participate in society it also produced new ways of thinking and acting, new traditions, and new possibilities for getting ahead.

Bibliography

Acheson, S.R. (1995) In the wake of the Iron People: A case for changing settlement strategies among the Kunghit Haida. *Journal of the Royal Anthropological Institute* 1: 273–299.

Acheson, S.R. and Delgado, J.P. (2004) Ships for the taking: Culture contact and the maritime fur trade on the northwest coast of North America. In T. Murray (ed.) *The Archaeology of Contact in Settler Societies*, 48–77. Cambridge: Cambridge University Press.

Amoss, P. (1978) Symbolic substitution in the Indian Shaker Church. *Ethnohistory* 25: 225–249.

Barnett, H.G. (1957) *Indian Shakers: A Messianic Cult of the Pacific Northwest.* Carbondale: Southern Illinois University Press.

Barnett, H.G. (1975) *The Coast Salish of British Columbia.* Westport, CT: Greenwood Press.

Barrett, J. (2000) A thesis on agency. In M. Dobres and J. Robb (eds.) *Agency in Archaeology*, 61–68. London: Routledge.

Barrett, J. (2001) Agency, the duality of structure, and the problem of the archaeological record. In I. Hodder (ed.) *Archaeological Theory Today*, 141–164. Cambridge: Polity Press.

BCLA PCILQ (1914) [1875] Papers connected with the Indian land question, 1850–1875. Victoria: R. Wolfenden.

Blackman, M.B. (1976) Creativity in acculturation: Art, architecture and ceremony from the Northwest Coast. *Ethnohistory* 23 (4): 387–413.

Boas, F. (1894) The Indian Tribe of the Lower Fraser River. *Report of the Sixty-fourth Meeting of the British Association for the Advancement of Science* 454–463.

Byrne, D.R. (2003) Nervous landscapes: Race and space in Australia. *Journal of Social Archaeology* 3 (2) :169–193.

Canada, Department of Indian Affairs (1877–1915). Black Series. National Archives of Canada, RG 10, vols. 3650 and 11021.

Carlson, C.C. (2006) Indigenous historic archaeology of the 19th-century Secwepemc village at Thomson's River post, Kamloops, British Columbia. *Canadian Journal of Archaeology* 30: 193–250.

Carlson, K.T. (1996) Early nineteenth-century Stó:lō social structures and government assimilation policy. In K.T. Carlson (ed.) *You Are Asked To Witness: The Stó:lō in Canada's Pacific Coast History*, 87–108. Chilliwack: Stó:lō Heritage Trust.

Carlson, K.T. (ed.) (2001a) *A Stó:lō-Coast Salish Historical Atlas*. Vancouver: Douglas & McIntyre.

Carlson, K.T. (2001b) Appendix 2: Stó:lō petitions and letters. In K.T. Carlson (ed.) *A Stó:lō-Coast Salish Historical Atlas*, 170–191. Vancouver: Douglas & McIntyre.

Carlson, K.T. (2001c) Expressions of collective identity. In K.T. Carlson (ed.) *A Stó:lō-Coast Salish Historical Atlas*, 24–29. Vancouver: Douglas & McIntyre.

Carlson, K.T. (2001d) Indian reservations. In K.T. Carlson (ed.) *A Stó:lō-Coast Salish Historical Atlas*, 94–95. Vancouver: Douglas & McIntyre.

Carlson, K.T. (2007) Towards an indigenous historiography: Events, migrations, and the formation of 'post-contact' Coast Salish collective identities. In B. Granville Miller (ed.) *Be of Good Mind: Essay on the Coast Salish*, 138–181. Vancouver: UBC Press.

Carlson, K.T., and Lutz, J. (1996) Stó:lō people and the development of the BC wage labour economy. In K.T. Carlson (ed.) *You Are Asked To Witness: The Stó:lō in Canada's Pacific Coast History*, 109–124. Chilliwack: Stó:lō Heritage Trust.

Clifford, J. (2001) Indigenous articulations. *The Contemporary Pacific* 13 (2): 468–490.

Comaroff, J.L. and Comaroff, J. (1992) *Ethnography and the Historical Imagination*. Boulder, CL: Westview Press.

Dornan, J. (2002) Agency and archaeology: Past, present, and future directions. *Journal of Archaeological Method and Theory* 9 (4): 303–329.

Duff, W. (1952) *The Upper Stalo Indians: Anthropology in British Columbia*. Memoir no. 1. Victoria: British Columbia Provincial Museum.

Duff, W. (1997) [1965] *The Indian History of British Columbia: The Impact of the White Man*. Victoria: Royal British Columbia Museum.

Ferris, N. (2009) *The Archaeology of Native-Lived Colonialism: Challenging History in the Great Lakes*. Tucson: University of Arizona Press.

Fisher, R. (1977) *Contact and Conflict: Indian-European Relations in British Columbia, 1774–1890*. Vancouver: UBC Press.

Fladmark, K.F. (1970) The Richardson ranch site: A 19th-century Haida house. In J.W. Smith and R.W. Smith (eds.) *Historical Archaeology in Northwestern North America*, 55–95. Calgary: University of Calgary Press.

Galloway, B. (1993) *A Grammar of Upriver Halkomelem*. Berkeley: University of California Press.

Gosden, C. (2001) Postcolonial archaeology: Issues of culture, identity, and knowledge. In I. Hodder (ed.) *Archaeological Theory Today*, 241–261. Cambridge: Polity.

Gosnell, R.E. (1897) *The Year Book of British Columbia 1897–1901*. Victoria: Government of British Columbia.

Hancock, R.L.A. (2001) The hop yards: Workplace and social space. In K.T. Carlson (ed.) *A Stó:lō-Coast Salish Historical Atlas*, 70–71. Vancouver: Douglas & McIntyre.

Harris, C. (1997) *The Resettlement of British Columbia*. Vancouver: UBC Press.

Harris, C. (2002) *Making Native Space: Colonialism, Resistance, and Reserves in British Columbia*. Vancouver: UBC Press.

Harrison, R. (2004) *Shared Landscapes: Archaeologies of Attachment and the Pastoral Industry in New South Wales*. Sydney: University of New South Wales Press.

Hobler, P.M. (1986) Measures of the accultrative response to trade on the central coast of British Columbia. *Historical Archaeology* 20 (20): 16–26.

Howay, F.W. (1941) The first use of the sail by the Indians of the Northwest Coast. *American Neptune* 1: 374–380.

Jenkins, R. (2005) *Social Identity*. Second edn. London: Routledge.

Jordan, K.A. (2009) Colonies, colonialism, and cultural entanglement: The archaeology of post-Columbian intercultural relations. In T. Majewski and D. Gaimster (eds.) *International Handbook of Historical Archaeology*, 31–49. Springer Science and Business Media: New York.

Knight, R. (1978) *Indians at Work: An Informal History of Native Labour in British Columbia*. Vancouver: New Star Books.

Kostuchenko, A. (2000) The unique experiences of Sto:lo farmers: An investigation into native agriculture in British Columbia. Masters research paper, Stó:lō Nation Archives.

Lefpofsky, D., Schaepe, D.M., Graesch, A.P., Lenert, M., Ormerod, P., Carlson, K.T., Arnold, J.E., Blake, M., Moore, P., and Clague, J.J. (2009) Exploring Stó:lō-Coast Salish interaction and identity in ancient houses and settlements in the Fraser Valley, British Columbia. *American Antiquity* 74 (4): 595–626.

Lightfoot, K.G. (1995) Culture contact studies: Redefining the relationship between prehistoric and historic archaeology. *American Antiquity* 60: 199–217.

Lightfoot, K. (2006) Missions, furs, gold, and manifest destiny: Rethinking an archaeology of colonialism for western North America. In M. Hall and S.W. Silliman (eds.) *Historical Archaeology*, 272–292. Oxford: Blackwell Publishing.

Lightfoot, K.G., Martinez, A., and Schiff, A. (1998) Daily practice and material culture in pluralistic social settings: An archaeological study of culture change and persistence from Fort Ross, California. *American Antiquity* 63 (2): 199–222.

Loo, T. (1996) Tonto's due: Law, culture, and colonization in British Columbia. In C. Cavanaugh and J. Mouat (eds.) *Making Western Canada: Essays on European Colonization and Settlement*, 62–103. Toronto: Garamond Press.

Lutz, J. (1999) 'Relating to the country': The Lekwammen and the extension of European settlement, 1843–1911. In R.W. Sandwell (ed.) *Beyond the City Limits: Rural History in British Columbia*, 18–32. Vancouver: UBC Press.

Lutz, J. (2001) Seasonal rounds in an industrial world. In K.T. Carlson (ed.) *A Stó:lō-Coast Salish Historical Atlas*, 64–67. Vancouver: Douglas & McIntyre.

Martindale, A. (2006) Tsimshian houses and households through the contact period. In D.E.A. Sobel, D.A. Trieu Gahr, and K.M. Ames (eds.) *Household Archaeology on the Northwest Coast*, 140–158. Ann Arbour, MI: International Monographs in Prehistory.

Martindale, A. (2009) Entanglement and tinkering: Structural history in the archaeology of the Northern Tsimshian. *Journal of Social Archaeology* 9 (1): 59–91.

Marshall, Y., and Mass, A. (1997) Dashing dishes. *World Archaeology* 28 (3): 275–290.

McIlwraith, T. (1948) *The Bella Coola Indians*. Two volumes. Toronto: University of Toronto Press.

Oliver, J. (2010) *Landscapes and Social Transformations on the Northwest Coast: Colonial Encounters in the Fraser Valley*. Tucson: University of Arizona Press.

Oliver, J. (forthcoming) Native-lived colonialism and the Agency of Life Projects: A view from the Northwest Coast. In N. Ferris, R. Harrison, and M. Wilcox (eds.) *The Archaeology of the Colonized and its Contribution to Global Archaeological Theory*. Oxford: Oxford University Press.

Ortner, S.B. (2001) Specifying agency. *Interventions: International Journal of Postcolonial Studies* 3 (1): 76–84.

Perry, A. (2003) From the 'hot-bed of vice' to the 'good and well-ordered Christian home': First Nations housing and reform in nineteenth-century British Columbia. *Ethnohistory* 50 (4): 587–610.

Prince, P. (2002) Cultural coherency and resistance in Historic-period Northwest-Coast mortuary practices at Kimsquit. *Historical Archaeology* 36 (4): 50–65.

Robb, J. (2010) Beyond agency. *World Archaeology* 42 (4): 493–520

Schaepe, D. (2001) The maps of K'hhalserten. In K.T. Carlson (ed.) *A Stó:lō-Coast Salish Historical Atlas*, 126–127. Vancouver: Douglas & McIntyre.

Silliman, S.W. (2001) Agency, practical politics and the archaeology of culture contact. *Journal of Social Archaeology* 1 (2): 190–209.

Silliman, S.W. (2009) Change and continuity, practice and memory: Native American persistence in colonial New England. *American Antiquity* 74 (2): 211–230.

Smith, M.W. (1955) Continuity in culture contact: Examples from southern British Columbia. *Man* 55: 100–105.

Stadfeld, B. (1999) Manifestations of power: Native resistance to the resettlement of British Columbia. In R.W. Sandwell (ed.) *Beyond the City Limits: Rural History in British Columbia*, 33–46. Vancouver: UBC Press.

Suttles, W. (1990) Central Coast Salish. In W. Suttles (ed.) *Northwest Coast: Handbook of North American Indians* 7, 453–484. Washington: Smithsonian Institution.

Taylor, W.A. (1975) *Crown Lands: A History of Survey Systems*. Victoria: Crown Land Registry Services, Ministry of Environment, Lands and Parks.

Tennant, P. (1990) *Aboriginal Peoples and Politics: The Indian Land Question in British Columbia, 1849–1989*. Vancouver: UBC Press.

Thom, B. (2009) The paradox of boundaries in Coast Salish territories. *Cultural Geographies* 16:179–205.

Vastokas, J. (1966) Architecture of the Northwest Coast Indians of America. Doctoral Dissertation, Department of Art, Columbia University, New York.

Wells, O.N. (1987) Edited by R. Maud, B. Galloway, and M. Weeden, *The Chilliwacks and their Neighbours*. Vancouver: Talonbooks.

Part IV

Confinement and Resistance

9 Resistance, the Body and the V-sign Campaign in Channel Islander World War II German Internment Camps

Gilly Carr

Introduction

Whilst held in civilian internment camps in Germany during World War II, the 2,200 Channel Islanders who were deported during the German occupation survived with the help of the Red Cross and the skills they had picked up during their two or more years of occupation before deportation. Chief among these coping mechanisms was the adoption and adaption of a mode of civilian resistance, the V-for-Victory campaign, which had been promulgated by the BBC in 1941. By utilizing the letter V, Channel Islanders boosted their morale and were able to make known expressions of their patriotism and resistance, both to fellow internees and to their guards, who were bribed to turn a blind eye. This chapter explores how this campaign was made manifest in the internment camps using the medium of the body as the prime locus of (safe) expression, supplemented by symbolic statements constructed from the recycled contents of Red Cross parcels.

In order to understand the forms of resistance or defiance carried out by Channel Islanders in their German internment camps, it is instructive to know how defiance was expressed in the occupied Islands themselves before the deportations took place, and where the capacity for resistance of the population was severely restricted. The vast number of soldiers deployed in the Islands, which was in the region of one soldier for every three Islanders at its height (Sanders 2004:128) compared to a ratio of 1:100 in France, meant that the activities of the islanders were constantly monitored. Many families also had soldiers billeted with them. Islanders thus became adept at disguising the forms of their resistance, or at concealing them upon their bodies.

The small size of the Islands themselves made it very difficult to have any kind of underground resistance movement, with nowhere to run and hide after any sabotage attempt. As well as issuing almost daily orders for the captive population, the Germans were able to threaten retaliation against family members or neighbours who lived in the area of any source of trouble. Thus, overt or active resistance of any sort was extremely dangerous, although small acts of sabotage were carried out—and punished (e.g. Sanders 2004).

Several forms of silent resistance emerged during the years of the occupation. After the order came from Berlin requiring all Islanders to hand in their wireless sets in June 1942, many Islanders either retained their old sets or began to make miniature crystal radio sets (also called 'cat's whiskers'; a simple radio without batteries which used a crystalline mineral as its most important component), which they kept hidden under floorboards and in hay lofts and also inside biscuit tins, hollowed-out books and inside bakelite light switches. Numerous other small-scale forms of resistance emerged. Among the most interesting for the archaeologist, and of relevance to this case study, were those acts which involved decorating the body with jewellery or symbols of patriotism and identity (Carr forthcoming, 2012). While these were among the safest forms of defiant action because they were easily hidden, other forms of resistance included speaking the local Norman-French *patois* in front of the Germans so that they could not understand, refusing to serve soldiers in shops, defying orders to declare any slaughtered animals (and thus keeping the meat for the family), and also volunteering to work for the Germans but 'going slow' on the job, thus claiming the money for little or no work. The first proper critical analysis of defiance and resistance in the Islands is only now in the process of being written (Carr *et al.* forthcoming 2014).

The most well-known act of silent resistance during the occupation began in the early summer of 1941, when the BBC started the V-for-Victory campaign, which was broadcast to occupied peoples in Europe (e.g. Rolo 1943; Tangye Lean 1943; Mansell 1982). Although the radio message was not intended for the Channel Islands because of their precarious and dangerous position with the occupiers, the Islanders nonetheless picked up the broadcast and took the message to heart. Soon, V-signs were being painted on walls, as instructed, in throughout Guernsey and Jersey (e.g. Cruikshank 2004:168) and people were tracing the letter 'V' in dusty windows and dropping carefully cut-out V-shaped pieces of newspaper in roads. The Germans issued a notice that if any Vs were seen, then the people living in the vicinity of the signs would be fined, have their radios confiscated and be forced to do civil guard duty (Sinel 1945:48); some of these penalties were indeed carried out (Cruikshank 2004:169).

Because of the increasing German crackdown on defiance, the V-sign campaign went underground in the Channel Islands, and began to move from the medium of ephemeral painted or paper Vs to small, hidden artefactual Vs, worn on the body. One of the most interesting items to be made in Guernsey at this time was the V-sign badge. People would take their British coins (which the Germans had decreed were no longer legal tender) to one of two Guernsey men, Alf Williams or Charles Machon, and these men would carefully file around the King's head, scoring a V underneath, and would solder a safety-pin to the back of the cut-out coin. Men would wear these home-made badges under their lapels whilst walking round town, lifting the lapel and flashing the 'V' to trusted friends in order to keep spirits high and boost morale (Carr and Heaume 2004; Carr 2010).

However, in September 1942, after the V-sign campaign had gone underground, the Germans issued a decree that all non-residents caught in the Channel Islands by the outbreak of war, and all English-born Channel Island men between the ages of 16-70, together with their dependents (including women, children and babies), were to be deported to Germany as a bargaining tool. Although the soon-to-be deportees didn't know it, this action had been demanded by Hitler in retaliation for the British internment of German civilians working in Iran (Harris 1979:4).

In February 1943, more Islanders were deported to Germany in retaliation for a British commando raid that had landed on Sark in October 1942. Not only did this round of deportations include some of those who had gained exemption and evaded deportation the first time round, but it also included registered Jews, high-ranking freemasons, former army officers, and the families of those who had upset the German administration in some way and were considered 'undesirable'. In all, some 2,200 men, women, children and babies were deported and the vast majority sent to civilian internment camps in Biberach, Wurzach, Liebenau and Laufen in southern Germany. There, conditions were primitive, food was scarce until the Red Cross parcels arrived, and diseases such as TB, scarlet fever and meningitis caused a total of 45 deaths. The majority were to stay in these camps until their liberation in April and May of 1945, although a very few were deemed too ill and were repatriated to the UK towards the end of the war.

Daily Life during Internment

The internees passed their time behind barbed wire engaged in a variety of activities designed to distract them from their situation. Theatre, sports, carnivals, musical bands and evening classes were set up with help from the Red Cross, the YMCA and the Channel Islands themselves. However, when not involved in these activities, many internees turned to artistic pursuits. Painting, sketching and making greetings cards were activities enjoyed even by those who had never shown much enthusiasm or ability before, and a variety of handicrafts and needlework items were produced, usually recycled from second-hand clothing or the contents of Red Cross parcels (Carr 2009). These absorbing hobbies and pastimes, coupled with various compulsory 'jobs' or duties around camp, appear to have kept most internees gainfully occupied. Additionally, many former internees still alive today acknowledge that working relations with the guards were, for the most part, good, established with gifts of Red Cross soap, chocolate or cigarettes, which persuaded the guards to turn a blind eye to some activities in camp.[1] While these selected facts might give the impression that the interned Channel Islanders were a contented lot, the resistant material culture and artwork that they produced tells a different story.

Resistance in Internment

There was a very limited range of resistance activities available to the internees. Overcoming the guards to steal their weapons and thus enable active or armed resistance was, of course, well-nigh impossible in enemy territory, especially in family camps containing pregnant women, babies and many children. Digging tunnels or escaping was also out of the question, because of repercussions for the family of the escapee, the withdrawal of Red Cross food parcels from the interned community as a whole, or the replacement of the 'Dad's Army' guards (the *Schutzpolizei* or German civilian police) with the more strict members of the *Wehrmacht* (army) who had guarded the camp for the first couple of months. The only form of escape possible was into the imagination; a place where Islanders certainly sought refuge, as can be seen by their vast output of creativity in all its many forms. And it is within this imaginative creativity that the Islanders expressed their resistance to captivity and to their German enemies by expressing their identity, their patriotism, and their solidarity with their family and friends back in the Channel Islands. This resistance was expressed primarily through the body as not only was bodily defiance among the most easily hidden, but it was also the only thing in the camp which was not communal and could, to a certain extent, be controlled. Despite having to stay within the barbed wire, and having to obey German rules and timetables, there was leeway within this for individual action and freedom, and this was taken advantage of.

When we consider the reasons for the resistance of the internees, we must remember that, although they had food, shelter and entertainment, they had been taken from their homes with sometimes as little as 12 hours' notice in which to pack only one suitcase, dispose of their pets, store their valuables, and leave their homes and jobs, with no idea of their destination or whether or when they would ever return to the Islands. Morale in the camps was often understandably low and some suffered from debilitating depression and anxiety. People lived in fear from one day to the next, not knowing what the next order would be, when their barracks would be searched, or when the war would end. Although initial letters were received back in the Islands from the deportees in early December 1942 and January 1943 (Sinel 1945:109, 117), by May 1943, three censored letters and four postcards a month were allowed to be sent to England or to the Channel Islands. People were frantic with worry, not knowing what was happening to their friends and family while war raged in Europe, especially after the change in fortunes of the Germans after the D-Day landings, which further cut off the Channel Islands from communication.

Under these circumstances, the retreat into the safety of their imaginations can be easily understood and appreciated. One of the main enemies of internment was boredom and the slow speed at which the days, months and years passed behind barbed wire. People did anything they could to pass the time in the ways already described. The Red Cross parcel provided the basic raw materials used by everyone in camp for almost everything. The metal tins, the parcel string, the cellophane packing material, the cardboard parcels themselves and the wooden parcel crates were recycled into everything from stage scenery for the theatre,[2] to jazz drums for the bands, and to chess sets for those who had no interest in outdoor sports. Everything produced was limited only by the imagination and geared around passing time and boosting low morale, and what better way to do this than by indulging in resistance activities?

Resistance and the Body

Like their compatriots back in the Channel Islands, the internees sought refuge in the V-sign campaign; however, the internees did this using their bodies as the main way to express their resistance and make their allegiances known in unspoken and creative ways. Vs were enacted bodily on several levels: through facial hair, clothing, adornment, gestures, walking, eating and drinking; and in interactions with others, such as in gift-giving and in decorating communal rooms.

Our evidence for such actions and interactions comes from camp portraits, artefacts, diaries and memoirs rather than oral testimony. Such ephemeral statements were perhaps too transient to stick in the memories of former internees today, the vast majority of whom were children or teenagers during their sojourn in Germany. It also suggests that these actions were perhaps too sophisticated and veiled to have been

Figure 9.1   Pencil sketch of Monty Manning by Eric Sirett (copyright and courtesy of Peter Sirett).

understood by, or trusted to, this age group at the time, although some still remember some of the key players who took part.

One such person was Monty Manning, the former scout master who was in charge of the boys' barracks at Biberach camp. A pencil portrait by interned graphic artist Eric Sirett shows Manning sporting both beard and moustache shaved into a V (Figure 9.1). The caption makes it clear that this was deliberate. It is not known who else in the camps copied this fashion.

At one remove from such V-inscriptions upon the body, others chose to incorporate it into their clothing. Several examples survive today of V-sign badges that were either made in Biberach or were taken to the camp from Guernsey, and worn with pride—perhaps openly (Figure 9.2). Other Vs worn on clothing are likely to have been more ambiguous or just a fortunate co-incidence. For example, in the same pencil sketch of Manning, he is shown wearing a suit with V-shaped lapels, his fastened double-breasted jacket and his shirt collar both making V-shapes at the neck. While Vs embroidered on clothing were possible in the camps—perhaps even likely—no record of it survives today.

Other symbols of patriotism were made in the camp and incorporated into clothing. Miniature Union Jacks were popular, made out of wool, beads, paper, cardboard, wood and canvas, and were worn as badges. One template for these badges was the Union Jack on Colman's mustard labels, no doubt taken from the contents of Red Cross parcels, and pasted onto wood. It is probable that for this very reason, the Germans eventually managed to get Colman's mustard banned from parcels; Wurzach internee Mike Shepherd[3] recalled that it was prohibited.

Figure 9.2   V-sign badge made by Alf Williams, courtesy of the Valette Military Museum, Guernsey (photo: author).

Figure 9.3   Brothers Neville and Ralph Godwin in Biberach with their parents, wearing their Union Jack badges (courtesy and copyright Ralph Godwin).

The buttons of children's clothes were sometimes painted with Union Jacks, as surviving examples show. This form of patriotism and resistance was in an obvious and unsophisticated form that children could easily understand and join in with, as shown in a photo of brothers Ralph and Neville Godwin, wearing their Union Jack badges with pride, taken around the time of liberation (Figure 9.3). These badges were also worn by the Channel Islands football team at Laufen during their matches with the Americans in camp. They also acquired a second use after the internees were liberated, enabling them to walk into the local town, wearing their badges to prove their identity, so that the liberating French or American armies would not mistake them for German civilians.

The V-sign campaign was also enacted daily through bodily movements and activities such as walking, eating and drinking. One of the most ubiquitous items made in the camps were parcel-string-soled shoes. They wore out quickly and were not suitable for wet or cold weather, so the high turnover meant that many were made in a variety of forms by a variety of people. One surviving example made in Wurzach has a clear plaited parcel-string V on the sole (Figure 9.4).[4] It would have left the most marvellous footprints around camp, especially when wet. The evidence of this resistance would soon dry and disappear, preferably before the guards had seen it.

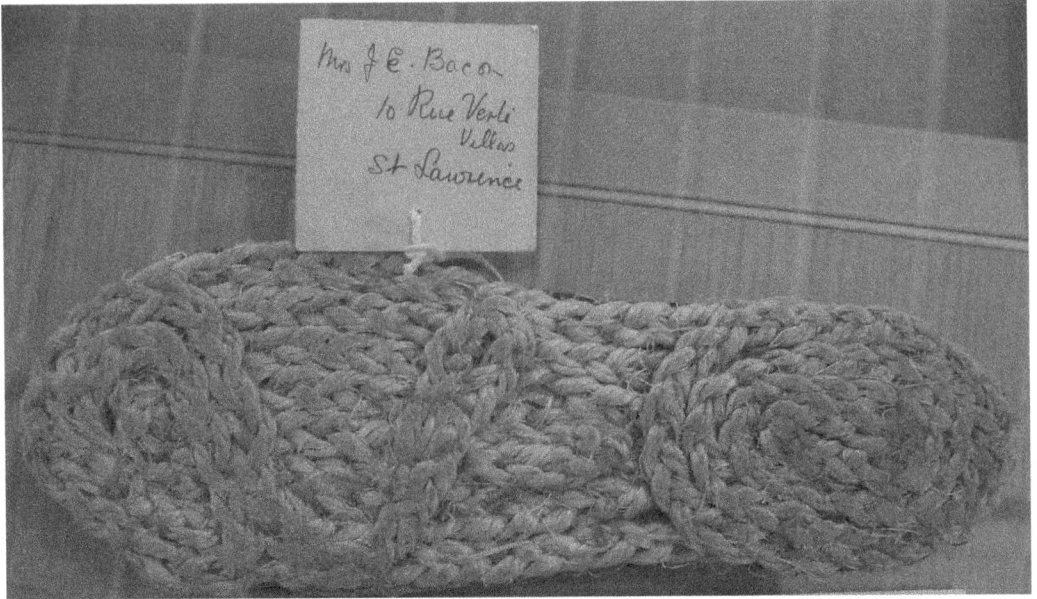

Figure 9.4   Parcel-string-soled shoe, courtesy of Jersey Heritage Collections.

Biberach internee Byll Balcombe introduced what might be termed a 'resistance toast' by engraving an army-issue steel mug with a V-sign, so that he could drink a toast to victory (Figure 9.5). Balcombe engraved a number of other mugs in the camp.

Figure 9.5   Mug engraved by Byll Balcombe, courtesy of Christine Bailey (copyright the author).

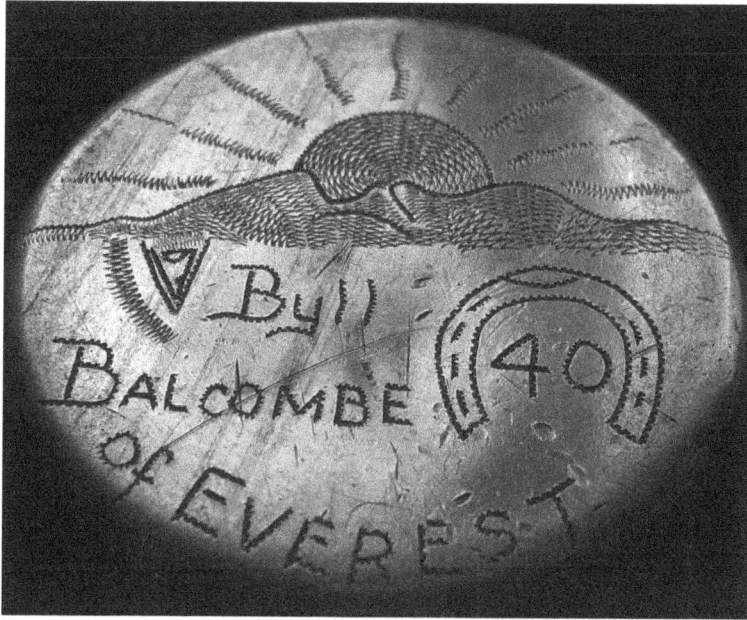

Figure 9.6   Mug engraved by Byll Balcombe, courtesy of Christine Bailey (copyright the author).

He would frequently 'sign' the bases by etching his own profile, the eye of which was actually a cleverly hidden V-sign (Figure 9.6). When turned through ninety degrees, the face would resemble a mountain range, behind which the sun would be rising, and he would often write his name underneath as 'Byll Balcombe of Everest'.

In Wurzach camp, a beautifully embroidered tablecloth[5] made by a Mrs Hadgetts was dedicated to George V by the use of his monogram and an image of a crown on a cushion in the centre of the cloth. Coloured Vs decorate the edges of the material (Figure 9.7). While this could have been explained away, if challenged by a guard, as a patriotic dedication to the king, George VI was actually the reigning monarch at this time and had been on the throne since 1936. Thus, by using this mug and tablecloth, internees could eat meals at, and drink out of, material culture that expressed their resistance and patriotic feelings.

Even the tools used in making this kind of item could bear the V-sign. In Liebenau camp, a protective plaited parcel-string case, currently in the Red Cross archives in London, was made for a pair of needlework scissors.[6] This case is embroidered with V-signs and is itself made in the shape of a V.

The 'resistance toast' was probably not the only gesture that enabled the V-sign campaign to be conducted in the camps. We can imagine that the two-fingered salute was popular, probably aimed at the backs of the guards with the palm facing either outwards or inwards, especially during the early days when the *Wehrmacht* still guarded the camp, before the *Schutzpolizei* had taken over, and before the prisoners and guards had come to an 'understanding'. However, the Victory sign (palm out) was also aimed *at* the internees during their long journey of deportation across Europe. As

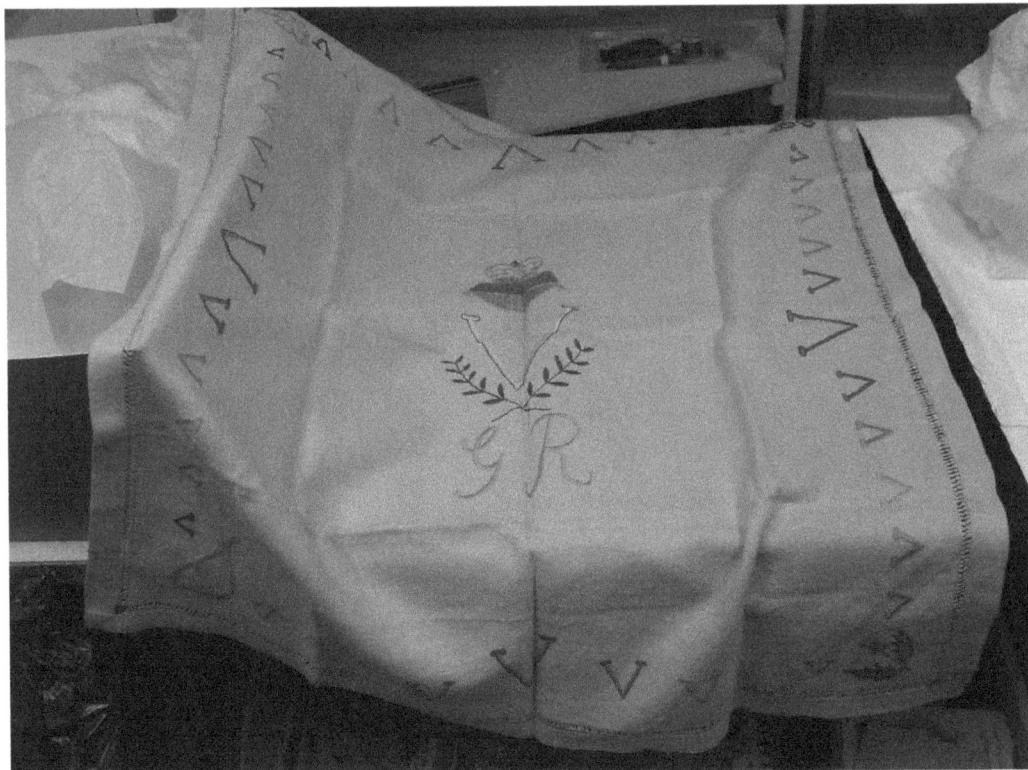

Figure 9.7   Tablecloth embroidered in Wurzach, courtesy of Jersey Heritage Collections.

they travelled through war-torn France and Belgium by train, the local civilians gave them the V-sign to help raise morale and signal their solidarity as occupied peoples, as recorded in the internment diary of Gerald Webb[7] on 28 and 29 September 1942.

Resistance was also enacted in gift-giving activities between internees. Apart from the V-sign mug made by Balcombe, which was given as a gift to fellow internees Edward and Texina Davis, the making of greetings cards was very much a craze in the camps, dampened only by periods of scarcity of paper experienced at the beginning and end of the period of internment. These cards created and reinforced bonds of friendship and community within the camps, and most former internees today own a modest collection of those that they and their parents received during the years of incarceration. Gift giving, especially through card exchange, was an important way for husbands and wives, who were segregated into single-sex barracks or rooms at night, to keep their romantic feelings alive. What could very rarely be expressed physically, nor often vocally, in a crowded camp where privacy was almost impossible, could be expressed in verse or prose inside greetings cards.

Images of barbed wire predominate in many greetings cards, as do the patriotic colours of red, white and blue. In some cards, these motifs coincide together. One greetings card made in Biberach, and belonging to the Channel Islands Occupation Society in Guernsey, sports a V-sign made of barbed wire and a thumbs-up symbol (Figure 9.8); another, from Wurzach, commemorates New Year 1944, and depicts a

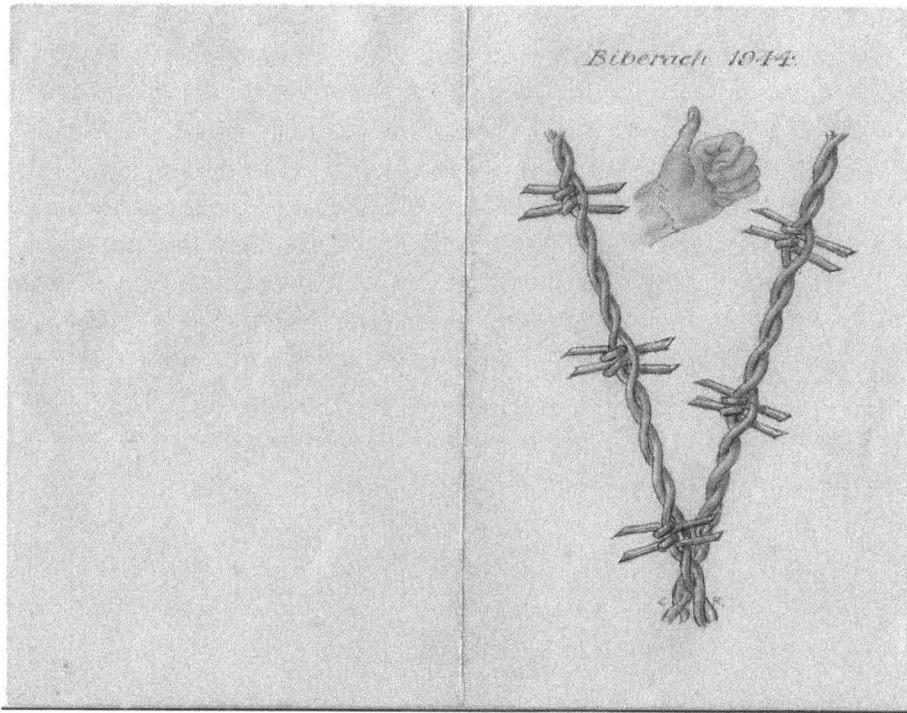

Figure 9.8   Card made in Biberach, courtesy of the Channel Islands Occupation Society (Guernsey branch).

red, white and blue V-sign, complete with bells at the bottom ringing out wishes for a peaceful New Year.[8] Barbed-wire brooches, complete with a barb, were worn by internees in Biberach camp. While none of the surviving internees remembers the symbolism of the brooch, it was likely to have been a way of producing something beautiful out of something ugly, or a way of communicating and making a statement about group identity among the interned.

In addition to the giving and receiving of greetings cards between friends and relatives, bonds were forged and camaraderie was created between other interned groups through the exchanges of V-signs. As Gerald Webb reported in his internment diary on New Year's Eve 1942, a group of Channel Islander internees in Laufen made a gift for the Greek contingent in their camp in the form of a *decorated box containing the Greek and British national colours in silk and a large V-sign with the year 1943 set in between*.[9] V-signs were also employed on other special occasions, such as Christmas. A solitary part of a Christmas decoration exists in a private collection in the form of a V-sign made of roundels of sailors' faces, cut from boxes of Player's Navy Cut cigarettes, slotted together and hung on the wall at a children's Christmas party.

We know from paintings and rare photos of barrack rooms that room decorations such as painted pictures and Union Jacks existed all year round. As a Biberach camp pencil sketch by John Merry of room 15 in barrack 6 testifies, internees also placed V-signs above the doorways of their rooms;[10] this same view is also rendered in embroidery by the same artist, and is in the German Occupation Museum in

Guernsey. Groups of people working together to brighten up communal rooms with flags, V-signs and other decorations would have further strengthened bonds between internees, showing the importance of resistant symbolism in all areas of camp life.

By early May 1945, all of the German civilian camps where Channel Islanders were interned were liberated. This, too, was an event commemorated and celebrated with the creation of art and artefacts and the use of subtle Vs. One particular example is a hand-made flan dish from Wurzach.[11] This was engraved with the name of the camp and the time and date of liberation. Underneath in large letters was written 'POW'. The 'O' is nestling inside a large V such that it resembles a head of a match-stick figure, with the V, its arms, thrown up in joy at being liberated.

V-like, too, are the rays of the sun rising above an image of the town of Biberach, engraved by Byll Balcombe on a shell-case, left behind by a fleeing German soldier just before liberation. The outstretched rays seem to melt the barbed wire, which is inscribed around the names of the internees to whom the shell case is dedicated. Below their names is an engraved prayer in *Guernesiaise*, the local Norman-French patois, and below that, an image of Guernsey, their island home.

Conclusion

In this chapter, I have argued that the V-sign, with all its connotations of resistance and pride in identity, became as important a symbol in Channel Islander internment camps as it was in the Channel Islands themselves, and boosted morale equally in both contexts. Moreover, this link with friends and family back in the Islands was explicitly evoked by use of the V, which forged unspoken and invisible bonds of solidarity, making possible the otherwise impossible: a co-ordinated campaign of silent resistance which could never be articulated or communicated back to the Islands, but which the internees kept alive, perhaps on behalf of their Island friends just as much as for themselves. They were thus able to draw upon modes of defiance from the occupied Islands, and to play upon cultural referents which were visible and meaningful to other Islanders in the camps, but which were otherwise 'invisible' or undecipherable to their bribed or unbribed German guards, who, like other people in Germany, were banned from listening to foreign radio stations in case they heard enemy propaganda (Rolo 1943:121; Sanders 2004:113).

In these contexts, the use of the V hardly constitutes silent nor passive resistance, as the V was proclaimed loudly to those who understood it, despite remaining ambiguous to those who did not. To inscribe, embroider and paint the Vs was also to take an active, albeit non-violent, stance against internment, despite the position of the internees as potentially powerless victims. Although they were unable or unwilling to physically fight their guards, they were not passive, silent prisoners.

Because the Vs would have been visible (though not necessarily recognised) to the guards in many contexts, they can perhaps be understood in terms of Scott's concept of the 'hidden transcript' (1990); the critique of power spoken or enacted by a subordinate group behind the back of those who have power over them. It is a discourse which takes place 'offstage', beyond direct observation by the power holders (in this case, the guards). This can be contrasted with Scott's 'public transcript', which is the subordinate discourse which takes place in the presence of the power holders (Scott 1990:4–5). More fitting still to several of the examples is Scott's third realm of 'subordinate group politics that lies strategically between the first two'; the politics of 'disguise and anonymity that takes place in public view but is designed to have a double meaning or to shield the identity of the actors' (Scott 1990:18–19). As we have seen, many of the Vs were deliberately ambiguous, including Monty Manning's beard and Mrs Hadgett's tablecloth. Others remained in less visible contexts, worn on the body and shielded from the gaze of the guards: very much 'hidden transcripts'.

It is also worth discussing briefly why the V-sign campaign remained mostly within the realm of the body during internment, while that which took place back in the Islands was much more publically visible, painted in large letters in strategic places, often in the capitals of Guernsey and Jersey. We must remember that, at the time of the deportations, the V-sign had already entered its second phase: that of going underground because of the German crackdown on and subsequent prosecutions of offenders. People were already confining their V-sign activities to wearing hidden badges. Second, in an overcrowded and communal camp, one's primary territory was one's own body, and that is where we find most V-resistance enacted. In these contexts, the confinement of the Vs to the body can be readily understood.

This chapter has shown how certain artefacts of internment can be crucial to understanding how resistance operated in civilian camps during WWII. While the testimony of those adults who might have participated in the V-sign campaign is now no longer available, the only traces of it must be gleaned through art, artefacts and, more rarely, memoirs and diaries. The degree of importance of the V-sign to the internees is, I argue, confirmed in the traces that survive which show how Vs were incorporated and inscribed into and onto the body at all levels: on the face, in clothing, in adornment, in methods of walking and gesture, in communal physical action, and in the prime cultural extensions of the body: artefacts used for drinking and eating. This link between body and V-sign was also evoked by using Vs to represent metaphorically parts of the body, notably eyes and arms.

I have shown that in the camps, the V-sign campaign was invigorated, becoming even more inventive and, at times, audacious in its use. It seems that to a certain extent the deported Islanders felt that, as they were already receiving the punishment of being interned, they were free to commit the 'crime' of displaying V-signs, although they were not unambiguously blatant in the way they used them. What is clear is that the use of Vs flourished in the camps and became part of the subtle language of resistance to internment and a source of pride at being unbroken in spirit despite living behind barbed wire. The importance of the V to internees and occupied Islanders alike was such that it remains a symbol that is still widely understood and used in the Channel Islands today, especially on the anniversary of Liberation Day on 9 May, to express not only the remembrance of victory against the Germans, but a part of the modern identity of Channel Islanders.

Acknowledgements

I would like to thank members of the Guernsey Deportee Association and former members of the Jersey ex-Internee Association for their help with my research. I would also like to thank Jersey Museum, Jersey Heritage Trust, the Valette Military Museum in Guernsey, Peter Sirett, the Channel Islands Occupation Society (Guernsey) and Christine Bailey, for permission to use images of their art and artefacts. This paper has also benefitted from comments from the audience of CHAT 2007.

Notes

1. Interview with Michael Ginns, Jersey, 6th April 2008.
2. Interview with Yvonne Osborn, Guernsey, 30th December 2009.
3. Mike Shepherd, *Behind Wire*, unpublished manuscript, Jersey Heritage Trust archives ref. L/D/25/A/70. p.115.
4. Jersey Heritage Trust archive ref. L/D/25/E/14.
5. Jersey Museum ref. 1992.224.
6. Red Cross Archives ref. 0551/18.
7. Gerald Webb, internment diary, Guernsey Archives ref. AQ 78/10.
8. Jersey Heritage Trust ref. L/C/01/B/A/19
9. Island Archives, Guernsey, ref. AQ 78/10.
10. Guernsey Museum and Art Gallery ref. 1979/314a
11. Jersey War Tunnels ref. 2003/929.

Bibliography

Carr, G. (forthcoming) Resistance material culture in occupied landscapes: The Channel Islands in World War II. In T. Clack (ed.) *Archaeology, Syncretism, Creolisation*. Oxford: Oxford University Press.

Carr, G. (2009) *Occupied Behind Barbed Wire*. Jersey: Jersey Heritage Trust.

Carr, G. (2010) The archaeology of occupation and the V-sign campaign in the Channel Islands during WWII. *International Journal of Historical Archaeology* 14 (4): 575–592.

Carr, G. (2012) 'Of coins, crests and kings: Symbols of identity and resistance in the occupied Channel Islands'. *Journal of Material Culture* 17 (4): 327–344.

Carr, G. and Heaume, R. (2004) Silent resistance in Guernsey: The V-sign badges of Alf Williams and Roy Machon. *Channel Islands Occupation Review* 32: 51–55.

Carr, G., Sanders, P. and Willmot, L. (forthcoming 2014) *Protest, Defiance and Resistance in the German Occupied Channel Islands, 1940-1945*. London: Bloomsbury Academic.

Cruikshank, C. (2004) [1975] *The German Occupation of the Channel Islands*. 2nd edn. Stroud: Sutton Publishing [OUP].

Harris, R. (1979) *Islanders Deported (Part I)*. Ilford: CISS Publishing.

Mansell, G. (1982) *Let Truth be Told: 50 years of BBC External Broadcasting*. London: Weidenfeld and Nicolson.

Rolo, C.J. (1943) *Radio Goes to War*. London: Faber and Faber.

Sanders, P. (2004) *The Ultimate Sacrifice*. 2nd edn. Jersey: Jersey Heritage Trust.

Scott, J.C. (1990) *Domination and the Arts of Resistance: Hidden Transcripts*. New Haven and London: Yale University Press.

Sinel, L. (1945) *The German Occupation of Jersey 1940–1945*. Jersey: The Evening Post.

Tangye Lean, E. (1943) *Voices in the Darkness: The Story of the European Radio War*. London: Secker and Warburg.

10 America's World War II Internment Camps: Japanese American Patriotism and Defiance at Manzanar

Jeffery F. Burton

The incarceration of almost 120,000 Japanese Americans by the US government during World War II is one of the more shameful episodes in American history. The 'Relocation', as it was euphemistically called, removed all persons of Japanese ancestry from their homes, schools and businesses on the West Coast of the United States and placed them under guard and behind barbed wire for most of the war. For decades after their release, many in the Japanese American community internalized the shame of this treatment. The Relocation still elicits very strong emotions and many former evacuees still have difficulty talking about the experience.

Some accounts suggested that the Relocation was passively accepted, per the Japanese concept of *Shikataganai,* which loosely translates as 'it cannot be helped' or 'there is nothing that can be done' (Figure 10.1). Indeed, the most obvious archaeological features at the camps, such as guard tower foundations and fence posts, suggest how difficult it would have been to defy the incarceration (Burton *et al.* 2001b). However, by looking more closely at the archaeological remains, it becomes clear that the Japanese American community did not, after all, passively accept the Relocation, or the negative identity promoted by this government-sanctioned racism. This essay summarizes the history of the Relocation, then describes some of the archaeological investigations the National Park Service has conducted at Manzanar, one of the relocation sites. The results demonstrate the ways that the internees kept faith, hope and charity alive throughout their imprisonment.

Japanese American Relocation

On 7 December 1941, the United States entered World War II when Japan attacked the US naval base at Pearl Harbor. The shock of a sneak attack on American soil caused widespread hysteria and paranoia. Sensationalistic newspaper headlines talked about sabotage and imminent invasion. Such stories had no factual basis, but fed the

Figure 10.1   Barracks at Manzanar (National Archives).

growing suspicions about Japanese Americans. While the military debated restrictions on Japanese Americans and limited their involvement in the war, public opinion was growing in support of interning all persons of Japanese ancestry. The anti-Japanese-American sentiment in the media was typified by a February 1942 editorial in the *Los Angeles Times*: 'A viper is nonetheless a viper wherever the egg is hatched—so a Japanese American, born of Japanese parents—grows up to be a Japanese, not an American' (Okihiro and Sly 1983).

Leaders in the Japanese American community were arrested, bank accounts were frozen, short-wave radios and cameras were seized, and restricted and prohibited zones were established. While some argued for the protection of Japanese Americans' constitutional rights (Irons 1993:363), negative public opinion prevailed. There had been a long history of anti-Asian feelings and legislation on the West Coast and since 1924 Japanese immigrants had been barred by law from becoming citizens or owning land (Niiya 2001:111–112). But even those Japanese Americans who were born in the United States and were therefore US citizens were subject to restrictions once the war began.

On 19 February 1942, President Franklin D. Roosevelt signed Executive Order No. 9066, calling for the removal of Japanese Americans from restricted areas. No person of Japanese ancestry living in the United States was ever convicted of any serious act of espionage or sabotage during the war. Yet in 1942, the United States incarcerated almost 120,000 American men, women and children in 'relocation centers', 'assembly centers' and other prison camps without formal charges or trials.

The 'crime' of those incarcerated was their Japanese ethnicity. Over two-thirds of them were American citizens, who had been schooled in the ideals of equality, democracy and justice, as embodied in the US Constitution. In fact, the percentage of citizens would have been much higher if immigrants born in Japan had not been barred from becoming citizens through the naturalization process available to other immigrants. 'Evacuees' included people from all walks of life; native-born citizens, the elderly, World War I veterans given citizenship by an act of Congress and children, even half-Japanese babies living in Caucasian foster homes.

The first evacuation under the auspices of the Army began on 24 March 1942, near Seattle, Washington, and was repeated all along the West Coast. In all, 108 'Civilian Exclusion Orders' were issued (DeWitt 1943). After initial notification, Japanese American residents were given six days in which to dispose of nearly all of their possessions. They were told they would need to bring bedding, toilet articles, clothing and eating utensils, but should pack only 'that which can be carried by the family or the individual'. Shops, homes and belongings all had to be quickly sold, usually for pennies on the dollar. Adjusted for inflation, their losses are estimated to have been over a billion dollars (Ng 2002:100).

After reporting to collection points near their homes, each group was moved to hastily contrived reception or assembly centres, most of them located at racetracks or fairgrounds. By 2 June 1942, all Japanese Americans on the West Coast, except for a few left behind in hospitals, were in assembly centres (DeWitt 1943). Living conditions at the assembly centres were chaotic and often squalid. Privacy at the assembly centres was next to non-existent with communal lavatories and mess halls. Often, many families were placed together in one large room with makeshift partitions constructed of blankets or sheets. At some of the assembly centres, temporary barracks were erected with thin walls and small rooms. However, these were considered inferior to the converted horse stalls at racetracks. Shortages of food and deplorable sanitation were common at many of the centres. The evacuees fixed up their new homes as best they could with salvaged lumber and other supplies that they could find in an attempt to make them more livable.

The US government initially hoped that many of the evacuees, especially citizens, could be resettled quickly, either directly released from the assembly centres and sent back to civilian life away from the military exclusion areas, or sent to small unguarded subsistence farms. However, anti-Japanese racism was not confined to the West Coast. No governor wanted any Japanese in their state, and if any came, they wanted them kept under guard. The common feeling was expressed by one of the governors: 'If these people are dangerous on the Pacific coast they will be dangerous here!' (Daniels 1993:57).

Milton Eisenhower, the head of the War Relocation Authority, the agency created to implement the Relocation, was forced to accept the idea of keeping the Japanese Americans in camps for the duration of the war. The idea of interning innocent people bothered him so much, however, that he resigned in June 1942. He recommended his successor, Dillon S. Myer, but advised Myer to take the position only 'if you can do the job and sleep at night' (Myer 1971:3).

Casella (2007:3) describes three reasons why a state would imprison members of its own citizenry: rehabilitation, segregation and punishment. The relocation centres appear to have served all three functions: the government wanted to 'rehabilitate' the Japanese Americans by relocating them from the West Coast to places in the interior of the country where they would not be so dangerous. Some argued that the 'segregation' of Japanese Americans was for their own good: they were put into centres to protect them from potential racist violence. But to those interned, the relocation amounted to punishment for the crime of being of Japanese descent. In January 1942 newspaper columnist Henry McLemore wrote: 'Herd 'em up, pack 'em off and give them the inside room of the badlands. Let 'em be pinched, hurt, hungry and dead up against it' (tenBroek *et al.* 1954:75).

Ten relocation centres were established in isolated inland areas. Although still in California, Manzanar was far from the coast, located at an abandoned town site in the high desert east of the Sierra Nevada. The one-square-mile centre, holding 36 blocks of barracks, was completed in six weeks, and within three months 10,000 people were interned there (Unrau 1996).

The relocation centres were designed to be self-contained communities, complete with hospitals, post offices, schools, warehouses, offices, factories and residential areas, all surrounded by barbed wire and guard towers. Administrative offices and houses for the Caucasian staff were also located within the barbed wire. The residential core was surrounded by a large buffer zone that also served as farmland. Internees came from all walks of life, and included doctors, nurses, teachers, fishermen, farmers, architects, artists, and businessmen; some were called on to continue their professional work to serve their incarcerated community. The Military Police guards had a separate living area adjacent to the relocation centre.

The layout of the relocation centres varied, but certain elements were fairly constant. The perimeter was defined by guard towers and barbed wire fences. There was generally a main entrance leading to the local highway, and auxiliary routes to farming areas outside the central core. Some of the major interior roads were paved, but most were simply dirt roads that were dusty or muddy depending on the weather.

The buildings and other features were organized by blocks. Each residential block consisted of ten to fourteen barracks, each divided into four or five rooms. Families would be assigned a single room in a barracks. Partitions between the rooms extended only to the eaves, leaving a gap between the walls and the roof. Each room, euphemistically called an 'apartment', had a heater, a single drop light, army cots, blankets and mattresses. Manzanar was the only relocation centre with an orphanage, called 'Children's Village'. It eventually housed over 100 children.

Each block had a mess hall, where internees served as cooks, servers and dishwashers. Internees vividly recall waiting in long lines three times a day for meals. Each block had separate latrines for men and women, a laundry, an ironing room, and a community building. The lack of privacy was painfully embarrassing for many internees. Because the land had been completely cleared for construction, strong winds created sand and dust storms at many of the camps. The hastily constructed barracks, with cracks in the walls and the floors, offered little protection and former internees tell of often waking up under a layer of sand.

During the war, the cases of three Japanese American citizens who had protested different aspects of the internment reached the US Supreme Court. The Court decided that the internment was based on military necessity and thus justified. However, the Court also determined that Japanese Americans who were undeniably loyal to the United States could not be interned indefinitely. Therefore, on 17 December 1944, the War Department announced the lifting of the West Coast exclusion orders, and the War Relocation Authority simultaneously announced that the relocation centres would be closed within one year.

Evacuees had to relocate on their own; the government provided only minimum assistance: $25 per person, train fare, and meals for those with less than $500 in cash. Many left when ordered and by September 1945 over 15,000 evacuees a month were leaving the various centres. But many had no place to go, since they had lost their homes and businesses because of the relocation. In the end the government had to resort to forced evictions.

After Manzanar was closed, the wooden barracks and other buildings were sold at auction and removed. Rubbish and camp equipment were disposed of in shallow pits west of the camp. The auditorium was used by Inyo County as a garage for the repair of large vehicles and equipment. Of the over 800 buildings originally at the site, only the auditorium, two sentry houses, and the cemetery with its monument remained. The rest of the site was seemingly abandoned. However, at least a couple of former internees returned to the site every year and beginning in 1969, the Manzanar Committee sponsored annual pilgrimages. In 1972 Manzanar was designated a California State Historic Landmark and in 1985 Manzanar was designated a National Historic Landmark.

Although during World War II the Relocation was justified as a 'military necessity', decades later evidence surfaced that the War Department and the Justice Department had altered blatantly racist reports and submitted false information to the Supreme Court about the potential danger posed by the Japanese Americans. With this newly discovered information Federal District Courts overturned the convictions of the three Japanese Americans who had used civil disobedience to protest the internment (Niiya 2001:145–146). A federal commission determined that there had been no true threat to national security (Commission on Wartime Relocation and Internment of Civilians [CWRIC] 1997). The commission found that the incarceration of Japanese Americans was due to war-time hysteria, racial prejudice and failed political leadership. In 1988 Congress passed the Civil Liberties Act of 1988, signed by President Ronald Reagan, which provided a formal apology and redress for all Japanese Americans interned during World War II.

On 19 February 1992, the US Congress designated the Manzanar Relocation Center a National Historic Site to be managed by the National Park Service. Since then, two more internment sites have been set aside as National Park Service units to provide opportunities for public education and interpretation of the internment of Japanese Americans. In 2007 the US Congress authorized the funding of a $38 million grant programme for the preservation and interpretation of internment sites (Public Law 109–441).

Archaeology

For many years it was believed that little remained from these ephemeral cities of confinement. Empty landscapes aptly evoked internees' remembrance of desolation and exile. And it was also believed that perhaps archaeology would be extraneous. Thanks to the typical government propensity for paperwork, the archival record was voluminous; internees and others had produced numerous books; and many internees were still alive to seemingly provide all anyone might want to know about the experience.

However, the development of the sites for visitors and public interpretation triggered the National Historic Preservation Act requirements for archaeological investigations. In the spring of 1993 the National Park Service began archaeological work in the Manzanar Historic Site. The first goal was to determine what was left of the relocation centre and the condition of any features.

In all 84 archaeological sites have been discovered and recorded at Manzanar. Many of these sites relate to the relocation centre, but many predate it, including 12 Native American Indian sites and dozens of sites and features associated with the early twentieth-century town of Manzanar and late nineteenth-century ranches. Archaeological testing was undertaken at four Native American Indian sites, four sites associated with the town of Manzanar, three relocation centre features and a late 1940s dump (Burton 1996). By documenting this earlier use of the area, the survey also elicited more support for the National Historic Site from the nearby tribes and the local residents, who were pleased that the site could preserve and interpret what they saw as 'their' diverse histories. The results of the survey were used to expand the boundaries of the National Historic Site. Later, archaeological investigations were conducted to mitigate the effects of proposed developments, such as parking lots for visitors, and to provide information and examples of features for public interpretation.

Archaeological data debunked inaccurate memories and myths that had developed. Some people in the local population contended that the relocation camp was not much different than a resort: internees were coddled and ate better than the general population during the war. Some even claimed there had been no guard towers. Although the towers themselves were removed after the war, the very substantial foundations remained, some buried by sediments. Portions of the barbed wire fence were also identified, symbolic of the incarceration, and of the threat these immigrants and citizens were perceived to represent (Burton 1999). Artefacts in the camp dump reflect institutional food, with large containers and simple condiments, and abundant bleach bottles to help reduce contamination in the crowded conditions. Thick military-issue dish fragments testify to the mess hall experience.

Archaeological features also indicate clear status differences between the internees and the staff. Concrete steps leading to Caucasian apartments and patio walls located at the camp director's house and at the Caucasian recreation club mark the more substantial buildings and greater number of amenities in the staff area. The traces of the 10,000 Japanese Americans who lived at Manzanar are more ephemeral. Scattered foundation blocks are all that remain at the barracks. Here only wooden steps led to the board-and-batten frame buildings, and concrete slabs occur only at the communal latrines and wash rooms. Stubs of communal outdoor water faucets remain; barracks had no indoor plumbing.

Other archaeological investigations provided information to identify grave sites and allow the accurate reconstruction of the fence at the long-abandoned cemetery (Burton et al. 2001a). The excavation of ponds and gardens has uncovered the love of beauty that internees carried with them into camp, and the will and freedom they had to improve their harsh surroundings (Burton in prep.). Volunteers have helped provide labour, which has turned the archaeological investigations into a facet of the

Figure 10.2　Joan (Uchida) Watanabe holding a photo of her mother, Setsuko (Nishi) Uchida, sitting on the same rock, taken during archaeological excavations at Manzanar's Pleasure Park.

public interpretation as the volunteers learned a little about archaeological techniques and methods. Some of our volunteers have been former internees, who provided first-person accounts of the features uncovered during the excavations

Artefacts reflect the internees' daily life in the relocation centre, with paper clips found in the administration area, and buttons, coins, toys and other personal items throughout the residential blocks (Burton 2002, 2005). In some cases, the pre-war life that was abruptly ended is also reflected in artefacts, such as the large fish hooks found in the block where a former fisherman lived. Toy cars and marbles, record fragments, and bobby pins show that inmates strove for a normal life even within the barbed wire. They set up a co-op to order food that suited their taste. Abundant abalone and fish bones, for example, were found during archaeological investigations. Rice bowls trace the efforts to reassert family traditions (Branton 2004). All in all, the features and artefacts encountered during the archaeological work indicate how the Japanese Americans maintained faith, hope and charity during their incarceration.

Faith

If faith is defined as belief without evidence, faith is well represented at Manzanar. Japanese Americans retained faith in their country, even while they were being persecuted by it. Internees worked hand-in-hand with the administration to construct the camps and make them run smoothly (Figure 10.3). The internees maintained American institutions, such as basketball, baseball and Boy Scouts, and baseball field remnants, including bases, home plates and back stops, were found during the

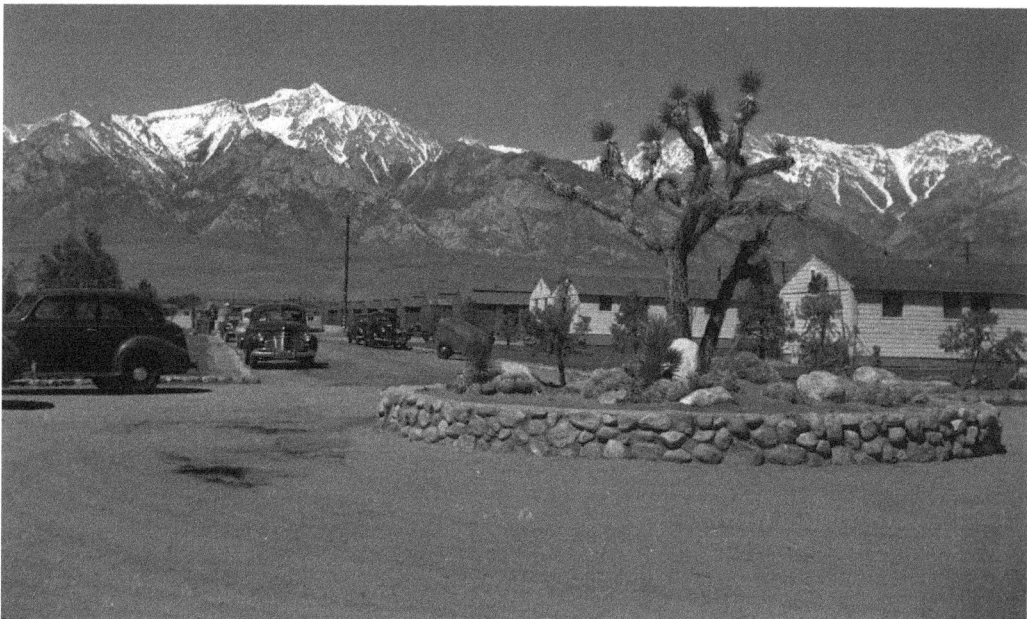

Figure 10.3   Traffic circle (historic image) constructed by internees in the administration area.

archaeological investigations. In support of the war effort, internees grew victory gardens, and made camouflage nets for the military. Metal is almost completely absent from the dump, since metal was recycled for the war effort. Remnants of grease traps show that waste fat was captured for recycling. Faith is also manifest in patriotic symbols: internees erected flag poles at the grade school, at the high school auditorium and at the administration building, and built landscaped gardens around them.

Even more dramatic is the fact that many Manzanar internees served in the military. Japanese American citizens were initially barred from the military. But in January 1943 President Roosevelt declared that:

> Americanism is not, and never was, a matter of race or ancestry.... Every loyal American should be given the opportunity to serve this country wherever his skills will make the greatest contribution - whether it be in the ranks of our armed forces, war production, agriculture, government service, or other work essential to the war effort. (CWRIC 1997:191)

Approximately 1,200 Japanese Americans volunteered from the relocation centres at the initial registration. Manzanar was one of the few camps that had no draft resisters. These volunteers and the later draftees became the 442nd Regimental Combat Team. The 442nd combined with the 100th Infantry Battalion of the Hawaii National Guard, which had originally been transferred to the US mainland. The government had hoped that creating a predominantly Japanese American unit would help impress the general public with Japanese American patriotism and bravery, but some opposed joining the army in a segregated unit.

Figure 10.4   Traffic circle (modern image) constructed by internees in the administration area.

The combined 100th and 442nd became the most decorated regiment in American history, with 18,143 individual decorations and 9,486 casualties in a regiment with an authorized strength of 4,000 men (Chuman 1976:179). Both units fought in Italy and France, and were responsible for the rescue of the 'Lost Battalion' of the 36th Texas Division. In addition, more than 16,000 Japanese Americans served in the Pacific and in Asia, mainly in intelligence and translation, performing invaluable and dangerous tasks. Japanese American women served with distinction in the Women's Army Corps as nurses and for the Red Cross.

Hope

If many of the Japanese Americans maintained faith in their country in spite of the way their country was treating them, hope is the flip side of that faith. Hope, manifest in defiance and protest, highlighted the distinctions between the reality of their incarceration and the dream of freedom and justice. Schooled in the American values of equality and fairness but imprisoned for their ethnicity, many of the Japanese Americans embraced their Japanese heritage in defiance.

Elaborate landscaping and pathways constructed at the Judo Dojo show its importance to the internees. They created other Japanese gardens and ponds, played Japanese games and sports, and practiced Japanese arts and crafts. Abundant Japanese ceramics show that family heirlooms were brought to the camps even when luggage was strictly limited and military-issue 'hotelware' was provided at mess halls. Lost *goh* pieces reflect the popularity of a traditional Japanese game, even while the children were playing with American-style army toys and marbles. Wire stems found at the cemetery indicated that Japanese-style paper flowers adorned grave sites. Most pervasively, traces of internee-built rock alignments, gardens and ponds reflect not only the Japanese ideals of order, beauty and harmony, but also the social cohesiveness and organization required to construct such features. Internees made their own soy sauce, tofu and other Japanese foods.

The modifications the internees made to improve and personalize their barracks and mess halls also exhibit hope. The physical changes the evacuees made in their environment were important ways of taking control over their own lives. Although little of the vegetation planted by the internees has survived the harsh climate, traces of their gardens have been found in rock alignments and even structural remains of a trellis. Although some of the internees' improvements are documented in photographs, others, such as basements constructed under barracks and mess halls, were discovered only through archaeological excavation.

As part of camp operations and maintenance, internees constructed improvements to the water system and agricultural facilities using concrete (Figure 10.5). The archaeological investigations discovered much graffiti inscribed in the concrete, including names, dates and poetry (Figure 10.6). One graffiti-writer with an indomitable

Figure 10.5   Internee crew working outside of the security fence (NPS).

spirit clearly resisted internalizing the shame of the internment: in addition to an inscription, 'I Love Myself Tommy M.', Tommy's name appears five more times on the same wall. At the farthest point from the relocation centre is an inscription on a pipeline support expressing pride in workmanship: 'Finished by Tom Fujisaki & Crew Mar. 23, 1944'. Writing Japanese characters was itself defiant, since the Japanese language was banned at the camps, and most of the Japanese graffiti found is located outside the fence and in hidden areas. Some inscriptions found in the concrete at the reservoir, below the normal water level, suggest that the humiliation of centre life turned some internees against their country: 'beat US and Britain', 'Manzanar Black Dragons Group Headquarters'. Another one nearby, which translates as 'Peace', may be the ultimate expression of hope.

Charity

Charity, a concern for the good of the community beyond the individual or family, was also manifest at Manzanar. The War Relocation Authority had not originally provided schools for the children. Internees converted barracks into schools, volunteered as

Figure 10.6 Inscription on pipeline support translated as 'Pleasantly we will reap all spikes / If you want to be proud. be proud for now / Ugly rice (ugly despicable Americans)'.

teachers, scrounged for books and cobbled together teaching supplies. With materials provided by the camp administration, internees even built a large auditorium for high school and community events.

Attention to the greater good is also manifest in the physical remains: community gardens, created to improve the prison environment, were uncovered during archaeological investigations. Mr Harry Ueno, who served as a cook at Block 22, created a garden at the mess hall so that the internees would have something beautiful to look at as they stood in the long lines awaiting meals. This was the first of many mess hall gardens. Mr Ryozo Kado, a Methodist landscaper interned in Block 34, constructed an elaborate garden with a fish pond for the Buddhists at Block 9 to revive the morale of the Japanese American fishermen who lived there. No historic photos have been found of the Block 9 garden. During archaeological excavation it was discovered to have been much more extensive than originally thought.

The largest and most elaborate garden at Manzanar was Merritt Park, a Japanese stroll garden named after the camp director who allowed its construction. Covering 1.5 acres, the park incorporated tons of decorative boulders, most of which had to be

Figure 10.7 Teahouse at Pleasure Park (Ansel Adams Photograph, Library of Congress).

brought in from miles away. With ponds, waterfalls, bridges, an island and a tea house (Figures 10.7 and 10.8), Merritt Park became a showplace, as well as a place for young people to go on a date. Not only was the park a source of pride during the internment, it remains so today: the Japanese American community identified its restoration as a priority during public hearings for the park management plan.

Conclusion

Taken together, the overall patterns at Manzanar indicate the persistence of Japanese culture and its integration with 'American' culture, even in the face of persecution, even when the dominant culture had defined 'Japanese' as something to be afraid of and ashamed of. In retrospect the faith maintained by the Japanese Americans in their country, and the hope manifest in the material remains of daily life, was at least to some extent justified, given that the executive branch of the government apologized for the internment, the judicial branch overturned the convictions of those who had protested against it and the legislative branch authorized compensation for the victims.

As important as faith and hope are, the moral in the relocation story could be said to focus on charity. As described above, charity served to improve the conditions within the camp, for the entire incarcerated community. However, if charity is defined as

Figure 10.8   Excavation of tea house foundation at Merritt Park.

extending compassion to individuals beyond our immediate kith and kin, the charity of the Japanese American community has extended even further. Japanese Americans have fought to have their story remembered and told, not for personal vindication, but rather because they do not wish other groups to experience the same prejudice and discrimination. Having seen how easy it is for United States Constitutional rights to be abrogated, they do not want it to happen again. The lessons learned from the Japanese American internment still resonate and merit discussion, as the United States attempts to protect itself from today's threats without diminishing the principles it stands for.

Bibliography

Branton, N.L. (2004) Drawing the Line: Places of Power in the Japanese-American Internment Eventscape. PhD Dissertation, University of Arizona, Tucson.

Burton, J.F. (1996) Three Farewells to Manzanar: The Archeology of Manzanar National Historic Site, California. *Western Archeological and Conservation Center Publications in Anthropology* 67. Tucson, Arizona: National Park Service.

Burton, J.F. (1999) *Trip Report, Excavation of Security Features (MANZ 1999A), Manzanar National Historic Site, Inyo County, California.* Tucson: Western Archeological and Conservation Center, National Park Service.

Burton, J.F. (2002) *Trip Report, Block 8 Investigations (MANZ 2002 A), Manzanar National Historic Site, Inyo County, California.* Tucson: Western Archeological and Conservation Center, National Park Service.

Burton, J.F. (2005) *Archeological Investigations at the Administration Block and Entrance Area, Manzanar Relocation Center.* Tucson: Western Archaeological and Conservation Center, National Park Service.

Burton, J.F. (in prep.) The Archeology of Trees and Stones: Excavation and Restoration of Merritt Park and the Block 9 and 34 Mess Hall Gardens, Manzanar National Historic Site.

Burton, J.F., Farrell, M.M., Lord, F.B. and Lord, R.W. (2001a) *Confinement and Ethnicity: An Overview of World War II Japanese American Relocation Sites.* Seattle: University of Washington Press.

Burton, J.F., Haines, J.D. and Farrell M.M. (2001b) I Rei To: Archeological Investigations at the Manzanar Relocation Center Cemetery, Manzanar National Historic Site, California. *Western Archeological and Conservation Center Publications in Anthropology* 79. Tucson, Arizona: National Park Service.

Casella, E.C. (2007) *The Archaeology of Institutional Confinement.* Tallahassee: University Press of Florida.

Chuman, F. (1976) *The Bamboo People: The Law and Japanese Americans.* Chicago, Illinois: Japanese American Research Project.

Commission on Wartime Relocation and Internment of Civilians (CWRIC) (1997) *Personal Justice Denied: Report of the Commission on Wartime Relocation and Internment of Civilians.* Seattle: University of Washington Press.

Daniels, R. (1993) *Prisoners without Trial: Japanese Americans in World War II.* New York: Hill and Wang.

DeWitt, J.B. (1943) *Final Report, Japanese Evacuation from the West Coast, 1942.* Washington, DC: Government Printing Office.

Irons, P.H. (1993) *Justice at War: The Story of the Japanese-American Internment Cases.* Berkeley: University of California Press.

Myer, D.S. (1971) *Uprooted Americans: The Japanese Americans and the War Relocation Authority during World War II.* Tucson: University of Arizona Press.

Okihiro, G.Y. and Sly, J. (1983) The Press, Japanese Americans and the Concentration Camps. *Phylon* 44: 66–83.

Ng, W.L. (2002) *Japanese American Internment during World War II: A History and Reference Guide.* Westport, Connecticut: Greenwood Press.

Niiya, B. (ed.) (2001) *Encyclopedia of Japanese American History: An A-to-Z Reference from 1868 to the Present.* New York: Checkmark Books.

tenBroek, J., Barnhart, E.N., and Matson F.W. (1954) *Prejudice, War, and the Constitution: Causes and Consequences of the Evacuation of the Japanese Americans in World War II.* Berkeley: University of California Press.

Unrau, H.D. (1996) *Manzanar National Historic Site, California: The Evacuation and Relocation of Persons of Japanese Ancestry during World War II : A Historical Study of the Manzanar War Relocation Center.* Washington, DC: National Park Service.

11 Manifestations of Hope in a Place of Fear: Long Kesh/Maze prison, Northern Ireland

Laura McAtackney

Long Kesh/Maze prison site in Northern Ireland, long considered one of the icons of the Troubles, is not a place normally associated with hope. Since opening in 1971 until it closed in 2000 Long Kesh/Maze has been synonymous with imprisonment, conflict, protest and even illegality, brutality and injustice. By virtue of its initial use as an internment camp it became central to controversial methods used by the British and Northern Irish governments to control the bloody civil conflict and deal with the perpetrators of violence. Despite internment being abandoned as a method of controlling paramilitary groups by the mid 1970s, this taint remained with the site throughout its usage. Whilst it has been associated with dubious and reproachful tactics, it could be claimed that Long Kesh/Maze has made a positive contribution to the numerous peace processes. It was during imprisonment in this structure that many of the paramilitary bodies involved in the escalating conflict began to explore political means to pursue their aims, as can be seen in the consolidation of Sinn Féin from being the official mouthpiece of the Provisional Irish Republican Army (PIRA) to the second largest political party in Northern Ireland by the 2007 general election. Furthermore, on a symbolic level this infamous prison has evolved during its 30-year history from an unusual but functional prison to a place of myth and misunderstanding. This paper aims to illuminate the site by examining the significance of Long Kesh/Maze and its role in the recent conflict before exploring its evolution in character from a place associated with injustice and death to a potential symbol of hope.

Long Kesh/Maze and the Troubles

'The Troubles' is the euphemism that is frequently used to describe the bloody civil conflict that afflicted Northern Ireland from c.1969 at least until the signing of the Good Friday Agreement in 1998. Long Kesh/Maze prison was intimately connected with the course of the conflict as it was used to contain primarily paramilitary prisoners from 1971 to 2000. As well as the prison and conflict co-existing, a close examination of the relationship between the two indicates that they were involved, to an extent, in a cyclical relationship of cause and affect. Whilst paramilitary activities connected to the Troubles resulted in huge increases in prisoner numbers, many of whom were placed in Long Kesh/Maze prison, actions within the prison shaped the activities of active paramilitaries, appealed to the sympathies of the wider public and thereby impacted on the course of the conflict. Indeed, one need only consider the impact of the deaths of ten Hunger Strikers on the nationalist community during the summer of 1981 to recognise that a new dynamic and impetus was added to the conflict thus ensuring its continuation. The British government files from the time accepted that the Hunger Strikes were 'one of the greatest propaganda successes of all time' for Republican paramilitaries and their attempts to gain local, national and international support and recognition (INF 12/1400, 1981, The National Archives).

The Troubles claimed the lives of over 3,600 people from 1968 to 1998 (McKitterick *et al.* 1999), and the archaeological landscape that continues to be associated with this dark period of the recent past contains few positive elements. Indeed, it has been noticeable that many of the most prominent buildings and constructions associated with the recent conflict—army bases, police station, road checkpoints and associated security infrastructure—have been demolished in the years directly following the Good Friday Agreement. Long Kesh/Maze is significant in this regard as it remained standing for a number of years despite, or perhaps because of, its most vivid associations with the conflict (by 2011 only representative elements remain *in situ*). A number of commentators, including the journalist Liam Clarke, have noticed the growing public unease regarding the swift disposal of the remnants of conflict: 'some of Ulster's vanishing fortresses are now regarded with something approaching nostalgia' (Clarke 2005:2). Long Kesh/Maze is significant in this regard. As the largest ex-security site in the province, it was transferred to the Northern Ireland government for regeneration under the Reinvestment and Reform Initiative in May 2002. This transferral indicates an acceptance by central government that the future of ex-security sites should be decided on a local level, that those special category zones should be handled with some delicacy and that these sites are to be regenerated rather than to be kept in their current form. It is clear that whilst public opinion is strongly divided about the future of the site—with a marked preference for retention by Republicans and for destruction by Loyalists—the government clearly want its past associations to be neutralised.

It is against this evolving, unresolved and emotive background that one must attempt to explore the site as an archaeological site. Delving into a problematic and contentious recent past will never be a straightforward task; as well as exploring, recording, interpreting, incorporating and discarding the vast numbers of physical remains, one has to contend with the impact of living memory and evolving stories of hardship, conflict, loss and pain. Whilst the archaeologist can never be immune from the effect of their subjects—both human and material—or their sensitivities and perspectives, they can be self-reflexive about how this is incorporated into the story of place. When exploring a site that was in use during living memory, the gathering of oral testimonies is vital and one must grapple with the difficulties of attempting to present the interviewees' perspectives faithfully. In this regard, Alessandro Portelli (1998:40–41) describes the interviewer as not only 'the stage director' but he states that 'the impartiality traditionally claimed by historians is replaced by the partiality of the narrator'. Archaeologies of the recent past are enlivened and complicated by such considerations and often one-sided and even unpleasant personal perspectives need to be included to exemplify the multiple realities of what the site meant and continues to mean to those entwined with its history.

Long Kesh/Maze Prison

Long Kesh/Maze prison was the primary container of paramilitary prisoners in Northern Ireland for much of the Troubles, holding at least 10,000 prisoners over the course of its operational life (Purbrick 2004:91). Whilst these numbers alone are testament to its significance in a previously law-abiding society, the physical remains of the prison are also important. Long Kesh/Maze is a unique prison site due to the nature of the prison population and also because it contains the remnants of two very different prisons systems on the one site: the communal Nissen huts synonymous with prisoner of war camps and the cellular H Blocks, which are associated with modern criminal institutions. *Long Kesh Internment Camp* was the original name given to the Nissen hut element, which pre-existed the prison as the long-abandoned remains of a World War II Airforce base, and *HMP, the Maze* became synonymous with the H Blocks, built to replace them. These two names continue to be associated with the two forms of prison, despite *HMP, the Maze* actually being used in official parlance at least from 1972, with the introduction of non-internee, remand and convicted prisoners to the site. Loyalist and Republican prisoners frequently call both elements of the site 'Long Kesh' as they associate the name change with government attempts to replace their special categorisation, effectively as prisoners-of-war, with criminal status. To further complicate matters, not only did the remnants of both prison buildings, with their different regimes, remain in place until long after closure but they also functioned side-by-side for a substantial period—from 1976 to 1989—due to the right of those imprisoned before March 1976 to serve their time in the crumbling internment camp. Prison officers assigned to the older prison after the official opening of the newly constructed H Blocks claimed they were 'like a forgotten army', despite initially having 750 inmates to control (Gaynor 1987:10). Whilst archaeologies of the recent past are in some respects assisted by the vast number and range of sources that are accessible to study, when sites are contested the complexities and nuances of the understandings that they reveal can be almost overwhelming.

What can be said about Long Kesh/Maze with certainty is that it continues to occupy a prominent place in the now post-conflict state of Northern Ireland. Despite closing its doors to prisoners in September 2000, the controversy surrounding its future life encompasses debates on more fundamental issues: how does society resolve and deal with a divisive past whilst attempting to create a more cohesive future? How can places that are central to the identities of specific groups be incorporated into the more general experiences of society? Whilst so strongly associated with the Republican experience of the Troubles, can Long Kesh/Maze move beyond its current position as a 'sum zero heritage site' (Graham and McDowell 2007:363) to reveal multi-perspectives? Can a place associated with imprisonment, sectarianism, brutality, fear and death become a symbol of hope? I believe that even sites such as Long Kesh/Maze, with very difficult and contested pasts, can evolve in meaning and identity from negative to positive places in relatively short timescales; the case study of the Hunger Strikes of 1981 will be used to explore this contention.

Case-study: The Hunger Strikes of 1981

With the change from Nissen hut to cellular block in the mid to late 1970s the government initiated a number of strategies to re-situate the conflict from political and international to criminal and local through processes of criminalisation, normalisation and Ulsterisation (Mulcahy 1995:450). The change of status that was associated with the purpose-built prison at Long Kesh/Maze was manifest in a number of material changes from the necessity to wear a prison uniform, reduced visits and parcels to the integration of paramilitary groupings onto assigned wings and the loss of freedom of association. Protests by Republican prisoners began with a refusal to wear prison uniform (the blanket protests) that heightened to defecating and smearing faeces around their cells (the dirty protests) eventually leading to hunger strikes. Therefore, the Hunger Strikes of 1981 were not an isolated incident, rather they were the culmination of a campaign of escalating protests that began as soon as the H Blocks were occupied. Indeed, it has been claimed that the significance of these protests were not merely related to prisoner rights but they 'offered an alternative interpretation of the nature of the conflict, and even of the Northern Irish state itself' (Mulcahy 1995:450).

Hunger strikes are not an unusual form of protest for the Republican movement. There are numerous examples of hunger strikes being used by Irish Republican prisoners dating back throughout the history of British involvement in Ireland. The most recent precedent before the hunger strikes of the early 1980s at Long Kesh/ Maze are those of isolated Irish prisoners being held in British prisons who partook in hunger strikes in an attempt to pressurise for transferral to prisons in Ireland. Throughout the 1970s there were high profile individual examples of this practice, including Frank Stagg who died in Wakefield Prison, West Yorkshire, in 1976, which had tested the resolve of the authorities in dealing with such personalised and emotive means of protest. Through these precedents, it was established by the 1980s that the British government and their agents would not medically intervene in hunger strikes. By this time it was only when hunger strikers lapsed into a coma that their family could be prevailed upon to allow feeding tubes to be used to prevent self-starvation.

Whilst these rules of engagement had been previously negotiated and set, it was the sheer scale and communal focus of the Hunger Strikes of 1981 that was unique.

In 1980 a group of Republican prisoners held at Long Kesh/Maze partook in the first organised communal hunger strike relating to the long-running campaign for the return of special category status. This hunger strike, by seven men simultaneously, was halted on 17 December 1980 as one prisoner, Sean McKenna, entered the critical phase. Conflicting reports stated that the prisoners believed that they had been assured by government officials that their conditions would be met in exchange for the cessation of the immediate hunger strike, whilst the authorities claimed that no such deal had been done (Mulcahy 1995:453). Regardless of the accuracy of either claim, this background of distrust ensured that when a reformulated set of organised hunger strikes were begun in the spring of 1981 there was a renewed determination by the prisoners to continue to their logical conclusion.

The Hunger Strikes of 1981 were a seminal moment in the life of the H Blocks and in the Troubles in general. Over the course of six months, from 1 March to 3 October 1981, ten men died in this orchestrated campaign of extreme non-cooperation. The sheer volume of casualties involved was unparalleled in Irish Republican tradition and indicated the entrenched nature of both sides: the British and Northern Irish governments and their desire to confront the paramilitaries and the Republican prisoners and their campaign to be treated as political prisoners. This hardened resolve did not augur well for negotiation, reconciliation and understanding—both at a political level and within society in general. The Hunger Strikes polarised opinion at large on a local, national and international level and ensured widespread and violent reactions as each new staggered hunger strike began and death was announced. The Hunger Strikes of 1981 remain a contentious issue within Northern Irish society: those who died were considered and remembered as martyrs by the nationalist community and as unrepentant terrorists by their unionist neighbours.

The reaction to the Hunger Strikes in wider society initially was violent and widespread, with riots, destructive protests and a general escalation of civil unrest greeting the deaths, but it continues to have relevance today, even after the end of the Troubles. During 2006, the 25th anniversary of the Hunger Strikes, nationalist areas commemorated this occasion proudly—with festivals, films, concerts, poetry readings and debates—whilst they were essentially ignored by the majority of the unionist community. The prominence of wall murals in nationalist areas that depicted the hunger strikers, and particularly the most famous and first man to die—Bobby Sands—were noticeable throughout the year. For not only were new murals erected in prominent locations but old ones that had continued to stand since the twentieth anniversary in 2001 or before were redecorated and replicated. This includes a particularly striking example—a freestanding wooden 'H' (the recognisable aerial image of the H Blocks associated with media reports) with images of all the hunger strikers complete with the dates of their self-starvation—which pre-existed 2006 but was updated and was replicated at main thoroughfares and prominent locations throughout nationalist west Belfast (see

Figure 11.1). Small, green wooden 'Hs' with '1981' written on them were nailed to trees on the main thoroughfares in this area. Wall murals of Bobby Sands and the other hunger strikers were constructed through different media, including paint, mosaic and wood inlay. The content of the murals had transitioned beyond commemoration connected to military activity, defiance and overt violence to be replaced with less confrontational content including quoting of poetry, and even associating the figureheads with local business and the concerns with ex-prisoners' situations in contemporary society. It

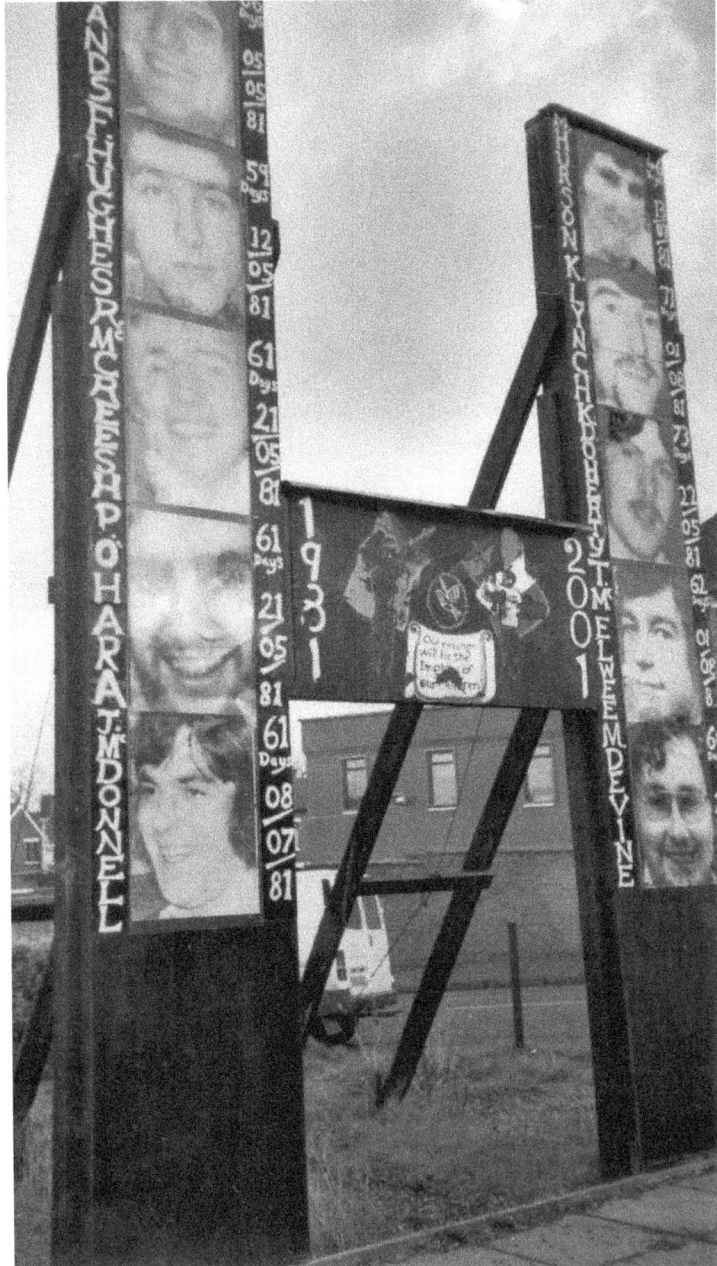

Figure 11.1 Wooden 'H' Hunger Strike mural.

was clear that Bobby Sands and the Hunger Strikers of 1981 were not merely being commemorated in Republican historical iconography in 2006 but their position was being reaffirmed—what Jonathan McCormick and Neil Jarman describe as 'embedding memory' (2005:51)—and officially installed whilst revising contemporary nationalist identity. These commemorations coincided with the continued mainstream nationalist move from paramilitary to essentially political organisation, and the need to reaffirm their connections to their past, reformulated for a very different present and future.

Alongside the archaeology of commemoration many other material remains connected to the Hunger Strikes continue to exist. LuAnn DeCunzo states in her recent work on institutions that there is a need to scour archives, museums and private collections to explore the artefacts of prisoners, due to them frequently being ignored (2006:184). This need is particularly relevant in relation to Long Kesh/Maze. The prison hospital, where all the Hunger Strikers died, is still standing and continues to contain within its sparse walls the metal frames of the beds and some medical paraphernalia. No doubt other artefacts have been moved and now reside in the hangars—remnants from its past-life as an airforce base—that act as on-site storage. Contraband artefacts, which were confiscated from prisoners, lie in the small museum room and attic store of the Northern Ireland Prison Service museum in Millisle, Co. Down. This museum holds confiscated materials from all the prisons in Northern Ireland with the largest collection relating to Long Kesh/Maze at over 300 individual artefacts (McAtackney 2008:116). In the numerous community museums that have appeared since the end of the Troubles in mainly working-class nationalist areas, artefacts connected to the Hunger Strikers and their struggle are being displayed. Whilst one may question the authenticity of some of the examples, including blood pressure gauges that purportedly were used by the doctors of the prison at this time, there are prized ephemera that are undoubtedly 'real' to those who present them. Of particular relevance in the wider community is the existence of collections of tiny 'communications' [known by the prisoners as 'comms.'], whether for personal or propaganda purposes, which contained the writings from and about the Hunger Strikers. The obvious care manifest in their ongoing survival and maintenance is indicative of their continued, indeed heightened, value.

However, an archaeology of the Hunger Strikes cannot merely be restricted to cataloguing the vast array of material remains connected to this event. To truly conduct an archaeological study one has to attempt to understand the meaning, importance, emotional impact, the evolution of these places and things and their multi-connections to society from their inception through to present day. Historical and contemporary archaeologies are not about recording the ephemera of our current situations, they are about being able to explore the vast complexities of meaning and understandings that exist and evolve in things and places over time. It is in this respect that the changing meanings associated with the material remains of the Troubles, of the Hunger Strikes, of the most intimate connections to those who died, should be explored.

The Hunger Strikes of 1981: The Prison Hospital

After 1981, the previously nondescript prison hospital at Long Kesh/Maze began to irretrievably change in a symbolic sense and gain heightened significance to a substantial section of society in Northern Ireland. This previously functional building gained a strong social, cultural, even spiritual dimension due to its connections with the Hunger Strikes. The change of meaning cannot solely be attributed to physical interaction rather, this change has multiple and convoluted roots. Of the significant numbers who claim a connection to the site, only a small number have actually entered it. I will argue that the events that occurred within the prison hospital changed the relationships of the prisoners, and indeed many of their communities, with the buildings and site without any physical alteration or indeed interaction with the material remains being necessary.

After the H Blocks of Long Kesh/Maze were built in 1976 the prison authorities were careful to ensure that no element of the site was connected to any particular paramilitary group or person. To ensure this occurred prisoners were frequently moved between wings and even H Blocks, with those considered most dangerous—and on the so-called 'red book'—being moved at least every two weeks.[1] This disruption was not only to ensure that plots and plans for escape could be foiled but also so that there were no individual or communal associations to specific areas of the site. However, when the Hunger Strikers became critically ill, it was to the prison hospital that they had to be taken and where they all ultimately died. The myths and legends surrounding the prison hospital began at this time. Initially it was viewed as a place of despair and grief, particular in the immediate aftermath of the Hunger Strikes. When the Hunger Strikes were called off in the autumn of 1981 they were seemingly defeated, without winning any concessions. Whilst the Hunger Strikes appeared to have been unsuccessful, they had created a heightened stand-off that the authorities did not want repeated and many conditions were granted in the following years to avoid the return of such tumultuous scenes. Indeed, all the conditions that the Hunger Strikers requested were eventually granted, often without public knowledge, by the late 1980s. Demands for paramilitary segregation were one of the first concessions granted, although in direct response to a Loyalist prisoner riot in 1983.

By the mid to late 1980s the prisoners' life was one of relative freedom due to the relaxation of the prison regime. With prisoners now celebrating the *de facto* return of special category status, their relationship with the prison hospital changed. One ex-prisoner remembers being housed in the prison hospital overnight when he broke his ankle playing football in the late 1980s and he recalled wanting to know if he was in the hospital cell of one of the hunger strikers, 'Obviously you didn't ask the screw or maybe you didn't have the confidence to ask him or whatever. But I remember, but there was a calm feeling … It wasn't as if you were frightened or anything like that'.[2] The movement of the hospital from site of despair to reverence and wonder mirrored that of the role of the Hunger Strikers themselves, who became frequent subjects of wall murals and campaigns of commemoration in wider nationalist society. Whilst memory and place are important constituent elements of identity, the connection of Long Kesh/ Maze, and specifically the prison hospital, with the final weeks, days and moments of the Hunger Strikers' lives ensured that the physical remains grew in significance.

The impact of this place is only truly apparent on physical inspection in the presence of those emotionally connected to the Hunger Strikers and the Republican experience of the recent period of conflict. Indeed, the continued empathy that many in the Nationalist community feel towards the Hunger Strikers is a diluted version of how Republican prisoners relate to those who died within the prison. It has been of particular interest when interviewing prisoners from different—often diametrically opposed—nationalist paramilitary organisations that there exists consensus regarding the significance of the prison hospital in relation to the Hunger Strikers and in particular the figurehead, Bobby Sands. Prisoners who had left before the Hunger Strikes occurred, such as an ex-Official IRA prisoner who departed the Nissen Huts in 1975, spoke in awe and reverence of those individuals who died. The most intimate physical remnant of their final moments—the hospital and its contents— were discussed with heightened interest.[3] On entering the hospital with a group of ex-Republican prisoners, the physical impact of the building, and the individual hospital cells specifically, on the ex-prisoners was immediately apparent. It is this 'human experience of place' that Michael Bell (1997:813) highlights when discussing the specific and personal phenomenon in transforming a space into a place. To those ex-prisoners this building was no longer the prison hospital of Long Kesh/Maze, it had transcended its functional role to encompass cultural, personal and even sacred meanings. The surfaces and structures took on a heightened significance; 'the artificial light that shone off the shiny black floor and clean, speckly cream walls created a cold airless atmosphere. An eerie place' (Gorman 1994:190). The 'ghosts' of this place were hard to ignore, whilst walking around the building with ex-prisoners and talking to those who had shared their hardships and privations.

The heightened significance of the prison hospital relates on many levels, as both a communal and individual experience. Individual connections to the Hunger Strikers and their associated remains are particularly evident amongst ex-prisoners. These more intimate connections relate not only to the empathy that one can feel towards men who died by such a means and the human suffering this would have entailed—which is strongly felt amongst the nationalist community at large—but specifically to the parallels between their lives and the Hunger Strikes. Such associations allow the ex-prisoners to make sense not only of the ultimate sacrifice of their fellow prisoners but also to their relationship with paramilitary conflict, the prison and ultimately the Troubles. On entering the cell that Bobby Sands was purported to have died in one ex-prisoner stated: 'I don't want to be melodramatic about it, this is the cell in which an icon died. A person whom, when he died I was 15 … I was 15 when he died and I found his death shaped a lot of my life'.[4] However, these individual memories are couched in the communal remembrance of the Hunger Strikes and as such are not an organic occurrence. For whilst individual remembering is largely involuntary, communal memory is by necessity 'deliberate, purposeful and regulated' (Lowenthal 2001:xi). Means of ensuring continued remembrance of such an internalised means of protest are highly directed and connected to physical *aides de memoire* in wider society. This intervention can be seen in the treatment and continued use of the Hunger Strikers in wall murals, which have been highlighted by McCormick and Jarman (2005) and Kenney (1998). The Hunger Strikers have continually been used in tandem with current concerns and campaigns within nationalist circles as a means of legitimisation, especially by Republican organisations who use their images to support policies of more recent vintage. The Hunger Strikers are further commemorated through the placement of the physical remnants most intimately connected to the protest and the individual men in community museums. The sheer volume of artefacts both intimately and fleetingly connected to the event indicates the continued significance to wider society. In this context what could be more relevant and precious than the place of death?

It was apparent whilst moving around the prison hospital that despite the site being closed, and access officially controlled, interactions with the building and its scant remains were ongoing. In the cell that Kieran Doherty had occupied before he died on the 73rd day of hunger strike on 2nd August 1981, a small floral tribute and card had been left by his family and remained from its initial deposit in the summer of 2006 until at least November 2007 (my last visit to the site). This act of commemoration displays the building's ongoing symbolic transformation, to those most intimately connected to its most famous occupants, from a functional prison building to a sacred site. Its sacredness relates to its human connections, for as Bell has stated, 'the experience of place is the experience of people, and for us, nothing could be more holy' (1997:821), but also to its evolving role as a place of cultural significance. The majority of visitors to the site since closure are those active within and connected to Republican prisoners groups; Loyalist ex-prisoners currently display a little, if cautious, interest in places of past incarceration. Whilst being conducted on the official tour of the site, there is no doubt that the prison hospital is the primary area of interest and the focal point of the visit. The results of these visitations have not only resulted in the additions to this officially defunct site—such as the floral tribute—but there have been numerous, stealthy subtractions from the hospital and the site in general. This is most evident in the changes to the frame of 'Bobby Sand's' bed. Springs have been removed one-by-one, evidencing minute, repeated interactions with place (see Figure 11.2). Tiny trophies are secreted in pockets and bags, cumulatively stripping the frame of its constituent parts, now recast as moveable artefacts. Their removal answers multiple needs. They are taken due to their intimate connection with those who died on Hunger Strike, to act as sacred artefacts, ensure remembrance, diffuse into wider society and continue to subvert the authorities.

Conclusion

As an institution that has been mediated for millions through the lens of the media, Long Kesh/Maze prison would appear as an unusual but functional institution that

Figure 11.2   Bobby Sands' bed.

provided little happiness, humour or hope. However, the realities of this place, as evolving and experienced individually and communally, are much more complex. Undoubtedly this prison hospital—if not the site it is situated within—has many meanings, both negative and positive, to the vastly different groups that constitute Northern Irish society. The prison hospital not only identifies with the communal Republican prisoner experience but has proved cathartic for individuals. By exploring the evolution of meaning of the remnants of the recent conflict, through the example of the prison hospital, it is apparent that within a short amount of time a place of function, control and desolation can transform to be identified as significant, sacred, meaningful and ultimately uplifting. Domestic and industrial artefacts that would not normally hold any significance are prized possessions to be secreted away by those who connect most strongly with the place and the events that occurred therein.

Whilst the prison hospital acts as evidence of the changing meaning of place and the context-related significance of seemingly banal artefacts, how does this relate to hope? On the most obvious level, it shows how the negative connotations initially associated with the prison hospital have been dissipated and replaced with positive remembrances relating to steadfastness and pride. However, the prison hospital also is a symbol of hope for the many places, buildings and things that relate to the Troubles and continue to exist in Northern Ireland. If a place of death can transform in meaning so swiftly and completely it provides hope that divisive and complicated places can undergo many evolutions and metamorphoses in meaning. It indicates that for society to move on from conflict there is not necessarily a need to destroy every physical trace, as if they never existed, as their meaning shifts with the needs and concerns of contemporary society. Instead, changing contexts, interactions and contemplations with place have the potential to allow changing relationships with the past, whilst not forgetting the often distasteful events associated.

Notes

1. M. M., oral testimony conducted at Long Kesh/Maze, January 2006.
2. D. A., oral testimony conducted at Long Kesh/Maze, January 2006.
3. G. L., oral testimony conducted January 2007, Belfast.
4. D. A., oral testimony conducted at Long Kesh/Maze, January 2006.

Bibliography

Belfast (Good Friday) Agreement (1998) *The Agreement*. Belfast: NIO.

Bell, M.M. (1997) The Ghosts of Place. *Theory and Society* 26 (6): 813–836.

Clarke, L. (2005) Introduction. In J. Olley, *Castles of the North*, 2–3. www.coldtype.net/irish.html

DeCunzo, L. (2006) Exploring the institution: Reform, confinement, social change, boundaries and crossings. In M. Hall and S. Silliman (eds) *Historical Archaeology*, 167–190. Oxford: Blackwell.

Gaynor, S. (1987) Maze Compound—formerly Long Kesh. *Gatelodge: the Prison Officers' Magazine*, 10–11. Belfast: HMSO.

Gorman, M. (1994) In B. Campbell, L. McKeown and F. O'Hagan (eds) *Nor Meekly Serve My Time: The H Block Struggle (1976–1981)*. Belfast: Beyond the Pale Publications.

Graham, B. and McDowell, S. (2007) Meaning in the Maze: Heritage of Long Kesh. *Cultural Geographies* 14 (3): 343–368.

Kenney, M.C. (1998) The Phoenix and the Lark: Revolutionary mythology and iconographic creativity in Belfast's Republican districts. In A. Buckley (ed.) *Symbols in Northern Ireland*, 153–168. Belfast: Institute of Irish Studies.

Lowenthal, D. (2001) Preface. In A. Forty and S Küchler (eds) *Materialising Culture: The Art of Forgetting*, xi–xiii. Oxford: Berg.

McAtackney, L. (2008) The Archaeology of Political Prisons: Long Kesh/Maze, Northern Ireland. Unpublished PhD thesis, University of Bristol, UK.

McCormick, J. and Jarman, N. (2005) Death of mural. *Journal of Material Culture Studies* 10: 49–71.

McKittrick, D., Kelters, S., Feeney, B. and Thornton, C. (1999) *Lost Lives: The Stories of the Men, Women and Children Who Died as a Result of the Northern Ireland Troubles*. Edinburgh: Mainstream Publishing.

Mulcahy, A. (1995) Claims-making and the construction of legitimacy: Press coverage of the 1981 Northern Ireland Hunger Strikes. *Social Problems* 42 (4): 459–467.

Portelli, A. (1998) What makes oral history different. In R. Perks and A. Portelli (eds) *The Oral History Reader*, 32–43. London: Routledge.

Purbrick, L. (2004) The architecture of containment. In D. Wylie (ed.) *The Maze*, 91–110. London: Granta.

Part V

Death and Remembrance

12 Faith in Action: Theology and Practice in Commemorative Traditions

Harold Mytum

Theological developments in faith during the historic period greatly affected the literate population. The debates and controversies were argued out in pulpits, sitting rooms and coffee shops, and profoundly influenced people's aspirations and actions. This edited volume is a welcome part of a movement to recognise the importance of religion and belief to past communities by historical archaeologists who have hitherto been surprisingly reticent in examining some of these issues.

As an archaeologist and an active Reader in the Anglican tradition,[1] the author is acutely aware of the importance of faith, but also how Biblical interpretation at a theological level, and its application in daily life, is highly contextualised. Whilst there is now a significant ecumenism amongst some denominations at least, at many times in the past religion was a major defining characteristic of difference. Moreover, all denominations have changed over time, and we need to be careful, as in other aspects of our interpretation, not to put our current theological interpretations back into the past. We also need to be aware of local interpretations and variations within each denomination, by the clergy themselves and by those within their disparate congregations.

Death and bereavement are times when many consider their lives and their faith. Commemorative monuments through their texts and symbolism revealed, but were also designed to enhance and reinforce, specific religious attitudes. These were often reinforced by regular church or chapel attendance, and by reading, prayer and contemplation at home—where many items of material culture reinforced religious values, sometimes linked to commemoration. Commissioned and erected by those closely concerned with these issues, most monuments until the mid-nineteenth century were placed in a clearly Christian context of church or churchyard. How strong faith may have been, and to what extent social convention and physical context of burial affected memorial and text choices, remains at times uncertain. Nevertheless, when combined with patterns of church attendance, chapel building, and overt resistance by religious minorities often in the face of oppression or discrimination, there can be confidence that trends in popular faith can be identified and studied through the memorials.

This chapter briefly examines certain theological debates and how they were worked through in different denominations, using gravestone data from New England, Britain and Ireland. These are necessarily brief and therefore at a certain level simplistic, but they do at least indicate the potential variability in theology and its practical, material manifestation. The data sets are everywhere more limited for much of the eighteenth century and exponentially rise throughout the nineteenth century (Mytum 2006a), but through appropriate sampling strategies many clear trends are visible for the whole of this period. These various studies reveal how faith was manifest in people's lives and in their attitudes to death and commemoration. These monuments do not represent some postscript to life, but were active in providing exemplars of lives lived and evidence of faith in action. They need to be read as those reading at the time would have read them, imbued with Christian faith that was vibrant and central to many lives at that time.

The Protestant treatment of death and commemoration was centred around the concept of judgement based on the life and faith of the deceased which, on death, could not be further ameliorated. The role of the monument thus became one of celebration of the social persona of the deceased and had a didactic role in warning those still alive of the fate that awaited them (Llewellyn 2000). There were, however, different perspectives on the nature of judgement and the chances of salvation based on denominational interpretations, though these denominational emphases have often changed over time.

Most gravestone studies considering archaeological and art-historical interpretations of symbolism have predominantly considered Protestant monuments, especially when examining the period before the nineteenth century. Reformation theology is appropriately applied to explain meanings of symbolism on these memorials, but this is only part of the picture. These limitations in analysis (partly caused by bias survival and partly caused by cultural practices regarding commemoration and grave space reuse) could be taken to imply that the symbol systems were a uniquely Protestant manifestation. This was certainly not the case, as many of the same motifs were widely applied within a Counter-Reformation context, and in a few parts of Europe, such as Ireland, sufficient evidence survives for the Catholic context to be studied. Therefore the present interpretations within Protestant theologies need to be balanced with a Catholic perspective, and some Irish data is provided below to illustrate the potential for more nuanced and comparative analysis.

The Counter-Reformation, bringing new theological emphases and correspondingly modified requirements from iconography, is clearly a process that should be incorporated within mortuary monument studies. Although some of the worst excesses of medieval practices in relation to Purgatory were removed in the Counter-Reformation, its theology did not remove this concept, which still therefore affected mourning and commemorative practices (Ariès 1981:463). Prayers could reduce the time spent by the soul of the deceased in Purgatory, a contrast to Protestant theology where no acts by the living could influence the fate of the deceased. This makes the sites of Catholic memorials more active locales, where the practices of visitors and observers could have an impact on the fate of the deceased's soul. Even into the nineteenth century, actual skeletal material could be displayed in Catholic chapels to create environments where prayer was encouraged (Ariès 1985:190–92), but often mortality symbols were used instead, and on the funerary monuments themselves these were frequent. Thus, Catholic mortuary art emphasized prayer by those still alive, balancing the morbid symbolism of physical decay provided by the mortality symbols with exhortations to action through prayer. They served a dual purpose of a warning for the living as in the medieval Catholic tradition of the Three Living and the Three Dead, and which continued in the Protestant didactic, warning messages, and in the active pursuance of more rapid ending of any torture to the soul.

Eighteenth-century Puritan New England

Puritan perspectives on death have been well studied and integrated with evidence from mortuary monuments (Messer 1990; Stannard 1975, 1977; Watters 1981). Dethlefsen and Deetz (1966:508) saw the skull as linked to a strong Puritanical concern with judgement and mortality (Figures 12.1a and b), unlike the later use of the cherub that epitomized a more optimistic anticipation of resurrection (Figure 12.1c). Ludwig (1966) also placed the use of the mortality symbols firmly within the Puritan tradition, with the decay of the flesh carrying with it the possibility of eternal damnation for those who were not within the elect, destined for a place amongst the saints. Here we have a theology which in its early phases emphasized salvation for a limited and selected group, not for all who had faith. Many colonial revivals of the early eighteenth century were within strongly Calvinistic traditions that emphasized the saving of only the elect (Taylor 2001:344–346). On the other hand, the revival known as the Great Awakening led by George Whitfield, an English evangelizer linked with Wesley (though they later disagreed) encouraged a more positive emotional reaction to faith and salvation, and this could be seen as part of the shift to more positive imagery of the cherub, already well established in England by this time. Whitfield was a very successful preacher, but combined this personal appeal with marketing of books and pamphlets, including his sermons (Lambert 2001). Deetz's simple model of stylistic change has been effectively critiqued from a historical viewpoint by Hall (1976), where the diversity within New England theology and social structures is emphasized. However, it is likely that cherubs do reflect a more positive attitude than Death's heads (and many other mortality symbols), but the timescales over which they became popular, and the ways in which they are depicted, are so variable it is only through regional and local studies that the ways in which the agents commissioning and making the stone operated is becoming clear.

A large amount of work in recent years has concentrated on the identification of particular carvers and their products, stylistic changes in their outputs over time, and to a lesser extent the influence of one carver on another, much reported in the pages of the journal *Markers*. A few studies have tried, however, to consider some

Figure 12.1 (a) Winged Death's Head with crossed bones above, (b) Winged Death's Head with heart in mouth, and (c) Winged Cherub, all at Kingston, Massachusetts.

of the theological drivers behind production of particular designs, though with little reference to the commissioners of the monuments. The broad pattern of change from Death's Heads to Cherubs and then Urns and Willows still holds, but some of the stylistic changes within and between these can be further dissected for theological significance. For example, Peter Benes notes in his Plymouth County study that the most important stylistic innovations took place during the Great Awakening, which took place in the part of New England he studied in the years 1740–45 (1977:150–151), but then emphasizes how this acceleration is part of a longer-term trend in theological changes that involved a weakening of core Puritanical theology from the late seventeenth century onwards, and one that was variable over both time and space. He has a set of descriptions of what he terms the death masks, caricature-like images linked to feelings and expectations of the afterlife, but behind these lie an increased optimism concerning the Resurrection, and the ability of the sinner to repent and be saved, rather than be in angst-ridden doubt as to membership of the Elect and therefore whether they were eligible for salvation. Another study (Brooke 1988) has examined how various Connecticut sects reacted differently to the symbolic choices available for memorials, selections that were clearly not linked to wealth but to denominational affiliation and therefore presumably dominant local theological viewpoints.

Most New England inscriptions include brief details of the name, age and date of death of the deceased, and are usually for one individual. A minority of stones carry theological information in the text, and these largely match the iconography, with an early emphasis on mortality (with 'Here lyes buried' or 'Here lyes ye body'), but some of the later eighteenth-century monuments are more likely to include some optimistic reference to the deceased's eventual resurrection (Tashjian and Tashjian 1974). These may be clear statements of theology. Some of the symbolism may have been read by different individuals in very different ways. Some of the art-historical interpretations of the symbolism imply a great sophistication on the part of the carvers (though possibly of the commissioners if they gave detailed instructions). Whether this was the case, or symbols and designs were copied with only generalized or vague understanding of the multiple meanings, it is difficult to ascertain. It is possible that many members of the congregations were well aware of the symbolic meanings due to hearing sermons explicating Scripture, and through the reading of religious tracts, some illustrated with woodcut designs.

David Watters (1999) has studied Ulster Scots stones in the Merrimack River valley, New Hampshire, to reveal the theological importance of avoiding the forms of representation developing in the Massachusetts and Rhode Island stones noted above. Instead mortality symbols such as coffins, combined with hearts and a particular form of cross design, emphasized certain ethnic affiliations but also a particularly Presbyterian symbolism regarding love, membership, acceptance and participation. These associations were cemented at Biannual communion services, often involving several churches coming together for these services, and sometimes taking place outside in the churchyards themselves. The iconography on these monuments reflects a particular set of theological emphases and their concomitant behaviours, ones linked to the Ulster Scots heritage, but not merely a copying of it. These reflect a normative set of values, beliefs and associated symbolism rather than individualistic interpretations, though particular monuments reflect the selection of certain designs from the repertoire, thus allowing some individuality. A consideration of some Ulster evidence, where some of the imagery and meanings emphasized in New Hampshire were derived, is therefore appropriate. It also allows consideration of symbolism in a more overtly and politically charged multi-denominational context.

Eighteenth-century Scotland and Ireland: Protestants and Catholics

The use of mortality symbols was extremely widespread in Scotland, and this can also be linked to the Presbyterian tenor of the church that developed out of a range of factions with varying Protestant inclinations (Dunbar 1996). This Scottish Calvinist emphasis provides a clear parallel to the New England situation, and so the popularity of mortality symbols can be explained in a similar manner. Indeed, Betty Willsher (1996:15) notes that the Church in Scotland emphasized that death of the sinful body was inevitable, but balanced this with hope of salvation through grace on the Day of Judgement. In Scotland, the cherub therefore often can be found to counterbalance the mortality symbols even from an early date. Rather than combine these themes in one symbol, the winged skull, two elements were often present on memorials, with headstones featuring the mortality symbols low down and the cherub towards the top. Thus, Scottish stones often provided visually complex iconographical schemes, but ones that were similar in theology to those of New England, though often combing the dangers of decay and damnation with the hope of eternal salvation. They were more complex than the New England monuments, however, and demonstrate far greater variability, reflecting both theological differences and the patterns and scales of production.

Only a subset of the Scottish symbols was widely accepted by the Scots in Ulster, derived from a package of symbols that occurs as one of many combinations there. The selected repertoire has an emphasis solely on the mortality aspects, through the use of five symbols: skull, long bones, coffin, hourglass and bell (Figure 12.2a). Here there has been a loss of optimism in the saving power revealed through the cherub, and which reappears in New Hampshire and parts of Massachusetts with the heart (Figure 12.1b). We can thus see how the selection, combination and emphasis of different symbols can both reflect and help to form theological emphases. It is worth noting, however, how the same symbols in different contexts can carry with them alternative associations and theologically inspired responses.

Ulster Catholics suffered oppression and discrimination in many ways, but during the eighteenth century a class of successful merchants, tenant farmers and those associated with the linen trade were able to make sufficient surplus to commission mortuary monuments. The limited set of mortality symbols used by the Protestants for their theological interpretations could be appropriated and applied within the largely hidden Counter-Reformation Catholic church theology (Mytum 2009a). For example, mortality symbols were widely used on the rear of the wheeled cross headstones found in west Ulster (Mytum 2006b), being exactly the same symbols used by the Protestants in the same burial grounds. One group (Protestants) emphasized that with the inevitability of death came judgement based on the life and faith of the deceased, whilst the other (Catholics) used the mortality symbols to remind those alive that by prayer the living could expedite the deceased's time in Purgatory. Although there was considerable variety in the stylistic representation of the symbols, and how they were arranged on

Figure 12.2   Irish gravestone symbolism. (a) Mortality symbols, Errigal Trough, Co. Monaghan; (b) IHS with cross designs from Irish gravestones, Termonfeckin, Co. Louth.

the monuments and in which combinations, this was due to carver preferences rather than to theological or social emphases as the symbols largely repeat the same theological message and the symbol combinations or arrangements do not correlate with the age or gender of the deceased.

Within the Counter-Reformation movement, the Jesuits were one order that promoted the IHS with cross symbol (Smith 2002), and this became one of the most significant, and no doubt widely understood, markers of Catholic affiliation and devotion in Ireland (Figure 12.2b). It was also an appropriate symbol to be incorporated with gravestone design as the cross indicates Christ's sacrifice in death but also his rising again, giving to all a chance of resurrection at the Second Coming. The IHS is usually, though not exclusively, depicted with a cross rising from the horizontal cross-bar of the H, the cross itself having a strong Catholic association in the eighteenth century (Protestants at that time tended to avoid it, though it became popular again at least for

Anglicans in the nineteenth and early twentieth centuries). What the IHS specifically meant to the Catholic viewers is itself instructive. The fluidity of meaning can be well illustrated through this symbol.

When, according to Eusabius, Constantine looked up to the sun before the Battle of Milvian Bridge in 312 he saw a cross and the Greek words *Εν Τούτω Νίκα* (in this, be victorious!). He later had a dream that explained the Christian meaning of the phrase, which was subsequently translated into Latin as *In hoc signo vinces*, though IHS standing for the first three letters of Jesus in Greek was also being used on early Christian inscriptions. It is likely that it is the Latin phrase that is being recognized on most Irish gravestones as some have that phrase written in full on the stones, and the cross coming off the horizontal bar of the H further supports this interpretation. The use of Latin evoked a Catholic context, even though the basic theological message was a universal Christian one. The placing of the IHS on the stone was related to prayers for the deceased in Purgatory, and such praying at graves is depicted in nineteenth-century Irish illustrations. However, other meanings including *Jesus Hominum Salvator*, 'Jesus, Saviour of People', may have also been evoked, and in contemporary Anglican understanding it has been explained as meaning 'In His Service'. We can therefore see that symbols such as IHS, or those of mortality, can have variable meanings across time, space and denomination. This is their power; if we can understand the context of their creation and use they can open up subtle aspects of theological emphasis.

The IHS could be used as a symbol of resistance in Ireland, and indeed with the few families in Scotland that remained resolutely Catholic (Bryce and Roberts 1993, 1996), but it was largely used as a focus for prayer and devotion. Indeed, the way in which both Protestant and Catholic could use the same burial grounds throughout the seventeenth and eighteenth centuries, and erected their distinctive monuments within sight of each other, indicates that some of the emphasis on conflict, resistance and intolerance needs to be tempered with a certain acceptance of parallel if not socially or politically equal communities, as evidenced in the way that graveyards such as Aghalurgher, County Fermanagh was used, with clear spatial separation as a way of managing tensions (Mytum 2009b).

In some Irish regions, the use of other Biblical scenes was common. Crucifixion images and symbols of the Passion were popular in areas such as Louth and Tipperary, and these were alternative potent symbols of Catholic belief as well as identity (Longfield 1943; 1954; Tait 2002). Other scenes, such as the Nativity, also occur, though why these are appropriate to a commemorative context is less clear, and more research is required on the meanings implied by their use. During the nineteenth century, Catholics obtained more rights, and separate burial grounds were established by denomination, as well as denominationally segregated larger urban cemeteries. All denominations developed different strategies of commemoration in the nineteenth and twentieth centuries, partly because of these different locales, and partly because monument fashions on a larger scale were changing (due to a range of social, economic and cultural factors). This period of change has received less attention thus far in

Ireland, though fieldwork is ongoing, but has been the focus of attention in Wales and some patterning relevant to the themes discussed here are apparent.

Nineteenth-century West Wales: Multidenominational Protestant Traditions

West Wales offers the opportunity to examine the varied emphases exhibited in burial grounds of Anglican and a number of different nonconformist denominations during the nineteenth and early twentieth centuries. Language, symbol and monument form all may be seen to create complex physical manifestations of faith within a contested environment based on language use. Whilst there was greater use of the Welsh language on rural sites and in chapel rather than Anglican church contexts (Mytum 1994), our interest here focuses on relative popularity of monument form, symbolism and theology, rather than language *per se*, though the last may be indicated through text in a consciously chosen language, particularly Biblical quotations.

Graveyard surveys in north Pembrokeshire reveal theological differences in attitudes to death in the relative popularity of different introductory terms such as 'Here lies the body of' and 'In loving memory of', with their equivalents in Welsh incorporating *bedd*, 'body', and *er cof am* (Mytum 2002). Perhaps unsurprisingly seeing some of the earlier preoccupations of the Ulster Scots and the New England congregations, the Calvinistic nonconformists, such as those at Brynberian Independent chapel, were those who held on longest to the mortality phrases in the nineteenth century (though no mortality symbols are present this late), compared with those commemorated in the Anglican churchyard in Newport.

Monument form is also indicative of denomination and theology. Just as the cross was a Catholic symbol in Ireland and not used by the Ulster Scots, so in nineteenth-century Pembrokeshire the cross is almost exclusively the preserve of the Anglicans. This monument form, and the IHS which frequently occurs on such memorials, both occur widely in Protestant memorial contexts in the later nineteenth and early twentieth centuries, especially where Anglo-Catholic High Church traditions developed, and can be seen in some numbers at Newport and the nearby rural parish of Nevern, with only tiny numbers at the nonconformist sites (Mytum 2002). The cross was not considered appropriate in most Protestant contexts and has indeed been removed from the repertoire once again from Anglican graveyards under normal circumstances.

A major Protestant concern that is well illustrated in the west Wales evidence is the powerful place of the Word of God, as revealed through scripture, and then interpreted through preaching which was itself heavily informed by the theology of the particular sect. Many Welsh believed that the revelation of God's word in their language had a unique significance (Jones 1980:53). This is visible on monuments through both quotations and depictions of the physical book, both open and closed. The Bible is normally depicted in the centre top of the stone, and when shown closed was often painted with a black cover and gilded edges to the page, just like many actual Bibles. In some cases it was actually inscribed 'Y Bibl' on the cover, but often this was not always thought necessary. Where a book is displayed open, there may be no text visible, or a Biblical verse may be inscribed across the pages (Mytum 1999: Fig. 7.6).

The Biblical texts can be tabulated according to their place in the Bible (Table 12.1), and patterns can be seen to emerge when comparing different sites. Thus far, only the Anglican churchyard of St Mary's Newport has received detailed published attention (Mytum 1999), but the evidence from the Calvinistic Independent Brynberian chapel is instructive and is presented here in comparison. A smaller but still significant number of stones displayed Biblical quotations compared with Newport, but there were nearly as many different verses chosen and with a wider variety of Books from the Old Testament.

Table 12.1 Biblical quotations on nineteenth-century gravestones at two graveyards: Newport, north Pembrokeshire (data from Mytum 1999) and Brynberian.

	St. Mary's Newport Anglican		Brynberian Independent	
Book	No. Occurrences	No. Different verses	No. Occurrences	No. Different verses
Old Testament				
Deuteronomy	2	1	1	1
2 Samuel	2	2	0	0
1 Chronicles	3	1	1	1
Job	13	8	11	11
Psalms	30	19	15	12
Isaiah	0	0	3	3
Jeremiah	0	0	1	1
Proverbs	6	4	1	1
Ecclesiastes	0	0	1	1
Lamentations	2	2	0	0
Ezekiel	0	0	1	1
Amos	0	0	1	1
Malachi	0	0	1	1
New Testament				
Matthew	13	7	3	2
Mark	3	2	3	3
Luke	4	4	1	1
John	2	1	2	1
Romans	2	2	1	1
Philippians	8	3	0	0
1 Corinthians	0	0	2	2
1 Thessalonians	3	1	1	1
Hebrews	0	0	2	2
James	2	2	0	0
1 Peter	2	2	0	0
2 Peter	0	0	1	1
Revelation	14	4	3	3

Overall there are slightly more Old Testament than New Testament quotations, but in both graveyards that is largely due to the overwhelming popularity of the Psalms and Job. However, there is not much repetition between sites in the particular verses selected. Of the Job verses, only three of the eight chosen in Newport are repeated at Brynberian, and in the Psalms, only four out of the nineteen Newport quotations are also found at Brynberian; the others are all different. This indicates a wide use of the Bible, not just a few stock phrases, as may be suggested by the mason cutting the memorial, a practice that took hold through patterns and quotation books used from the mid-nineteenth century onwards.

The messages can be divided into those which relate to religious issues and those which would seem to have particular relevance for the deceased. In the former category come those concerned with suffering and death on the one hand and salvation on the other. The latter include personalized choices which relate to the age or activity of the deceased. Comments on the mortality and suffering of man are common, often with a warning for the living; indeed, these are the majority at Brynberian. Some were appropriate for children or the relatively old. Not all verses are now easy to interpret, but may relate to the character and behaviour of the deceased or the attitudes of others to him or her. Much of this context cannot be known, but for most verses the emphasis of the sermon is clear.

Biblical quotations are often set out following the main commemorative biographical details with the verses in upper and lower case (Figure 12.3a and b) and usually consist of one verse. After the Biblical quotation, there is a reference to the source, normally the chapter is given in Roman numerals and the verse in Arabic, though variation is common. The need to record the Biblical source for the quotation on the stone is in itself significant, and relates to the use of the Bible in society. Moreover, it has a special significance with regard to the funeral service and the process of grieving, remembrance and memorialisation.

Figure 12.3 Two pedimented headstones from Newport, Pembrokeshire. Each person commemorated has their own Biblical verse inscribed beneath their biographical details.

Occasionally the Biblical quotations are annotated to indicate that they were used to form the focus for the sermon or address at the funeral of the deceased, as with Lettice Lewis, died 1821 and buried in Newport St Mary's. Although the main commemorative text is in English, the Biblical quotation, 1 Corinthians 15.58 is in Welsh, followed in English by 'The above verse was her Text preached by the Revd. W.G. Hughes. The Memory of the Just is blessed'. This indicates the importance of Welsh for the Bible but English for other aspects of commemoration at Newport. The funeral was an important religious experience, but also was of prime social significance. Funerals were often attended by many members of the local population and assembled relatives, and were linked to acts of hospitality that formed a stage in the grieving process. The display of the body and its coffin, their journey from home to place of worship and the form and nature of the service there, the subsequent interment and finally the wake was of great importance to the survivors of the deceased.

The funeral service, and particularly the sermon, formed a central part of the whole experience. The presiding minister, guided by a carefully chosen reading from Scripture, would tailor the address to meet the needs of the occasion, bearing in mind both the character of the deceased and the attitudes of the family and community. Whilst the quality of preaching could vary greatly, the most impressive orators would have provided the most moving sermons that would be long remembered and commented upon. That the executors of Lettice Lewis considered naming the minister on the stone suggests that this was a particularly famous and eloquent preacher, and worthy of record. In most cases the Biblical quotations have no supporting explanatory text, but probably many if not all represent those used at the funeral. That the Biblical text associated with the funeral was so often given in Welsh indicates the language used for the funeral service itself, demonstrating the social centrality of Welsh and its role in rites of passage.

Conclusions

Through studies in various Protestant and also Catholic contexts, it is possible to see how theology, belief and practice are interwoven. In these examples of commemorative practice, certain strands of Christian belief, particularly eschatological concerns with judgement, redemption and eternal life at the Second Coming, dominate. Nevertheless, the archaeological evidence is important in that it reveals popular reactions to theological trends, rather than relying on the tracts and sermons published by the clergy and others active in theological debate. Most historical research has concentrated on the producers of theology, rather than the consumers. Gravestone symbolism and texts reveals the popular reception and pronouncement of theology, albeit within a socially constrained context associated with one particular set of liturgies and practices. Given the numbers of monuments surviving in graveyards across the English-speaking world, it is possible to identify trends and degrees of variation within congregations that would not be possible from documentary sources. The texts on the monuments are more confidently interpreted in terms of popular theology than the symbols, which could have carried unorthodox associations not recorded in standard theological texts. However, text and symbol together allow for subtle and at times conflicting messages to be constructed. In situations as varied as Puritan New England with its strong social conventions, and the contested landscape of Ulster, monuments could be used to challenge and extend meanings as well as reinforce dominant theological orthodoxies.

Gravestones concentrate on judgement and redemption. Other theological concerns such as love, compassion, sacrifice or forgiveness may be more dominant in other arenas, such as in the home or at church or chapel. These could be represented materially through books, pamphlets, prints and display ceramics, but are not discussed here. Gravestones display both symbols and texts which were used in the exposition of theology and its application in death, bereavement and commemoration. Individual monuments reveal certain aspects of theology, but the assemblages in burial grounds reveal trends over time, space and denomination. These symbols and texts also could be read and interpreted differently across time, space and denomination, just as the Bible is today—they are even more powerful and important for that reason.

Acknowledgements

Much of the data used in this paper was collected during many seasons of the Castell Henllys Field School, with graveyard supervision by Robert Evans and Kate Chapman. Some of the Welsh data was collected by Earthwatch volunteers and part of the Ulster data was collected on fieldwork as part of a small grant (no. 119562) from the Arts and Humanities Research Council as part of the Diasporas, Migration and Identities Programme.

Note

1. A Reader is a lay person trained to preach, lead public worship and offer pastoral care after being authorized by an Anglican bishop.

Bibliography

Ariès, P. (1981) *The Hour of our Death*. Translated by H. Weaver. New York: Knopf.

Ariès, P. (1985) *Images of Man and Death*. Translated by J. Lloyd. Cambridge, MA: Harvard University Press.

Benes, P. (1977) *The Masks of Orthodoxy: Folk Gravestone Carving in Plymouth County, Massachusetts, 1689–1805*. Amherst: University of Massachusetts Press.

Brooke, J.L. (1988) 'For honour and civil worship to any worthy person': Burial, baptism, and community on the Massachusetts near frontier, 1730–1790. In R. B. St. George (ed.) *Material Life in America, 1600–1860*, 463–485. Boston: Northeastern University Press.

Bryce, I.B.D. and Roberts, A. (1993) Post-Reformation Catholic houses of north-east Scotland. *Proceedings of the Society of Antiquaries of Scotland* 123: 363–372.

Bryce, I.B.D. and Roberts, A. (1996) Post-Reformation Catholic symbolism: further and different examples. *Proceedings of the Society of Antiquaries of Scotland* 126: 899–909.

Dethlefsen, E. and Deetz, J.F. (1966) Death's heads, cherubs and willow trees: Experimental archaeology in colonial cemeteries. *American Antiquity* 31 (4): 502–510.

Dunbar, J.G. (1996) The emergence of the reformed church in Scotland *c*.1560–*c*.1700. In J. Blair and C. Pyrah (eds.) *Church Archaeology: Research Directions for the Future*. CBA Research Report 104: 127–134. York: Council for British Archaeology.

Hall, D.D. (1976) The gravestone image as a Puritan cultural code. In P. Benes (ed.) *Puritan Gravestone Art*, 23–32. Dublin Seminar for New England Folklife Annual Proceedings. Boston: Boston University.

Jones, I.G. (1980) Language and community in nineteenth-century Wales. In D. Smith (ed.) *A People and a Proletariat: Essays in the History of Wales, 1780–1980*, 47–71. London: Pluto Press.

Lambert, F. (2001) *Inventing the 'Great Awakening'*. Princeton: Princeton University Press.

Llewellyn, N. (2000) *Funeral Monuments in Post-Reformation England*. Cambridge: Cambridge University Press.

Longfield, A.K. (1943) Some eighteenth-century Irish tombstones. I. Introduction and Dennis Cullen of Monaseed. *Journal of the Royal Society of Antiquaries of Ireland* 73: 29–39.

Longfield, A.K. (1954) Some eighteenth-century Irish tombstones. VII. Clonmel, Kiltoom, Seir Keiran, etc. *Journal of the Royal Society of Antiquaries of Ireland* 84: 173–178.

Ludwig, A.I. (1966) *Graven Images: New England Stonecarving and its Symbols, 1650–1815*. Middletown: Wesleyan University Press.

Messer, S.C. (1990) Individual responses to death in Puritan Massachusetts. *Omega: Journal of Death and Dying* 21 (2): 155–163.

Mytum, H. (1994) Language as symbol in churchyard monuments: The use of Welsh in nineteenth- and twentieth-century Pembrokeshire. *World Archaeology* 26 (2): 252–267.

Mytum, H. (1999) The language of death in a bilingual community: nineteenth-century memorials in Newport, Pembrokeshire. In R. Blench and M. Spriggs (eds.) *Language and Archaeology*, 211–230. London: Routledge.

Mytum, H. (2002) A comparison of nineteenth- and twentieth-century Anglican and Non-conformist memorials in North Pembrokeshire. *Archaeological Journal* 159: 194–241.

Mytum, H. (2004) Local traditions in early eighteenth-century commemoration: The headstone memorials from Balrothery, Co. Dublin and their place in the evolution of Irish and British commemorative practice. *Proceedings of the Royal Irish Academy* 104C: 1–35.

Mytum, H. (2006a) Popular attitudes to memory, the body, and social identity: The rise of external commemoration in Britain, Ireland, and New England. *Post-medieval Archaeology* 40 (1): 96–110.

Mytum, H (2006b) The wheeled cross headstones of West Ulster: Towards a definition of the type. *Church Archaeology* 10: 39–56.

Mytum, H. (2009a) Mortality symbols in action: Protestant and Catholic early eighteenth-century West Ulster. *Historical Archaeology* 43 (1): 160–182.

Mytum, H. (2009b) Scotland, Ireland, America: The construction of identities in mortuary monuments by the Scotch-Irish in the seventeenth and eighteenth centuries. In A. Horning and N. Brannon (eds.) *Ireland and Britain in the Atlantic World*, 235–252. Society for Post-Medieval Archaeology Monograph. Dublin: Wordwell.

Smith, J.C. (2002) *Sensuous Worship: Jesuits and the Art of the Early Catholic Reformation in Germany*. Princeton, NJ: Princeton University Press.

Stannard, D.E. (ed.) (1975) *Death in America*. Philadelphia: University of Pennsylvania Press. Originally published with some chapters in 1974 as *American Quarterly* 26.

Stannard, D.E. (1977) *The Puritan Way of Death: A Study in Religion, Culture and Social Change.* Oxford: Oxford University Press.

Tait, C. (2002) *Death, Burial and Commemoration in Ireland, 1550–1650.* London: Palgrave Macmillan.

Tashjian, D. and Tashjian, A. (1974) *Memorials for Children of Change: The Art of Early New England Stonecarving.* Middletown, CN: Wesleyan University Press.

Taylor, A. (2001) *American Colonies: The Settling of North America.* New York: Penguin.

Watters, D. (1981) *Eschatological Themes in Puritan Literature and Gravestone Art.* Ann Arbor: UMI Research Press.

Watters, D. (1999) Fencing ye Tables: Scotch-Irish ethnicity and the gravestones of John Wright. *Markers* 16: 174–209.

Willsher, B. (1996) *Scottish Epitaphs: Epitaphs and Images from Scottish Graveyards.* Edinburgh: Cannongate Books.

13 The Changing Memories and Meanings of the First World War Expressed through Public Commemorations in Exeter, Devon

Samuel Walls

Introduction

The commemoration of the First World War is frequently expressed in public locations and in monumental forms. The choices made in the forms, timings and locations of these memorials helped to determine how the conflict was rendered meaningful, considered and remembered (Winter 1995). Public war memorials are usually acts of compromise and conflict between different interest groups, the consequence being that they frequently express the dominant views and memories of the social elites, particularly landowners, churchmen, industrialists and politicians (Bartlett and Ellis 1999). These groups often use commemoration not only as a means to articulate the ideals of honour, bravery and sacrifice which they wish the public to follow, but also in justifying their own roles in the conflict and in its remembrance (Grieves 2001). They may also embody overt expressions of other desires and aspirations, such as the regeneration of public space or for funding the building of hospitals or halls (Mansfield 1995; Webster 2008). Therefore, public war memorials of the First World War can be investigated to understand not only the ways in which communities remember the conflict and those that fought and died, but also the social realities of those wishing to negotiate and evoke memories of the war dead (Winter 1995; Mansfield 1995; Grieves 2001). The shifting choices in monumental forms and locations informs us of the instabilities that exist after the end of the conflict, as the meanings of the war are negotiated within and between communities, both on national scales and locally.

First World War memorials have received an increasing amount of attention from researchers in a variety of fields. They have been regarded as valuable sources of information on inter-war society (King 1998), the processes of commemoration (Winter 1995), the biographies of the monuments (Rainbird 2003), and the construction and reconstruction of identities (Gordon and Osborne 2004). A number of these studies have emphasized the importance of the context of war memorials, especially in terms of their location (Tarlow 1997; Osborne 2001), but also in relation to the timing of their construction (Black 2004; Gough and Morgan 2004). However, most of the studies to date have focused upon individual memorials or a single type of memorial (for example, Gough and Morgan 2004), with the majority only touching upon the wider commemorative landscapes of which they were a part of (for example, Grieves 2000). Studies have rarely addressed the interaction between either contemporary or successive monuments in the same vicinity or landscape.

This paper attempts, therefore, to move away from focusing upon single memorials, their messages and biographies, and instead to focus on the changes in the commemorative forms chosen over time within one community and involving multiple memorials. In such instances, the various public commemorative strategies adopted can be seen as both reacting to each other and wider commemorative strategies, but also as reflective of the changing meanings and memories of the First World War. In this sense, the identities and memories of the community created and remembered through public war memorials exist not only at the memorials, but in the physical and conceptual spaces in between them (see Walls and Williams 2010).

In order to investigate how public monuments embody a variety of different interpretative strategies this paper focuses upon the commemoration of the First World War within the city of Exeter, Devon. A variety of memorial practices were utilized, and the nuances of choice in location and form can be seen to provide details on how the war was continually reinterpreted and re-remembered in various ways, and how these shifting memories were negotiated by different people and groups within the city. The range of commemorative monuments can be seen as reacting not only to the changing memories of the conflict in relation to the present political and social situations, but also as considered and strategic responses to the designs and locations of each previous monument and other commemorative practices in Exeter, its immediate environs and nationally. The monuments were also utilized by the city and county elites to convey a variety of concerns and objectives unrelated, or only loosely connected, to the conflict. These objectives changed over time and can also be fruitfully investigated to understand the memories these public monuments attempted to embody. This detailed and contextual appreciation of public war memorials can shed new light on a seemingly well-studied aspect of twentieth-century commemoration and the nuances of changes in the commemorative practices in both their form and iconography, on the one hand, and their landscapes and topographies on the other.

Earlier War Memorials

Exeter, like the majority of British cities or towns, has a variety of different forms of war memorials (for example, Inglis 1992). The earliest of these relate to patriotic memorialisation during the Victorian period and are regimental memorial tablets and plaques to the Crimean Campaigns (1854–1855), the India Mutiny (1857) and the Second Anglo-Afghan War (1878–1881). These memorials and the numerous plaques set up to individual officers within the cathedral set the tone for the locations and forms of memorials which were to follow in the city in the aftermath of the First World War. It was, however, the county memorial to the South African Wars (1899–1902) which was to have the greatest impact upon the commemorations of the Great War. This was unveiled on 30 May 1903 in the Cathedral and took the form of a large stained-glass window with two large tablets below listing the names of the county's dead, which was placed directly opposite the Crimean memorial on the southern wall of the nave. The South African War Memorial was subject to some criticism by the cathedral authorities and the public, which seems to have greatly influenced the form of the city's First World War memorials. The main criticism was the illegibility of the names listed on the memorial (*The Exeter Express & Echo* 23/11/1918 and 5/3/1919) which resulted in the tablets of the memorial being moved from beneath the window to a much less prominent and dominating position prior to the erection of any of the city's First World War memorials. The movement of the South African War Memorial at this time may reflect the diminishing value of this conflict in the immediate aftermath of the 'war to end all wars' which had made the South African wars seem a very minor skirmish in comparison. It is therefore not surprising that the majority of First World War memorials in the city did not take the same locations or forms as the county's South African memorial. In fact few public war memorials commemorating the First World War were located within the cathedral, with the exception of the continuing erection of regimental memorials, which culminated in the 1936–37 reconstruction of the St Edmund Chapel to the Devonshire Regiment. The forms of either cream marble tablets or stained glass windows as war memorials are rare throughout Exeter despite being common in the rest of the county (Walls 2010) and country as a whole (Furlong *et al.* 2002). This memorial therefore helped determine the location and forms of the First World War memorials in the city, with the community leaders and cathedral authorities (in particular) wanting to construct something very distinct from the South African War Memorial and the other war memorials in the cathedral. This perhaps included the desire, especially amongst the public, to create a memorial of a more permanent nature, which would not be moved, as well as one that was outside the exclusively religious and denominational context of the cathedral itself, whose authorities had decided to move part of the South African Wars memorial, despite some of the public objecting (*The Exeter Express & Echo* 8/3/1919).

Also influential upon the forms of the war memorials erected after the First World War was the 1905 statue of General Sir Redvers Buller, which was unveiled in front of thousands including the General and his family at the junction of Hele Road and New North Road. The location was a popular one, being the main road from Exeter to Crediton (the family home). However, many individuals in Crediton felt that it was a deliberate snub that the statue was orientated away from their town and facing into

Exeter. The location also caused problems for the statue in later years, as although it was frequently saluted by Australian troops and others during the First World War who remembered the General fondly, it also became a focus for some vandalism. For example, on Armistice Day 1920 the statue was painted red by students (Clapp 1982) and this high profile attack upon the statue seems to have acted as a stimulus for the careful choices and orientation of Exeter's First World War memorials. There was a desire for public locations, but ones which would allow for a greater level of respect, already having an aura of quietness, reflection and peace rather than being near major road junctions.

The Devon War Memorial

Exeter cathedral had been seen as the logical choice for the county's South African War Memorial, partly as Exeter is the county town, and was the base for many of the county's troops and the county authorities. This situation persisted at the end of the First World War and in late 1918, shortly after the Armistice, the idea of a county memorial was first discussed (*The Exeter Express & Echo* 22/11/1918). These discussions immediately presumed that Exeter would be the location of this county memorial, with no strong objections about this choice amongst the officials who planned the memorial (*The Exeter Express & Echo* 22/11/1918). This was partly because the initial impetus for the construction of a county memorial came from the Devonshire Patriotic Fund Committee, which did not include representatives of the county's other large city, Plymouth, which had formed its own Patriotic Fund during the war, and who were thus not consulted upon the initial idea of a county memorial. Lord Fortescue (the Lord-Lieutenant of Devon) developed the initial proposal for the form that the county's memorials should take (*The Exeter Express & Echo* 11/1/1919). At first, the proposed memorial was to be of a functional nature with the combined aims of renovating the dilapidated cathedral cloisters, helping to fund hospital improvements and the construction of a new memorial wing dedicated to servicemen and their families (*The Exeter Express & Echo* 22/11/1918; Russell 1977). These suggestions were proposed at the same time that initial fundraising efforts and publicizing the need for improvements to these buildings were taking place, which had included approaching Lord Fortescue (Caldwell 1972; *The Exeter Express & Echo* 11/1/1919). The improvements to the cathedral were to be completely funded by the proposed memorial scheme and alongside the nearby Royal Devon and Exeter Hospital were seen by the authorities as useful and symbolic to the whole county. Once funds began being raised in late 1918, it soon became clear that the majority of residents in the county were not interested in funding a county memorial, being more concerned with local acts of war commemoration and their returning service personnel (*The Exeter Express & Echo* 22/2/1919). It seems that in particular the cathedral cloisters renovation was an unpopular plan and only a fraction of the required funds were raised. It was decided by Lord Fortescue and the Devon Patriotic Fund in

February 1919 that the scheme for the county memorial should be changed and that the cathedral cloister renovation should seek funding from another source (*The Exeter Express & Echo* 19/2/1919). The memorial fund would still finance the hospital's new wing, as this was the smaller and cheaper project, as well as being more useful to the war veterans and their families and thus receiving greater support from the public.

The altered memorial scheme monies would not only be used for a hospital wing but also be used to erect some form of public monument. The choice of its location was inevitably to be associated with the cathedral, especially as the original plans had involved this location. However, an external memorial rather than an internal monument was selected, which took the form of a large granite cross located on the smaller of the cathedral's two greens. The choice of an external memorial may not only reflect an attempt to move away from the 'ill chosen' South African War Memorial (*The Exeter Express & Echo* 8/3/1919), but also the more general regional and national pattern of town, city and county memorials being placed externally to religious buildings, with surprisingly few municipal memorials being located inside cathedrals (although they remained a focus for regimental memorials). The preference towards an external memorial can be seen as an attempt to be more inclusive by not being in an enclosed Anglican space (although it was still located within a distinctive and historic ecclesiastical space) as it was a memorial to all who died in the Great War and not just Anglican casualties (Walls 2010). The choice of the smaller of the two greens was partly determined by the orientation the memorial could then have with the main entrance of the cathedral, and also its closeness to the Broadgate entrance to the cathedral yard. It may also have been determined by the location of a statue erected in 1907 to Richard Hooker, the sixteenth-century theologian on the other green, which would perhaps have been seen as detracting from the significance of a war memorial (Walls 2010). The green created a sacred space for the war memorial. It is notable that to fulfil this aim several trees were removed and the green was partially railed off from the surrounding paths. The location is replete with historical associations of local, regional and national importance, and this partly determined the choice of placement, although the monument's east-west alignment with the cathedral's main entrance was probably the main determining factor. This placement also aligns with the graves of the dead whom the memorial commemorated whose inscriptions (heads) face east. This evoked the role of the memorial as a cenotaph allowing those who had no grave to have a symbolic grave in the county's symbolic centre.

In this context it is noteworthy and perhaps unsurprising that an eminent architect was commissioned, namely Sir Edwin Lutyens, who was not only involved with the War Graves Commission, but who also designed the national war memorial (the Cenotaph) amongst others. The choice of the designer of the national memorial for the county's project shows how the organizers were attempting to create added significance to the county memorial. Adding to these aspirations for prestige and authority, it is also noteworthy that it was unveiled by the Prince of Wales (later Edward VIII). Further significance was created by the choice of material used; not only is granite the material

Figure 13.1 The Devon War Memorial Cross with Exeter cathedral in the background (photo by the author).

typically used for the majority of the county's medieval crosses, but also it is the stone that perhaps reflects the county more than any other. A unique piece of granite, it was mined from Haytor Quarry on Dartmoor, which was reopened for the sole purpose of quarrying the stone for this memorial. This quarry was run by an Exeter firm and had been put out of business mainly by the competition of the Cornish granite quarries, which were used for the majority of the other war memorials in the county, so its choice was therefore highly emblematic. Hay Tor itself can be seen as a symbolic place and, although not the highest of Dartmoor's tors, it is one of its most imposing, especially when viewed from the eastern (Exeter) approaches to Dartmoor (Harris 1994). Therefore multiple elements of the monument's form and location reflected attempts to add to the sacredness of what was being commemorated. This creation of new symbolic rituals in the commemoration of the First World War was exceedingly common: for example, the invented rituals associated with the burial of the Unknown Warrior at Westminster Abbey; the casket of the Unknown Soldier being made of oak from Hampton Court Palace; the transportation of the body back to Britain in HMS *Verdun*, thereby linking this battle to the soldier, while many other famous battlefields were linked by their soils being included in the internment (Hanson 2005).

The form of the memorial also reveals some of the motivations of the organizing committee. As it took the shape of a cross, one can discuss the connotations of the widely employed association between the sacrifice of the soldiers and that of Christ (see Saunders 2003 for further discussion of this). But it is particularly interesting that the cross was the form initially suggested by the proposer of a county memorial (Lord Fortescue), and that no debate about its appropriateness occurred. However, it is clear that not all of his suggestions were followed, as it was not made out of captured German Guns, as he had initially proposed (*The Exeter Express & Echo* 19/2/1919). The acceptance of Fortescue's design indicates that the cross was viewed as an appropriate symbol for the sacrifices of the British people in late 1918, particularly in Devon and Cornwall where such a large number of stone crosses were erected as war memorials (Moriarty 1990; Walls 2010). The choice of a cross was also common across the county, and many of the parishes on the outskirts of the city such as Alphington, Exwick and Topsham also erected war memorial crosses. The inner-city churches generally erected internal monuments (with some exceptions such as Newtown) due to a lack of space in their churchyards. This choice also reflects the fact that the medieval crosses, which strongly influenced many of the forms of Devon's war memorial crosses (Walls 2010), are generally located in the more rural areas, and were perhaps less well-known and regarded as less relevant to those living in Exeter itself.

The Devon War Memorial did not include any of the names of the dead but, as part of the memorial, a roll of honour was compiled which took over two years to complete with 11,601 names placed in alphabetical order under each town and parish. Three copies of this book were made, with one being placed underneath the cross in a casket of burnished copper by the Prince of Wales on its unveiling in May 1921 (*The Exeter Express & Echo* 16/5/1921). The other two copies were kept as records of service with one being placed in the cathedral and the other with the county authorities, also located in Exeter. This method of burying the register of names provided a symbolic funeral rite which the families of those killed could attend during the unveiling ceremony. This method was also copied for the Plymouth City War Memorial, which was unveiled on 19 May 1923. It could also be suggested that this was one way for the authorities to honour the deaths in an easier manner than permanently inscribing the huge number of names on what would by necessity have to be a very large memorial. After all it is arguably the process of gathering the names together that is possibly one of the most important elements of the process of commemoration (Inglis 1992). There are many examples elsewhere in Devon of external war memorials that initially did not include the names of the dead, which instead were included on memorial rolls of honour retained in the nearby churches. This practice was particularly common with repaired or re-erected medieval crosses which the county memorial imitated, as at Shillingford St George and Clyst Hydon, while Buckerell, Brampford Speke, Moretonhampstead and Exmouth erected new external monuments but did not inscribe the names upon them (Walls 2010). The process of burying the names or, as Holtorf describes it, 'incavation' (Holtorf 2004) was very much part of fixing disparate memories to a place, constructing and integrating these memories into the county's and city's narrative and history.

The Hospital Wing

The Royal Devon and Exeter Hospital was the other chosen focus for commemorating the county's war dead, the leftover money raised from the public subscriptions being used to partly fund developments to the hospital on Magdalen Street. It is worth noting that in early 1919, when this development was first suggested as a war memorial scheme (*The Exeter Express & Echo* 11/1/1919), there were six hospitals in Exeter treating service personnel, and there were major concerns as to the future requirement for this provision, especially when the majority of hospitals were returned to their normal uses (Caldwell 1972). The wounded, disabled and families of the dead were at this early stage a major concern to the authorities, and a new hospital wing and dedicated beds for service personnel were seen as one way of helping those who had given so much. Specifically, the money was used for building a new memorial wing with 40 beds for disabled and discharged soldiers, which helped supplement other redevelopment work being done at the time. The money for the new wing was only partially paid for by the county war memorial fund, with the Red Cross and the Ministry for Pensions also providing substantial grants.

In contrast to the memorial cross placed on the cathedral green which was the symbolic element of the county's public war commemoration efforts, the new hospital wing was utilitarian, although still containing symbolism of renewal and regeneration. It was named the 'Victory Wing', and almost immediately a second storey had to be added to accommodate nurses (Caldwell 1972). One ward was named after the former President of the Hospital, Sir Edward Channing Wills, who had died the previous year (Russell 1977), but who also had strong connections to the Devonshire Regiment, as he had served as the first President of the Devonshire Regiments Volunteer Training Corps in 1915. The Victory Wing was opened on 22 June 1922 by Viscount Hambledon, who also had strong links with hospital work, as well as having served in Gallipoli with the Devonshire Regiment during the war; the two men can perhaps be seen as embodying both the functional and symbolic roles of the new wing (Simkins and Simkins 1991; Caldwell 1972). In 1974 the hospital moved to new purpose-built facilities in Wonford, Exeter, and although the buildings initially continued as NHS offices, the buildings are in the process of being transformed into a hotel and accommodation. Built to fulfil a shortage of hospital beds in the city at the end of World War I, it seems ironic that it will now fill 'a shortage of bedrooms in the city' (Derek Phillips, chairman of the Chamber of Commerce quoted in *The Express & Echo* 24/9/08).

The Exeter and Devon War Memorial

The process of organizing and constructing a county memorial in Exeter ran parallel to the process of choosing a memorial scheme for the city itself. Initially a war memorial for the city of Exeter was suggested early in 1919 when the then Mayor, Sir James Owen, having been present at the first proposal by Lord Fortescue for a county memorial, invited a few prominent citizens to dine with him and discuss preliminary steps towards the erection of a memorial for Exeter. This led to a public meeting at which a committee was appointed to help the Mayor raise funds and select a suitable memorial. It is noticeable that this committee was mostly composed of the same prominent individuals who were invited to the dinner. The first major issue that was debated was the form the memorial should take – the completion of the cathedral cloisters and a new memorial hospital wing was favoured by many as both projects were already in hand and lacking finance. It is perhaps no coincidence that the same schemes for the Exeter memorial were considered as for the Devon War Memorial, especially as these two schemes were initiated at similar times and at the forefront of many peoples' minds at the time (*The Exeter Express & Echo* 26/2/1919). Neither of these schemes was overly popular with the public in Exeter, partly due to the Devon War Memorial Committee having already discussed raising funds for these schemes. The majority of the people who attended the public meeting favoured a public statue rather than functional memorials. The initiative was taken by two members of the committee to approach John Angel, a native of Exeter whose work was being exhibited in the Royal Academy, who was then commissioned to make a model for a memorial for the city. This contrast between a local architect for the Exeter memorial and the national figure chosen for the county memorial provides another example of the careful symbolic choices which both committees made.

Northernhay Gardens was eventually chosen as a suitable location for the Exeter War Memorial, providing a suitable historic setting near Exeter Castle and the City wall, and thereby linking the First World War to the historic defences of the City, especially during the Civil War (Stoyle 2003). The committee had originally attempted to obtain permission for a location in Bedford Circus; however, this was found to be impractical due to objections by adjoining landowners who viewed a memorial to the war dead as inappropriate to a business location. Northernhay Gardens was therefore a compromise which was suggested by the City Council and in many ways it imitates the Devon war memorial's location as being outside of the historic boundaries of the city yet in association with some of its oldest buildings and structures. This can be seen as reflective of attempts to ensure that both memorials appeal to wide audiences on not only a city scale, but county-wide. Northernhay Gardens was an important location in Exeter, especially within the Victorian era, when the majority of Exeter's statues were erected in this park leaving the rest of the city very sparse of public monuments in comparison. This park also has a very long history, having been used during the Roman period as a quarry for building stone, and being the first public park in the country. The long and important history of the location and the identity that the location possessed (i.e. strong links to defence and both the Roman and Medieval past) suited the aims of the Exeter War Memorial Committee, especially given the close relationship to the location of the National Volunteer Memorial. This memorial had been raised in the gardens in 1895 to commemorate the forming of the volunteer regiments (in 1852) and Sir John Charles Bucknell, who had played a very important role in their beginnings and who had been knighted in 1894. The First World War memorial was located near to this monument in the centre of the park, and this relationship seems to have been an important aspect of its location. It thereby drew upon memories of the formation of the volunteer forces and their role in the First World War, emphasizing the voluntary nature by which the men of Exeter (and Devon) had served in the war. The memorials do, however, have very different orientations; the Volunteer Memorial focuses on the Assize Hall at Exeter Castle to the southeast, while the Exeter and Devon War Memorial is orientated towards the southwest, looking over the entrance to the gardens, the southern part of the city, the Haldon Hills and Southern Devon. This orientation also differs to the easterly orientated Devon War Memorial.

The discussion around the proposed location continued for some time, but the design and estimated costs were received from the architect swiftly and the committee began raising the estimated £5000 needed. The costs did, however, rise to closer to £6000 by the time of the final commission (*The Exeter Express & Echo* 24/7/1923). A great effort was made to complete the fundraising before Sir James Owen left his post as mayor, and the committee (in particular the chairman and future mayor, Mr Plummer) helped achieve this by 13 November 1919. This rapid fundraising contrasted strongly with the Devon memorial, partly as a result of the competition, with the public unwilling to pay for two schemes and preferring to concentrate on the city war memorial. It may also reflect the public's preference towards sculptural schemes in the immediate aftermath of the Great War in Exeter, believing that the hospital wing scheme of the Devon War Memorial should not act as a memorial to those killed, even though they largely agreed that it should be carried out (*The Exeter Express & Echo* 11/1/1919). The city's memorial project was also aided by the fact that a large proportion of the costs were raised by the Mayoress and her supporters for the Prisoners of War, which raised £1,500 through the sale of surplus provisions, and which they wished to use to commemorate those who had died in captivity. They requested that one of the four figures around the base of the statue represent prisoners of war whom had died in captivity. This figure not only commemorates the bravery and sacrifices of the captured men, but also the Mayoress and her depot's work during the war.

Figure 13.2 The Exeter and Devon War Memorial in Northernhay Gardens (photo by the author).

The design of the Exeter and Devon War Memorial contrasts strongly with that which was proposed for the Devon War Memorial. It takes the form of a high central octagonal column on a cross shaped plinth with four seated figures on the four arms of the cross representing a 'Prisoner of War', a 'V.A.D Nurse', a 'Sailor' and a 'Solider'. On top of the central column stands the allegory of 'Victory' trampling a dragon and holding a laurel towards the heavens (*The Exeter Express & Echo* 24/7/1923). The choice of a more elaborate form for this memorial compared to the simplicity of the

Devon Memorial raises a number of issues related to the motivations and meanings each memorial attempted to express. First, the forms of both reflect and fit in with their location, with the medieval-style cross chosen for the Devon War Memorial reflecting the gothic cathedral, and medieval buildings nearby, while the more classical form of the Exeter and Devon War Memorial references the other statues found in the gardens and the history of the city wall. The Devon and Exeter War Memorial's elaborate form can be seen as expressive of the more unique and distinct identity which the city authorities were attempting to articulate and create, while the Devon War Memorial had to appeal to the county as a whole and be of a form and location that would be meaningful and significant to the greatest number of people possible. Second, although both memorials can be read as symbols of local pride and nationalism, the form of the Exeter and Devon War Memorial expresses this much more extensively, for example with the inclusion of the town crest and motto on the bow of the ship the sailor sits upon. Also, the inclusion of 'Devon' not only within the inscription on the memorial, but also through its location looking out over Devon reflects how the city wished to be remembered as having led the county's efforts in the war. It was also an attempt to make the Devon War Memorial second to this one in importance within the city and within the county. These inclusions attempted to justify the city's role, as well as strongly emphasizing the seafaring history of the city (and county). That this role had continued in the First World War was further emphasized by the unveiling ceremony being conducted by the Admiral of the Fleet, Lord Beatty.

The foundations for the Exeter and Devon War Memorial were laid from 1922 and as part of the memorial a scroll containing the 970 names of the dead was deposited inside the central pedestal in a lead casket. The list of names was deposited by the Mayor a month before the dedication, which contrasts to the Devon Memorial which included the deposition of a list of names during the dedication ceremony, although this was purely a practical concern. The Exeter and Devon War Memorial was finally unveiled on the 24 July 1923 after many years of planning, construction and some controversy (particularly in terms of the location). As the second main war memorial in the city it responded to the Devon War Memorial, and the choices made in terms of form, location, materials and in the use of names can all be seen as careful decisions made in relation to this and other war memorial schemes in the city, as well as the processes of commemoration which were occurring regionally, nationally and internationally.

In Exeter it seems that the initial views of the First World War by the authorities was as a convenient method of raising funds for practical concerns, for example the renovation of the cathedral cloisters. This idea proved largely unpopular with the public who wanted a more appropriate memorial, dedicated to the soldiers and their families, which the hospital wing was perhaps seen as fulfilling, especially by the authorities. These practical concerns for the returning soldiers largely evaporated shortly after they returned, as it was believed that the authorities should be the ones helping the returned service personnel and creating homes fit for heroes. Concerns for the families of the troops also faded slightly, but they were not completely forgotten in the commemorations, which still reflected their need to have a focus for their grief. What, however, increasingly became important were future generations and being able to teach them the example the fallen had set. The ways in which the conflict was viewed were very similar with importance placed upon the local contributions, reflected by the use of local materials and often craftsmen. Also it was felt that the names had to be included both inside the two main monuments and in more visual forms in each of the individual parishes' memorials and Rolls of Honour.

Other War Memorials

The other main forms of public First World War commemoration in Exeter existed at each of the parish churches in the city, with oak boards being the most common form of war memorial, as seen at Heavitree, St David's and St. Sidwell's. Also common were marble tablets which were located in many churches, as at St Leonard's and St Petrock's. Granite crosses were rarely used with only two of the city's parishes, Newtown and St Thomas, having crosses. The latter is on the outskirts of the city and is surrounded by villages which likewise chose to erect external crosses (Exwick, Ide, Alphington, Shillingford St George and Longdown). The majority of the nonconformist churches in Exeter also erected their own war memorials, which followed similar patterns, with brass plaques and marble tablets dominating. One other major city memorial was erected at Higher Cemetery, Heavitree. This is the main burial site of the city and located on its outskirts. This memorial was unveiled by the Mayor of Exeter and commemorated those individuals from the city who died of the effects of active service and were buried within the cemetery, the majority of whom had not been included on the other memorials in the city. This memorial displays the names of those who died, unlike the other main memorial projects of the city. All of these memorials can be seen as making up for the absences of names and groups from the larger memorial projects in the city, and each reflects a variety of motivations and concerns beyond remembrance.

Conclusion

Public commemoration of the First World War was not a straightforward process in Exeter or elsewhere (Walls 2010). As outlined in this article a large number of factors helped determine the forms such commemorations took, including when they were built, where they were built, who built them and what other commemorations were already built or being planned. It is important in the attempt to understand some of the meanings and significance placed upon any single memorial to appreciate the variety of different approaches communities adopted to commemorate the First World War and to move away from previous studies which often looked at a single war memorial or type of war memorial in isolation from the other public monuments and commemorative strategies adopted to remember conflict. This perspective offers the opportunity to analyse how public monuments and commemorations can be investigated to increase our understandings of the motivations, feelings and beliefs of the people who erected and interacted with these memorials. This can be utilized alongside the information gained from the increasing appreciation of private commemorative strategies (for example, Saunders 2003) to greater understand the roles of memory, materiality, identity, local pride and landscape in commemorative strategies.

Bibliography

Bartlett, J. and Ellis, K.M. (1999) Remembering the dead in Northop: First World War memorials in a Welsh Parish. *Journal of Contemporary History* 34 (2): 231–242.

Black, J. (2004) Thanks for the memory: War memorials, spectatorship and the trajectories of commemoration 1919–2001. In N.J. Saunders (ed.) *Matters of Conflict Material Culture, Memory and the First World War*. London: Routledge.

Caldwell, J. (1972) Notes on the history of Dean Clarke's hospital 1741–1948. *Report and Transactions of the Devonshire Association for the Advancement of Science, Literature and Art* 104: 175–192.

Clapp, B.W. (1982) *The University of Exeter: A History*. Exeter: University of Exeter.

Furlong, J., Knight, L. and Slocombe, S. (2002) They shall grow not old: An analysis of trends in memorialisation based on information held by the UK National Inventory of War Memorials. *Cultural Trends* 45: 3–42.

Gordon, D.L.A. and Osborne, B.S. (2004) Constructing national identity in Canada's capital, 1900–2000: Confederation Square and the National War Memorial. *Journal of Historical Geography* 30 (4): 618–642.

Gough, P. and Morgan, S. (2004) Manipulating the metonymic: The politics of civic identity and the Bristol Cenotaph, 1919–1932. *Journal of Historical Geography* 30 (4): 665–684.

Grieves, K. (2000) Investigating local War Memorial Committees: Demobilised soldiers, the bereaved and expressions of local pride in Sussex villages, 1918–1921. *The Local Historian* 30 (1): 39–58.

Grieves, K. (2001) Rural parish churches and the bereaved in Sussex after the First World War. *Sussex Archaeological Collections* 139: 203–214.

Hanson, N. (2005) *The Unknown Soldier: The Story of the Missing of the Great War*. London: Doubleday.

Harris, H. (1994) *The Haytor Granite Tramway and Stover Canal: A Guide to Retracing the Route of Dartmoor's Granite from Quarry to Sea*. Newton Abbot: Peninsular Press.

Holtorf, C. (2004) Incavation-excavation-exhibition. In N. Brodie and C. Hills (eds.) *Material Engagements: Studies in Honour of Colin Renfrew*. Cambridge: Mcdonald Institute for Archaeological Research.

Inglis, K.S. (1992) The homecoming: The War Memorial Movement in Cambridge, England. *Journal of Contemporary History* 27 (4): 583–605.

King, A. (1998) *Memorials of the Great War in Britain: The Symbolism and Politics of Remembrance*. Oxford and New York: Berg.

Mansfield, N. (1995) Class conflict and village war memorials, 1914–24. *Rural History: Economy, Society, Culture* 6 (1): 67–87.

Moriarty, C. (1990) The National Inventory of War Memorials. *The Local Historian* 20 (3): 123–125.

Osborne, B.S. (2001) Landscapes, memory, monuments, and commemoration:

Putting identity in its place. *Canadian Ethnic Studies* 33 (3): 38–77.

Rainbird, P. (2003) Representing nation, dividing community: The Broken Hill War Memorial, New South Wales, Australia. *World Archaeology* 35 (1): 22–34.

Russell, P.M.G. (1977) *A History of the Exeter Hospitals 1170–1948*, Exeter: Exeter Post-Graduate Medical Centre.

Saunders, N.J. (2003) Crucifix, Calvary, and cross: Materiality and spirituality in the Great War landscapes. *World Archaeology* 35 (1): 7–21.

Simkins, M.A. and Simkins, R.J.J. (1991) Lord Hambleden and Moretonhampstead. *Report and Transactions of the Devonshire Association for the Advancement of Science, Literature and Art* 123: 167–188.

Stoyle, M. (2003) 'Memories of the maimed': The testimony of Charles I's former soldiers, 1660–1730. *History* 88 (290): 204–226.

Tarlow, S. (1997) An archaeology of remembering: Death, bereavement and the First World War. *Cambridge Archaeological Journal* 7 (1): 105–121.

Walls, S.H. (2010) The Materiality of Remembrance: Twentieth-Century War Memorials in Devon. Unpublished PhD Thesis, University of Exeter, UK.

Walls, S.H. and Williams, H.M.W. (2010) Death and memory on the home front: Second World War commemoration in the South Hams, Devon. *Cambridge Archaeological Journal* 20 (1): 49–66

Webster, P. (2008) Beauty, utility and Christian civilisation: War memorials and the Church of England, 1940–47. *Forum for Modern Language Studies* 44 (2): 199–211.

Winter, J. (1995) *Sites of Memory, Sites of Mourning: The Great War in European Cultural History*. Cambridge: Cambridge University Press.

Index

www.ingramcontent.com/pod-product-compliance
Lightning Source LLC
Chambersburg PA
CBHW041431270326
41935CB00020B/1840